BUSINESS ETHICS

BUSINESS ETHICS

Making a Life,
Not Just a Living

GENE AHNER

ORBIS BOOKS

Maryknoll, New York 10545

Founded in 1970, Orbis Books endeavors to publish works that enlighten the mind, nourish the spirit, and challenge the conscience. The publishing arm of the Maryknoll Fathers and Brothers, Orbis seeks to explore the global dimensions of the Christian faith and mission, to invite dialogue with diverse cultures and religious traditions, and to serve the cause of reconciliation and peace. The books published reflect the opinions of their authors and are not meant to represent the official position of the Maryknoll Society. To obtain more information about Maryknoll and Orbis Books, please visit our website at www.maryknoll.org.

Library of Congress Cataloguing in Publication Data

Ahner, Gene
    Business ethics : making a life, not just a living / Gene Ahner.
        p. cm.
    Includes index.
    ISBN 978-1-57075-748-8
    1. Business ethics. 2. Free enterprise—Moral and ethical aspects. 3.
Free enterprise—Social aspects. 4. Moral development. 5. Social
justice. I. Title.
    HF5387.A43 2007
    174'.4—dc22
                                2007009632

To my wife, Nancy
To our children, Mark and Lisa
To our grandchildren, Nia, Imani, Rosey

Who give the fuller and richer meaning to "Making a Life"

Contents

Introduction   xi

1. **A Free-Market Economy**   1
The Solution or the Problem?

     The Issue   1
     The Purpose of Business   8
     Business as a Vocation   13
     A Christian Reflection   17
     Questions for Reflection   22
     Suggestions for Further Reading and Study   23

2. **A Better Way to Think about Business**   25

     An Alternate Vision   30
     Business as the Driver of World Prosperity   34
     Questions for Reflection   42
     Suggestions for Further Reading and Study   43

3. **Core Values and Culture**   44

     Core Values   44
     Our Employees Are Our Greatest Asset   52
     Corporate Social Responsibility   58
     Conclusion   64
     Questions for Reflection   65
     Suggestions for Further Reading and Study   65

4. **Leadership and Ethics**   66

     Personal Identity   66
     Leadership   76
     Questions for Reflection   81
     Suggestions for Further Reading and Study   82

5. **Personal Integrity**   83

     Ethics: Compliance or Achievement?   83
     Integrity/Authenticity   88

Integrity/Authenticity and Leadership   98
Questions for Reflection   103
Suggestions for Further Reading and Study   103

6. **Ethics as Culture**   **105**

Formal Elements of an Ethical Culture   108
Informal Elements   120
Conclusion   125
Questions for Reflection   126
Suggestions for Further Reading and Study   126

7. **Moral-Decision Making**   **128**

The Moral Dilemma   130
Three Moral Philosophies   139
Nine Steps to Sound Ethical-Decision Making   143
Conclusion   150
Questions for Reflection   151
Suggestions for Further Reading and Study   151

8. **Moral Development in a Business Environment**   **153**

The Workplace as an Opportunity for Development   153
Three Important Principles of Growth   158
Hindrances to Growth   168
Summary   177
Questions for Reflection   177
Suggestions for Further Reading and Study   178

9. **Globalization**   **179**

What Is Globalization?   180
Business Ethics in a Global Economy   190
Conclusion   211
Questions for Reflection   212
Suggestions for Further Reading and Study   212

10. **When More Is Not Enough**   **214**

The Dynamics of the Business Process   215
The Development of Personal Identity   218
The Meaning of the Common Good   226

The Impact of a Market Economy on Religion   230
Catholic Social Teaching   236
Conclusion   241
Questions for Reflection   241
Suggestions for Further Reading and Study   242

Index **244**

Introduction

When I was asked recently about how long I had been working on this book, I answered, without much hesitation, a lifetime.

Some forty years ago I began my professional career teaching the abstract and somewhat esoteric disciplines of philosophy and theology to college and graduate students. While the teaching was satisfying enough, I felt a personal need to move beyond the academic world and enter into the "real" world. What better way than to enter the world of business. What could be more real than business!

For the past twenty-eight years that decision has led me from being a personnel administrator to a director of human resources to an officer of a public corporation to the corporate secretary of a board of directors—and back to being a teacher of college and graduate students! The circle is complete, except it looks more like a spiral. While business is indeed about the specific and the concrete, it is also about purpose and meaning. And that brought me back to philosophy, ethics, and, ultimately, to theology.

There is a tension here that is usually relieved by focusing totally on one or the other extreme—either business *or* ethics. When I would tell anyone I was writing a book on business *and* ethics, I would usually be greeted with a laugh or a flip remark about oxymorons.

Business, by its nature, is about the nitty-gritty, the day-to-day struggle of making something very specific with a group of people who may hardly know one another, for a customer who may be far away and who has at least some idea what he wants, and for a predetermined amount of money. It is messy, full of approximations, if not actual mistakes, and riddled with ambiguity and all sorts of mixed motives. The problem comes when it is considered to be *only* that. On that showing, business is "just business," driven by impersonal "market forces," "competition," and "bottom-line profitability."

On the other hand, academic types, whether philosopher, theologian, or moralist, tend to keep their distance from the inner workings of business precisely because it is so messy, so ambiguous, and, to most people in academics, so far removed from their own interests. The result is a lot of general pronouncements that may be true but have little direct impact on concrete business operations. Christianity itself is much better at pronouncing on the generalities than giving directions on the specifics. On that showing, there is much talk about "justice and peace," "equality and fairness," and lofty moral principles.

My intention is to assist the reader to understand that the two poles find their unity in the human person. To do that, business must be seen first of all as a basic human activity that takes place within the larger human community. As human activity, it is—by that fact—moral activity that permeates everything business does, to such an extent that *for business to be successful in the long run it must be ethical.* If that sounds like a theme, you are right. You will hear it often, and I hope you will have come to the same conclusion by the end of the book. Business is a human science that has suffered from being reduced to an empirical science. As empirical science, it is limited to a set of mindless procedures that, if followed slavishly, will produce profits. On that reading, business ethics becomes a list of dos and don'ts for navigating through the business formula to success. At best, it ends up as a code of ethics promulgated by management and proudly displayed to all. There are more than enough books to cover that type of approach.

However, if business is indeed a human science, then business ethics becomes both more compelling and more complex. On this reading, ethics must deal with the full range of human values, motives, and purposes as they play out in all the managed processes and practices of the business community. For that reason all the dynamics that contribute to business success must be addressed. In the long run, the benefits should be more rewarding. We will not be giving a "formula (or slogan) for success" nor a set of principles for executives to follow. The book will not try to model an "ideal moral company"—something that can only frustrate any actual operating business. We will be examining all the various dimensions that make a company more or less moral. The reality is that businesses can only get better or worse in that regard. No company is completely moral or immoral, nor does any business just stand still. The basic elements of morality as discussed here apply to both "for profit" and "not for profit" organizations, to both small companies and large corporations. What we hope to achieve in this work is a new awareness and a new language of public discourse that will allow us to raise the questions of living well within the framework of making a living, a language that is neither naive, nor preachy, nor antiquated.

What then can we realistically hope for? If the reader is not already "morally converted" in the sense that he has moved beyond mere self-centered satisfaction to some basic orientation to value or "what is worthwhile," then something much more personal than reading a book will be required. If, on the other hand, one already has a sense of personal responsibility in a world larger than oneself, then is not business ethics just a case of common sense? Apart from the fact that common sense is not so common, there is the more basic fact that the moral life is itself a journey. We either continue to grow in caring about a larger and larger world or we find our world contracting into

ever-smaller circles until it revolves only around ourselves, and perhaps immediate family. Morality is never static since it expresses the orientation of one's
personal identity. To become more and more conscious of the full moral
implications of "making a living"—something that consumes so much of our
time and talent—is itself a significant achievement on the road to moral
maturity.

Just how important is this concern with ethics and business anyway? Is it
just headline news as a result of some highly publicized corporate scandals?
To the contrary, I would venture to say that ethics is at the heart of our concerns for the twenty-first century. I am reiterating what has been said so dramatically by Rushworth Kidder[1] when he concluded his interviews with some
outstanding leaders of our day. Six issues were considered central to the future
agenda of our world:

- nuclear threat
- environmental degradation
- population explosion
- North-South economic gap between the developed and developing
  worlds
- need for education reform
- breakdown of morality

In effect, ethics is no mere luxury; it is central to our survival. If this sounds
too alarmist, then consider this: For the first time in human history, we are
capable, through science, technology and business, to create the kind of world
we want to live in. Does the issue, then, of who we are and what we want not
become central?

I want to thank Bill Burrows, managing director of Orbis Books, for holding my hand during this labor. When he first approached me about writing
this book, I was very reluctant. Since then he has helped bring me to a point
where I feel grateful for the opportunity. He is an unusual combination of
being my student, my teacher, and my friend.

There are others who have contributed in various ways to seeing this work
in print. First of all, there are the many business colleagues I have worked with
over the years. They are the people who didn't speculate about business ethics
but lived it in the day-to-day decisions they had to make in the course of
doing their job. They showed me by their lives that most people in business
really do care about doing good by doing right. They far outnumber the

---

1. Rushworth M. Kidder, *How Good People Make Tough Choices: Resolving the Dilemmas of Ethical Living* (New York: Morrow, 1995), 7-8.

others. Second, there are my students. When I was asked to teach business ethics in the MA program at Dominican University, I wasn't sure how I was going to do it. There was some trial and error, but they hung in with me and continued to probe with their questions and their own experiences. I don't think I would have agreed to write the book if I had not experienced strong affirmation and agreement from them about the way we studied the subject. It is the basic pattern I have followed in this book. Third, there is a smaller group that I must acknowledge by name: Tom Bishop, Jack Boberg, Ed Carlson, John Dickman, Paul Knitter, and Ed Tennant. Some have been business colleagues; they have all been friends. They would help me through chapter by chapter with their personal support, their confirmation that I was on the right track, and with their criticisms. Finally, and most important, my deepest appreciation goes to Nancy, my wife. Not only did she put up with my oddity during the actual writing, but she took a crude and incomplete text, edited it, verified data, and turned it all into a book.

When is a book finished? When you get tired of revising it! I am more aware than ever of the incompleteness of this work. That is due partly to my own inability to comprehend thoroughly some of the issues involved and partly to the fact that many of these issues still need to work themselves out in our times. My hope is that I have been able to identify the significant factors and indicate general directions for resolution. I have also included exercises and further readings at the end of the chapters so that everyone can contribute their own thoughts and experiences to the task of understanding the role of a market economy in our world. While I have focused on making the presentations suitable for group learning, I believe the book can be read privately as well. The important thing is that we all move forward with a clearer vision of the tremendous challenge and opportunity we all share in bringing our world closer to its fullest potential.

1

A Free-Market Economy

The Solution or the Problem?

A morality that believes itself able to dispense with the technical knowledge of economic laws is not morality but moralism. . . .

A scientific approach that believes itself capable of managing without an ethos misunderstands the reality of man.

Today we need a maximum of specialized economic understanding but also a maximum of ethos so that specialized economic understanding may enter the service of the right goals.

Cardinal Joseph Ratzinger (Pope Benedict XVI)

THE ISSUE

Perhaps nothing creates greater extremist emotional response than terms like capitalism, big business, corporations, global economy. The range of opinions runs along similar extremes. There is much conflict and confusion. Consider the following indications.

- With the collapse of communism, some form of market economics remains the only viable alternative.
- A free-market economy is the best means of creating prosperity and lifting the largest number of people out of poverty.
- The heartland of the market economy, western Europe and the United States, is staggering under the weight of corporate scandals and cynicism about how "free" markets really are.
- India and China, following the earlier initiatives of Japan, Taiwan, and Korea, are demonstrating just how effectively a market economy can create prosperity. At the same time they are also witnesses to resultant social stratification, displacement of families, and cultural breakdown.

1

- In Africa, corporations harvest its natural resources but leave only a small percentage of the population (usually the political leaders) enriched.
- A free-market economy is only a cloak for the rich to get richer at the expense of the poor.
- Globalization is exporting the good jobs of the West to people willing to work for substandard wages.
- Humane cultural values are being wiped out by the relentless onslaught of impersonal market forces.
- A market economy creates jobs and careers that allow for a future beyond the self-perpetuating cycle of subsistence farming.
- A market economy creates the wealth that is necessary to improve education and health as well as to provide a necessary base for a free society.
- Corporations have more economic resources than some nations and so have the power to virtually enslave their populations.
- A free-market economy leads to a materialism that can suck the soul out of religion.

A number of issues become ever clearer. The question of a market economy is not a peripheral one. It raises issues that are central to our future. The issue is not limited to some one part of our world. It affects every person, every nation, and every part of the globe. No one today lives completely outside of a global market economy. The issue is highly charged emotionally, precisely because it gets to the core of our lives. Opinions about the nature and the impact of a market economy are wildly polarized and seem to be grounded more in personal character than in reasoned reflection. There is a need to find some understanding that can begin to make sense of some of the disparate knee-jerk reactions to the concrete effects of a market economy.

The focus of this book, then, is to work through an understanding of the nature of a market economy, how business works, what drives it, what kind of outcomes one can hope for, and what are its limitations. There can be no serious attempt to do theology in a global perspective without coming to grips with the fact that a free-market economy plays a key role in any global perspective. For that reason alone it would be worth our effort to deepen our understanding of the actual dynamics of a market economy.

Moral Options

Most people, I believe, want to do what's right. As we grow into adulthood we try to be decent, responsible people who take our word and our commitments seriously. We try to be fair and honest. We love those close to us, are considerate to those we meet casually, and maintain a basic respect for all people. All of this works fairly well at the level of our personal lives and activities. But how do we take that basic sense of decency into the larger worlds of work and business?

If we are religious we can turn to our Sacred Scriptures and find fairly well defined patterns of personal moral living. But what happens when we move out of our personal worlds to the vastly larger world of business and global interdependencies where our conduct involves not only ourselves, our families and friends, but the whole human race? How does our basic sense of decency play out in that world?

One of the cultural shocks I received when I returned to teaching after twenty years in the business world involved the general estimation of business itself. Here were adult students who had families and full-time jobs coming to evening courses to finish a bachelor's or master's degree at considerable personal sacrifice in order to advance their professional business careers. Business, they assured me, is sleazy, extremely suspect, and by and large immoral. How then, I asked them, could they devote so much of their time, talent, and energy to it? Even further, why would they commit even more effort to additional studies in order to move even deeper into the business world? Their answers were very straightforward—we want to make more money! Here were honest responses from people who were energetic, responsible adults with more than an average moral sense. How did they reconcile business and their own moral sense of right and wrong? Over the years I have recognized four general responses to that question.

I need to make a living.

This is the first and most common response. It is also the most unreflective. It states the obvious but doesn't go any further. The rationale goes something like this: Business is what it is, immoral or amoral, but I need a job to pay the bills, to provide for myself and my family as the case may be. Business is necessary to provide me with the money I need to stay alive, to be a responsible parent, a helpful neighbor, an honest member of society. In other words, my salary allows me to be moral and responsible in the rest of my life, an obligation that I take very seriously. However, that still leaves me with the conclusion that the engagement of most of my time, talent, energy is immoral either by cooperation or association. How does one justify or redeem so much evil? Does the end really justify the means? Another version of this position is to go along with doing what is necessary now, but with the intent of being more ethical and responsible once one gets established. This is a particular rationale of the young professional getting established in a career.[1]

---

1. Howard Gardner, Mihaly Csikszentmihalyi, and William Damon, *Good Work: When Excellence and Ethics Meet* (New York: Basic Books, 2001). The entire work is a profound study of the necessary conditions for a person to produce both excellent work and be ethical within a given profession.

I try to be moral in my own job.
This second pattern openly acknowledges the immorality that governs business activity but responds by trying to be moral in personal business dealings. The company might be corrupt, but I am honest and fair in what I do at work. "My desk" or "my department" is clean, whatever else might be going on. I try to carve out a little island of morality in my corner of the corporation. However, this stance also gives up on the larger picture. Morality retreats totally to personal morality. But is that really possible? Is my personal morality not always forced to the ugly compromises that are required by necessity in order to interact with the larger "immoral" operations of the company? At best, morality is always under siege and compromised while the individual is consistently in a no-win situation.

We don't do anything illegal.
A third position attacks the problem by recognizing that companies operate in the public domain and so are held responsible to the larger world by law and regulation. By observing the law, one's moral responsibility is fulfilled. In effect, business ethics becomes the equivalent of "staying out of trouble." Hence, an arsenal of lawyers, PR people, and human resource personnel are engaged in "keeping the corporate nose clean." Every dilemma is addressed as a legal issue. It becomes an issue of "risk management." Just as companies buy insurance for product liability and workplace injury, so corporate values and legal conduct become means for protecting the company from legal, financial, or adverse publicity risks. This position at least acknowledges some real accountability of the organization as such, especially by providing a basis for cooperation with other dimensions of the social order. However, it tends to do so by keeping that accountability to a minimum. What do we need to do to avoid problems? How far can we go? More fundamentally, this position assumes that morality is really something extrinsic to the important concerns of the business itself. The only recourse is to somehow fence it in legally so that the evil can be contained. On this basis business leaders will have no more than a passing interest in ethics since it is peripheral to the real concerns of business.

Government needs to regulate business.
This is a clear acknowledgment that business by its nature is suspect and the source of much that is wrong with the world. Only a greater power can keep business in check and set limits to the ever-expanding greed of the corporation that will devour anything in its path—natural resources, people, communities, nations. And that stronger (and more ethical?) power is government. Of course, that solution rests on the assumption that somehow, by nature,

business is immoral and government is moral—hardly a premise that will stand up to much scrutiny! More will have to be said on the relation of business and government in later sections of the book.

The fundamental problem with each of these patterns is that they position ethics *outside* of business. On the assumption that business itself is immoral, or amoral at best, then ethics can only have an incidental relation to what business is really all about. Basically then, the only moral response is some form of *containment*. Business must be contained either by (1) not letting it spread to other aspects of my life; (2) keeping my personal business activity honest; or (3) fencing it in by laws and regulations.

This picture of business has important consequences both for the corporation and for the individual. *For the corporation*, it means that the organization tends to become depersonalized. Companies are merely "legal fictions" defined by law and governed by economic abstractions such as global markets, return on investment, and the bottom line. However, the fact is that there is no such thing as a "multinational corporation." There is only General Motors, Intel, Abbott Labs, Sony, IBM, Unilever, Exxon, Citicorp, Philips, Toyota, etc. In other words, they are flesh-and-blood people organized to make something happen. They are thousands of companies and millions of persons making billions of decisions and choices each day. Most are decent persons, neither heroes nor monsters. They are not faceless forces. They are persons and relationships. Only persons make decisions and exercise choices. Only people are moral or immoral. Once that is lost sight of, "forces at work" and "economic realities" become the determining factors. And then morality is diminished to legal posturing with all its devastating and corrosive effects.

For the individual, the positioning of ethics at the fringes of business also has devastating effects. It implies that ethics really has little or nothing to do with successful business. It assumes that business is by its very nature immoral, greedy, trashy, cut-throat. At the same time, however, people everywhere are more and more consumed by their work. Two-income families, computers, Internet, cell phones, 24/7 work weeks all conspire to demand more time and devotion for the world of business. If business is really immoral, then how do we reconcile "making a living" with living a moral, and consequently human, life? If what takes up most of our time, energy, and talent is corrupt, how is human living not relegated to the periphery of our life? Or even more telling, how can we possibly not become what we give ourselves to so completely? We all tend to become what we associate with. If business is as consuming as it has become, do we really believe that we are not profoundly shaped by that reality? Many of our most creative hours and intense engagements occur at work. Do we really believe that they are not going to have an essential influence on who we are and what we do? Such are the issues we face. Far from going away, they are growing more central as economic realities become more dominant in defining our very existence.

> If you could know only *one* thing about a person,
> what would you want to know?

Try this on for size. Imagine yourself in a chat room on the Internet and you could only know one thing about the person with whom you are communicating. Remember, you cannot see this person and have no idea where in the world the person lives. What would be the *one* thing that would give you the best sense of that person—gender, nationality, marital status, religion, race, education level, age, neighborhood, etc.? Consider whether "what one does for a living" might not be the most defining. Increasingly, one's profession or work gives the best *single* perspective on a person's identity. Whether someone is a social worker, a doctor, farmer, an assembly-line worker, a certified public accountant, a manager, or a plumber will probably tell you more about the person than race, sex, or religion. For better or worse, contemporary society is delineated in economic terms. Different periods of history tend to be identified by their prevailing characteristic as, for instance, the Age of Religion or the Age of Reason. I believe our current age would have to be defined as the Age of Economics, or perhaps the Age of Business. "It's all about money, stupid" sums up much of our analysis of situations.

At the same time, we have perhaps never been more cynical about business. Opinions run from a "conglomerate of greedy behavior" to a "moral no-man's land" governed by impersonal (hence amoral) laws of market forces. As the joke goes: *What is the opposite of wrong?* Answer: *Poor.* You can test your own cynicism quotient. See table 1.

That business ethics is more than just common sense and goodwill should be evident by now. To say that either a person is moral and so knows how to be ethical in business or the person is immoral and there is nothing business can do about it is to duck the issue. James Rest, a scholar in professional ethics, has argued that "to assume that any 20-year-old of good general character can function ethically in professional situations is no more warranted than assuming that any logical 20-year-old can function as a lawyer without special education."[2] The world of business—as the worlds of medicine, law, and accounting—has its own particular dynamics and structures that must be understood if ethics is to have any internal relevance and not just be some type

---

2. Linda Klebe Treviño and Katherine A. Nelson, *Managing Business Ethics: Straight Talk about How to Do It Right*, 2nd ed. (New York, John Wiley & Sons, 1999), 10.

Table 1

Answer the following questions as honestly as you can. Circle the number between 1 and 5 that best represents your own beliefs about business.[3]	Strongly Agree			Strongly Disagree	
1. Financial gain is all that counts in business.	1	2	3	4	5
2. Ethical standards must be compromised in business practice.	1	2	3	4	5
3. The more financially successful the businessperson, the more unethical the behavior.	1	2	3	4	5
4. Moral values are irrelevant in business.	1	2	3	4	5
5. The business world has its own rules.	1	2	3	4	5
6. Businesspersons care only about making profit.	1	2	3	4	5
7. Business is like a game—one plays to win.	1	2	3	4	5
8. In business, people will do anything to further their own interests.	1	2	3	4	5
9. Competition forces business managers to resort to shady practices.	1	2	3	4	5
10. The profit motive pressures managers to compromise their ethical concerns.	1	2	3	4	5

Is there a pattern? Think about the reasons for your responses. Be prepared to discuss them.

of external constraint to unbridled immorality. The statements from Treviño and Nelson add an even more pessimistic confirmation: "Research has found that students in business ranked lower in moral reasoning than students in philosophy, political science, law, medicine and dentistry. And undergraduate business students and those aiming for a business career have been found to be more likely to engage in academic cheating (test cheating, plagiarism, etc.) than students in other majors or those heading toward other careers."[4]

The dilemma of making a life and not just a living can only deepen in this type of environment. How we position ethics becomes even more important

3. Treviño and Nelson, *Managing Business Ethics*, 18-19.
4. Treviño and Nelson, *Managing Business Ethics*, 11.

as we come to understand that our personal identity is the result of our moral being. Charles Taylor, in his monumental work on the making of the modern identity, has summed it up succinctly when he says:

> To know who you are is to be oriented in moral space, a space in which questions arise about what is good or bad, what is worth doing and what not, what has meaning and importance for you and what is trivial and secondary. . . . We are only ourselves insofar as we move in a certain space of questions, as we seek and find an orientation to the good.[5]

We are destined to a fragmented if not schizophrenic identity if the larger part of our time, talent, and energy is absorbed by activity that is, at best, suspect if not outright immoral.

THE PURPOSE OF BUSINESS

A further complication to our issue comes from the fact that the corporation has become the prevailing image of business. A corporation, by definition, is a legal entity, not a person. How then can a corporation be responsible since responsibility, or morality, is a distinctly human attribute? This notion of the amorality of the corporation has a long history that was expressed most colorfully in the question Did you ever expect a corporation to have a conscience, when it has no soul to be damned and no body to be kicked? This notion of the corporation as an obviously "artificial" and "intangible" entity makes it unsuitable for punishment or moral accountability. Since corporations are only "artificial persons," so the reasoning goes, they can only have "artificial responsibilities," better understood as "legal obligations." We need to remember that the corporate form of business is a rather recent phenomenon. It only came to be used extensively for business in England in the latter part of the nineteenth century. The size and influence of today's corporations far exceed anything even remotely imaginable by the initial proponents of what can be called the "corporate fiction" doctrine, which implies that the corporation is not a proper subject of moral assessment. It is only an instrument of commerce. Indeed the earliest corporations were set up in England under royal charters to develop foreign trade and colonies in other parts of the world. As such, they were merely neutral instruments of commerce, extensions of their shareholders' property rights. In some way, this ambiguity still lies at the heart of the two current and divergent views of the corporation and, by implication, of business in general.

---

5. Charles Taylor, *Sources of the Self: The Making of the Modern Identity* (Cambridge, Mass.: Harvard University Press, 1989), 28.

The first view, considered classic, is most often associated with the Nobel Prize–winning economist Milton Friedman. *A corporation's primary and perhaps sole purpose is to maximize profits for stockholders.*[6] His main arguments are twofold. First, stockholders are the owners of the corporation, and hence corporate profits belong to them. Second, stockholders have a different relationship to the corporation than all other participants. Other participants have some type of contract: employees get salaries; customers get goods; the community gets taxes. Once everyone gets what has been agreed to, the rest is what is called profit and rightly goes to the shareholders/owners. By the same token, if the business fails, the shareholders lose everything. It's a different type of commitment. It's like the relationship of the chicken and the pig to a ham-and-eggs breakfast—for the one it's a contribution; for the other it's a total commitment!

Before dismissing this position as being too crass and materialistic, let's consider its real strength. It is not an immoral position. It insists that contracts are to be honored. Goods and services are to be exchanged as agreed to by all parties. If anyone feels unfairly treated, they can enter into new contracts. Public laws are to be obeyed. If the common good of the community (e.g., clean water) is being threatened, then the community has a democratic process for creating laws and statutes that corporations have a duty to obey. What Friedman seems to be driving at is that business has a very important but also very specific purpose that becomes distorted if it is not clearly delineated. For example, should a company donate to charity? Not to any significant degree if it takes away from profits. This is money that the individual shareholders should be able to use or contribute as they see fit. Is it not better for each shareholder, rather than a CEO, to determine which charities are considered important or worthwhile? How can a company decide what a community needs: better schools, more parks, cleaner environment? Should not the community through its own democratic processes decide on its own common good? In other words, business needs to restrict its activity to maximizing shareholder value and not impose its will on the broader activities of the human community. To dilute the purpose of business with nonbusiness concerns can easily lead to business doing poorly on both scores. It becomes less profitable because of the lack of focus and intrudes arbitrarily into social concerns since it bypasses the democratic process. The specific focus of business on maximizing shareholder value has the effect of enhancing individual freedom and the democratic process. There are enough horror stories of company towns and company stores. Who should decide how much and to whom

---

6. Robert G. Kennedy, *The Good That Business Does* (Christian Social Thought Series 9; Grand Rapids, Mich.: Acton Institute, 2006), 88.

charitable contributions are to be made? Who should decide what a community needs for its own good? Is the current drift toward expecting that business justify itself by being responsible in some way for local schools, parks,
health care, elder care, and day care be really just an acknowledgment of the
ineffectiveness of society to handle these issues? And will any of this really
matter unless there are enough profits to create an economically free society?
There is much to be said for Friedman's position.

On the other hand there is a competing understanding of the responsibilities of business called the stakeholder theory, most often associated with the
name of R. Edward Freeman.[7] It begins with the recognition that there are
indeed many different parties with a legitimate "stake" in the corporation.
While their specific interests will vary, they must each be recognized if the
corporation is to thrive. These stakeholders and their interests are usually
identified as follows:

> *Stockholders* expect financial return on investment.
> *Employees* expect jobs providing decent livelihood.
> *Customers* expect products as promised.
> *Managers* expect empowerment to direct company activity.
> *Suppliers* expect reasonable payment.
> *Local Communities* expect tax base and social contribution.

While the stakeholder theory definitely broadens a narrow and one might say
distorted application of Friedman's understanding, it does not resolve the
issue of corporate purpose. The question still remains as to how one arbitrates
among the conflicting claims of the various stakeholders. What are the specific rights and responsibilities of each stakeholder group? And how does that
translate financially? It is a question that becomes concrete at every negotiation, whether that be to agree on a customer sale, on an annual budget, or on
a new union contract. A Friedmanite would still say that the only way to
resolve such conflicts is to keep focus on maximizing shareholder value. All of
the competing claims are legitimate enough but need to be settled on the
basis of what will make the most profit in the long run.

The stakeholder theorist would say the answer is to do the "right thing" for
each group. But how, for instance, is a CEO to determine what the right thing
is for each interest? Will not each interest group argue its own vested interest? Will the balance simply mean that each stakeholder will be equally disappointed? Is the theory too idealistic? What, for instance, is the right thing
if a company needs to cut costs (and jobs) to return to profitability? No one

---

7. R. Edward Freeman heads the (University of Virginia) Darden School of Business's Olsson
Center for Applied Ethics, one of the world's leading academic centers for the study of ethics.

well, a third to the study of things which are capable of demonstration."[13] The writer is now Clement of Alexandria called the founder of Eastern, or Greek, theology.

Each of the two theologians tells a part of the story. The one part is that the Kingdom of God and other-worldly values relativize all else. It is not wrong to hold fast to an other-worldly faith or to prefer it to a humanism or an economic activity that is entirely of this world. There is a dimension of the human person that cannot be reduced to economic terms.

The other part of the story is that faith is always embodied in concrete living. The church begins moving out of its closed circle of waiting for the Lord to living its faith within the larger world and engaging the culture of the Roman Empire. The history of the church can be understood as a shifting from emphasizing one part or the other of the two poles. Augustine's city of God and city of man play out their intrinsic tension in the history of the Western church—from monasticism to medieval Christendom, from pope to prince, from Crusaders to mystics, from Reformation to Reform, from faith to reason, from rebellion to reaction. There is no easy synthesis.

The Second Vatican Council was a definite shift back to Clement of Alexandria's part of the story. In perhaps the most important document of that council, the *Pastoral Constitution on the Church in the Modern World*, there is this opening statement:

> The joys and the hopes, the griefs and the anxieties of the people of this age, especially those who are poor or in any way afflicted, these too are the joys and hopes, the griefs and anxieties of the followers of Christ. Indeed, nothing genuinely human fails to raise an echo in their hearts.[14]

The document goes on affirming the genuine values of our age. Here is a sampling of issues closer to our business concerns:

> Laborers and farmers [read: all people involved in economic activity] seek not only to provide for the necessities of life but to develop the gifts of their personality by their labors, and indeed to take part in regulating economic, social, political, and cultural life. (*Gaudium et Spes* 9).

> God did not create the human person as a solitary. For from the beginning "male and female he created them" (Gen. 1:27) . . . For by our innermost nature we are social beings, and unless we relate ourselves to others we can neither live nor develop our potential. (*Gaudium et Spes* 12)

---

13. Crowe, *Appropriating the Lonergan Idea*, 165.

14. Vatican Council II, *Gaudium et Spes*, Pastoral Constitution on the Church in the Modern World, art. 1 (cited with the article number of the official edition following).

> Profound and rapid changes make it particularly urgent that no one . . .
> content themselves with a merely individualistic morality . . . the obli-
> gations of justice and love are fulfilled only if each person . . . also pro-
> motes and assists the public and private institutions dedicated to
> bettering the conditions of human life. (*Gaudium et Spes* 30)

> Through our labors and our native endowments we have ceaselessly
> striven to better our life . . . many benefits once looked for, especially
> from heavenly powers, we have now enterprisingly procured for our-
> selves. (*Gaudium et Spes* 33)

> Throughout the course of the centuries, people have labored to better
> the circumstances of their lives through a monumental amount of indi-
> vidual and collective effort. (*Gaudium et Spes* 34)

> For when we work we not only alter things and society, we develop our-
> selves as well. We learn much, we cultivate our resources, we go outside
> of ourselves and beyond ourselves. (*Gaudium et Spes* 35)

Yet, for all the glowing appreciation of earthly activity, the document does not
let us forget the other pole of the tension.

> We do not know the time for the consummation of the earth and
> humanity. Nor do we know how all things will be transformed. . . . But
> we are taught that God is preparing a new dwelling place and a new
> earth where justice will abide . . . the expectation of a new earth must
> not weaken but rather stimulate our concern for cultivating this one. For
> here grows the body of a new human family, a body which even now is
> able to give some kind of foreshadowing of the new age.
>   Earthly progress must be carefully distinguished from the growth of
> Christ's kingdom. Nevertheless, to the extent that the former can con-
> tribute to the better ordering of human society, it is of vital concern to
> the kingdom of God. (*Gaudium et Spes* 39)

The Pastoral Constitution on the Church in the Modern World does two
important things. First, it states unequivocally that there is an intrinsic connection between business and morality. It affirms that human activity, of
which business is an important instance, has a purpose and a meaning that is
ultimately both moral and religious. Second, it states that human activity has
lasting value. Business, in other words, is not just something to do while we
wait for the Kingdom. It doesn't just put food on the table. Rather our activ-

- wealth without work
- pleasure without conscience
- knowledge without character
- commerce without morality
- science without humanity
- worship without sacrifice
- politics without principle

Is this not similar to saying the activity of humans must always be moral if it is not to self-destruct? Give examples of each of these social sins.

3. The Judeo-Christian scriptures begin in nature (the garden of the book of Genesis) and end in the city (the Heavenly Jerusalem of the Apocalypse). Is this just accidental or does it say something about a human vocation to create or co-create? Explain.

4. Explore how your understanding of yourself, the world, and God will impact your attitude to work. Cultural and religious differences can play critical roles. If, for instance, human achievement is measured in how well one fits into the community (however that is defined), then one would take a dim view of work as changing the community and the environment.

5. U.S. culture, especially U.S. law, is strongly focused on individual rights and self-sufficiency. European and many other cultures have a broader focus on social interdependency. Consider how this affects the business environment; for example, laws about business lay-offs. Is one model better than the other?

6. Trust is a basic virtue for the conduct of business. If trust is extended only to the family or to the tribe (nation?), consider the difficulties this creates for the business enterprise.

SUGGESTIONS FOR FURTHER READING AND STUDY

Freeman, R. Edward, *Strategic Management: A Stakeholder Approach.* Boston: Pitman, 1984. A more detailed presentation of the stakeholder theory.

Friedman, Milton. "The Social Responsibility of Business Is to Increase Its Profits." *New York Times Magazine*, September 30, 1970.

———. *Capitalism and Freedom.* Chicago: University of Chicago Press, 1962.

Neafsey, John. *A Sacred Voice Is Calling.* Maryknoll, N.Y.: Orbis Books, 2006. A perceptive exploration of the meaning of vocation from a psychological, social, and biblical perspective.

Novak, Michael. *Business as a Calling: Work and the Examined Life.* New York:

Free Press, 1996. A deeper understanding of how a life in business can truly be understood as a vocation.

_____. *The Spirit of Democratic Capitalism*. New York: Simon & Schuster, 1982. An overview of a market economy within a democratic society.

_____. *The Catholic Ethic and the Spirit of Capitalism*. New York: Free Press, 1993. A further exploration of the relation of a market economy to a moral foundation.

Web site: workingknowledge@hbs.edu This site is a product of the Harvard Business School and continues on a weekly basis to explore business issues from many different perspectives. It is an excellent source for staying current with the latest concerns of business. The entry for February 9, 2004, by Carla Tishler gives an excellent short history of the relation of the corporation to ethics.

2

A Better Way to Think about Business

When business is cut off from the rest of the human enterprise, in such slogans as "business is business," for example, cynics suggest what is simply not true.

Business is not "just business." It is not self-contained, with its own rationale, its own rules, its own reason for being. It is, essentially, a part of human life and human community.

Robert C. Solomon, *A Better Way to Think about Business*

In chapter 1 we explored the relation of business activity to ethics and have come to recognize that business is essentially a human activity. If it is human, then by that fact, it has an ethical and, for many, an ultimately religious dimension. Ethics is not a mindless set of restraints imposed on a mindless set of amoral or premoral practices which we call business. In this chapter we need to take the next step and reexamine the function of business in human society. If business activity needs to be positioned solidly within human activity, then the role of business needs to be examined in its role within the larger human community.

This is all the more urgent because North Americans seem to have an unrealistic love-hate relationship to business. On the one hand we thrive on business. As the saying goes, "The business of America is business." Or as one Italian immigrant put it, "If I worked this hard in Italy, I could be rich there too!" The United States has some of the biggest and best business schools in the world. English is the common language of business. This country is admired worldwide for entrepreneurship and the ability to develop a steady stream of new inventions. For better or worse, the United States ranks at the top for number of hours worked per week among developed countries. Its heroes are the great "captains of industry," from the Carnegies, Fords, Rockefellers of history to the Welches, Waltons, and Gateses of our times. The American Dream is the rags-to-riches fantasy. Indeed, who is it that has come by the millions to this country to find a better life? It was largely the poor then, and it is the poor now, who come to find freedom and to break out of poverty. And how were so many people able to be assimilated into this country and reach their dream, if not in their own lives, at least in the lives of their children? What fed the dream that things would get better? It was, and is, the fact that business flourished. It is interesting to note that 1776 was the same year that the U.S. founders penned the Declaration of Independence, a charter of basic rights and freedoms, and Adam Smith penned *The Wealth of Nations*, a charter for a free-market economy—a historic moment indeed.

On the other hand we have this deep cynicism about business. Try the following exercise.

> How would you spontaneously imagine the purpose of the following professions:
>
>   a. doctor
>   b. teacher
>   c. scientist
>   d. lawyer
>   e. police officers
>   f. plumber
>   g. businessperson
>
> Quickly write out your own responses before checking against these common responses. a. Promotes healing; b. facilitates learning; c. seeks knowledge; d. promotes justice; e. protects the public; f. provides water flow; g. makes money.

But do not doctors and plumbers and lawyers also make money? Are not police officers and teachers concerned about making as much money as the market can reasonably bear? And yet we tend spontaneously to associate the businessperson with money and the other professions with some value to society. Once we allow this disconnect, we move almost spontaneously to the dichotomy of finding the morality of business in the fact that it provides me with a salary that allows me to be ethical in the other, "more human," dimensions of my life. Business itself falls into the same pattern when it seeks to justify its existence by financial contributions to worthwhile causes such as supplementing school funding, fighting Aids in Africa, etc. Not that there is anything wrong with these activities. The problem lies in business' use of these activities to justify or "redeem" itself—as if business had no worthwhile end in itself.

We are usually quick to add that money is not somehow evil. It's just not a value in the immediate sense that we identify with other professions. Rather, it is a means that can be used for any number of purposes. The problem is at least as old as Aristotle. The acquisition of wealth, he says, has three purposes. The first is the direct acquisition of goods needed to run a household. Its natural limit is what is required for the household to function well. The second purpose is to adjust for the inequalities of nature—the farmer and fisherman can exchange goods because of their different geographical locations. Again, it is limited by the realization of the goods of society. It was the third purpose of money that made Aristotle wary—the use of money to make money. For Aristotle, it is when money is cut off from the concerns of society that money becomes unnatural.[1] Granted that Aristotle's world did not know of an economy where capital formation was integral to genuine development, he did recognize an inherent danger of amassing a commodity that had no internal limit or intrinsic value. As he put it,

> The art of healing aims at producing unlimited health, and every other skill aims at its own end without limit, wishing to secure that to the highest possible degree; on the other hand the *means* towards the end are not unlimited, the end itself setting the limit in each case. Similarly, there is no limit to the end which this kind of acquisition [money making money] has in view, because the end is wealth in that form, i.e., the possession of goods.[2]

Since there is no internal end/control, one can use wealth simply to accumulate more wealth, in order to accumulate more wealth, in order to accumulate more wealth, and so forth. Contrary to other skills, the skill of making money has no term or built-in limit, no way to judge its own success (e.g., the doctor judges efforts by the resulting health of the patient). Unless one moves beyond the circle of making money, one can only judge success by making even more money. Or, to put it in a different way, as long as you stay in the framework of "making money," how do you answer the question of "when is enough, enough?" Aristotle identifies two unnatural conditions: the use of

---

1. For a summary history of the unnaturalness of accumulating money. see Robert G. Kennedy, *The Good That Business Does* (Christian Social Thought Series 9; Grand Rapids, Mich.: Acton Institute, 2006), 7–15.

2. Aristotle, *The Politics* 1257b25, trans. T. A. Sinclair; revised and re-presented by Trevor J. Saunders, in *Aristotle: The Politics* (London: Penguin Books, 1981), 84.

to show he didn't know how to swim! How much do we ourselves unconsciously buy into them and so justify business on some other basis? Seldom, if
ever, is there a theoretical framework to justify the accusation in a coherent
way. Somehow, whatever is wrong in the contemporary market economy is
uncritically attributed to the very nature of a market economy. The solution,
often uncritically accepted, is for government to control, regulate, even run
business and so to solve all the problems of a market economy.

One could make a similar list of accusations against, for example, the reality of a free press: sensationalism, manipulation, glorification of crime and
violence, sexual license, undermining of morals and religion, superficiality,
outright lies, and prejudices. Yet no one would want the government to be a
censor of everything printed! We accept the fact that some of the excesses and
failures of a free press need to be tolerated for two reasons: first, there is such
an intrinsic value to having a free press that it is worth the wrongs, and, second, there is a basically sound internal dynamism to a free press that it will
correct itself in the long run. Nevertheless, there is a large constituency of
politicians, religious leaders, and intellectuals who would abhor the thought
of government censorship of the press yet insist on government
censorship/control of economic activity in order to right its wrongs. Underlying this difference, I believe, is the perennial suspicion, or, perhaps more often,
ignorance of the very nature of business.

AN ALTERNATE VISION

Without doubt, business is the single largest institution of civil society. It is
larger than governments, churches, educational institutions. It unites more
people globally than any other type of organization. It would follow that the
moral health of a society depends to a great degree on the moral character of
business and its leaders. How one understands business and a market economy becomes a critical task of our age. It surely requires deeper and clearer
reflection than the current comments of most leaders, be they political, religious, or intellectual.

There are a number of emerging trends that provide the basis for a different perspective on the nature of a market economy. One important corrective
is the growing recognition that business is indeed a legitimate profession in
line with the notion of calling/vocation developed in chapter 1. The Harvard
Business School has as its motto To Make Business a Profession. Of course,
people in business are there to make money, but making money and the need
to make money are not restricted to businesspeople. Our doctor, teacher,
lawyer, plumber also make money and need to make money, but their work is

not *defined* by money. Only the hopeless cynic would say that the very *nature* of these professions is the quest to make money—except for business!

There is another reason to recognize business as a profession. A profession is usually defined by the specialized knowledge and skills required for its execution. The complexities of modern finance and accounting, global marketing and production, engineering and human resources call forth a level of knowledge and skill that rival any of the other professions. As a profession, then, business must assume responsibility to defend itself against fraudulent practice, to promote its social implications, and to pass on its skills and knowledge with integrity to the next generation. As a profession, it is called to develop a set of standards and practices by which its practitioners are measured.

More fundamental is a renewed focus on the nature of a market economy. There is a growing realization of the fact that business is really about something other than making money, while recognizing that making money is critical to any business. Three recent books, in particular, are very telling. The first, *A Better Way to Think about Business,*[5] subtitled *How Personal Integrity Leads to Corporate Success,* spells out in the first sixty-seven pages a total paradigm shift that grounds a comprehensive outlook on what business is really all about. The opening quote of this chapter is taken from that work.

The second work, *On Value and Values,*[6] outlines the realization that the world of value (money and wealth) is no longer adequate to the larger world of values we share, values that are no longer defined by geographical place.

> The world in which so many of us live [is]: a world of markets, networks, nations, organizations, friends and family. I call this a *world of purposes* and contrast it to the *world of places* our parents and grandparents inhabited. Billions of people on the planet continue to live—and to share fates—because of places. But not us. What we share with others—fates, ideas, roles, relationships—depends more on the purposes we bring to markets, networks, and organizations than the places we reside.[7]

The third work, *Development as Freedom,* is by the 1998 winner of the Nobel prize in economics, Amartya Sen.[8] In it he contends that the real measure of wealth cannot be calculated in dollars but in degrees of freedom achieved. In a telling summary he states,

---

5. Robert C. Solomon, *A Better Way to Think about Business: How Personal Integrity Leads to Corporate Success* (New York: Oxford University Press, 1999).

6. Douglas K. Smith, *On Value and Values: Thinking Differently about We in An Age of Me* (Upper Saddle River, N.J.: Financial Times Prentice Hall, 2004).

7. Smith, *On Value and Values,* xvi.

8. Amartya Sen, *Development as Freedom* (New York: Anchor Books, 2000; orig. published, New York: Knopf, 1999).

In fact, we generally have excellent reasons for wanting more income or wealth. This is not because income and wealth are desirable for their own sake, but because, typically, they are admirable general-purpose means for having more *freedom to lead the kind of lives we have reason to value.*[9]

What is taking place is more than just a variation on an old theme, more than just a rearrangement of individual parts while retaining old assumptions. What we are witnessing is a paradigm shift, a change in consciousness that colors all assumptions and questions every answer. It is a new framework for understanding everything. If there would be one word that captures this paradigm shift, it would have to be *interconnectedness.* Just as the shareholder theory is inadequate without the correction of stakeholder claims, so no part of business stands alone. Workers, customers, the environment, profits are all intrinsically interconnected. It is that interconnectedness that is being more and more consciously recognized.

Ancient societies are very instructive in this regard. They began with the assumption that one had to understand *everything* before one could understand *anything.* If indeed everything is interconnected, then religion and nature, history and seasons, roles and functions all had to be understood before one could understand oneself. One's life had to fit into the whole before it could make sense individually. In contrast, the Western analytic tradition since the Enlightenment took the opposite tack—the way to understand anything became a process of focusing more and more on individual objects. What was lost was the big picture. The current concern for interconnectedness, for ecosystems, for global economics and communication is a return to a more fundamental assumption that it is indeed necessary to understand everything before one can adequately understand anything. The new paradigm "takes ideas from quantum physics, cybernetics, chaos theory, cognitive science, and Eastern and Western spiritual traditions to form a worldview in which everything is interconnected."[10]

The paradigm shift that we are alluding to has implications on how we understand the nature of business. The real essence of business has been and continues to be about producing goods and services rather than about the one-dimensional simplification of "making money." Producing goods and services is not primarily a way of making money just as a doctor's focus on health is not primarily a way of making money. If one accepts that shift, as Robert Solomon argues so eloquently, then all sorts of general assumptions about business also shift. Here is what such a shift might look like.

---

9. Sen, *Development as Freedom*, 14 (italics added).
10. Linda Klebe Treviño and Katherine A. Nelson, *Managing Business Ethics: Straight Talk about How to Do It Right*, 2nd ed. (New York: John Wiley & Sons, 1999), 40.

Making Money	Producing Goods and Services
Competition driven by market forces	**Cooperation.** Competition actually demands more cooperation—with employees, suppliers, customers to produce a better product or service
Efficiency demands total control	**Human creativity** is the best means for promoting productivity
People are **replaceable parts**	People form a **group sharing common values**
People are **costs**	People produce **value**
Failure is equivalent to **defeat, destruction**	Failure improves chances of **future success**
Ethics is an external restraint on a free-for-all	**Virtue** is value/excellence embodied in action
Business is a **ruthless, cutthroat activity**	Business is **meaningful activity of adult life** and a major source of **self-worth and friendship**
"War, Game, Jungle"	"Meeting customer needs"
Greedy, self-serving individual	Honest, trustworthy team player
People **serve** purposes	People **have** purposes
"Business is business"	Goal of free enterprise is **general prosperity**

The implications of this shift in perspective will occupy us through most of the rest of the book.

BUSINESS AS THE DRIVER OF WORLD PROSPERITY

David Packard, cofounder of Hewlett-Packard, was ruminating on the reason why any company including his own would be in business:

> I want to discuss why a company exists in the first place. In other words, why are we here? I think many people assume, wrongly, that a company exists just to make money. While this is an important result of a company's existence, we have to go deep and find the real reason for our being. . . .
>
> As we investigate this, we inevitably come to the conclusion that a group of people get together and exist as an institution that we call a company so they are able to accomplish collectively what they would not be able to accomplish separately. *They make a contribution to society, a phrase which sounds trite but is fundamental.*[11]

To carry the question further one needs to ask, "And just what is the contribution that business makes to society?" Some statistical data can be instructive. In broad and overgeneralized categories, it is possible to identify three distinct types of human economic activity.

1. *Agriculture.* From about 3000 B.C., human activity moved from hunting and food gathering to herding animals and cultivating the soil. It was the first division of labor that allowed for specialization of roles in society. Subsistence farming and hunting were the major form of economic activity. While it did not increase productivity significantly, it did provide for a level of independence and self-esteem. In this type of economy the primary form of wealth was ownership of land.

2. *Industry.* With the development of the steam engine in the 1750s there is a further specialization of labor that initiated the great flow of manufactured goods to more and more people. It is the age of factories, machinery, and wages. The increases in productivity beyond mere survival were largely the result of equipment and technology. In this type of economy, wealth equates to the money/capital required to establish the means of production. The word "capitalist" comes from this era. Landowners became less relevant as the factory was not as dependent on land as the farmer was.

3. *Service/information.* Our own era can be dated to the 1950s with the spread of general literacy and the communication of ideas. The advent of computers and satellites only hastened its arrival. In this world, intelligence is

---

11. Jeffrey Hollender and Stephen Fenichell, *What Matters Most: How a Small Group of Pioneers Is Teaching Social Responsibility to Big Business and Why Big Business Is Listening* (New York: Basic Books, 2004), 202.

wealth. A good idea can procure the needed finance, and cyberspace trumps land (e.g., the dotcoms such as Amazon and Google). Knowledge workers are the new professionals. Six services are considered critical in a global economy: accounting, advertising, banking, insurance, law, and management consulting.[12]

Now the interesting correlation is to tie these three stages of activity to stages of prosperity. No doubt all three levels continue to be necessary, but the number of people involved in each level changes drastically. Sociologists speak of three general levels of socioeconomic status (SES) and identify countries that correspond to these levels. Although one could surely quibble about the exact numbers, the general pattern seems valid:

Table 2

	Agriculture	Industry	Service/info
Low SES/income countries (60 countries)	63%	15%	22%
Middle SES/income countries (90 countries)	32%	28%	40%
High SES/income countries (40 countries)	4%	28%	68%

What becomes strikingly clear is that countries grow in prosperity not by enriching farmers but by shifting the economy from agriculture to industry and service/information. In other words the specific contribution of business to society (in Packard's question) *is to increase the general prosperity of a society.*

Another statistical pattern, this one developed by the *Wall Street Journal*, is equally instructive. The *Journal* has developed what it calls an Index of Economic Freedom, which ranks the world's economies according to fifty economic variables in ten broad categories. They are banking and finance; capital flows and foreign investment; monetary policy; fiscal burden of government; trade policy; wages and prices; government intervention in the economy; property rights; regulation; and black markets. Although the *Journal* has a definite orientation to business, the statistical data are telling. While economic liberty has grown for seven straight years, most of the world's economies, eighty-two, remain mostly unfree or repressed, compared with seventy-three that are free or mostly free. Most significant is the fact that the world's poorest societies are also the most economically unfree. In other

---

12. *Chicago Tribune*, October 17, 2004.

words, they represent societies where business and free-market economics cannot flourish. Here is a sample of the ranking for 2005.

Table 3

Free	Mostly Free	Mostly Unfree	Repressed
1. Hong Kong	18. Germany	88. Colombia	145. Haiti
2. Singapore	27. Taiwan	91. Philippines	146. Venezuela
4. Estonia	30. Japan	92. Brazil	148. Iran
5. Ireland	31. Spain	123. Indonesia	149. Cuba
6. New Zealand	53. Sri Lanka	124. Russia	150. Laos
11. Chile	63. Mexico	134. Pakistan	153. Libya
12. United States	70. Malaysia	142. Nigeria	155. North Korea

Some of the *Journal*'s observations include the fact that the United States went from sixth to twelfth place in four years; that Latin America was moving in the direction of greater freedom, while North Africa and the Mideast actually declined; that Sub-Saharan Africa remains the most economically unfree region—and by far the poorest; and that the Asia-Pacific region contains some of the freest as well as most repressed economies. In summary, eighty-six countries are freer in 2005; fifty-seven are worse off; and twelve remain unchanged. A final statistic shows the freest economies have a per-capita income of $29,219, more than twice that of the "mostly free" at $12,839, and more than four times that of the "mostly unfree."

> This data is updated every year. As an exercise, go to the *Wall Street Journal* Web site at index.heritage.org and review current standings. Notice changes and try to discover new trends.

While individual points might be argued, the central link of business and prosperity can hardly be denied. There is a further implication here. Why are there rich nations and poor nations at all? Did the human race begin poor or rich? By some accounts the answer is obvious: the rich nations became rich by stealing from the poor nations, just as the wealthy became so by stealing from the poor. After all, if wealth is a defined and limited quantity, then the only way for one to have more than the other is by taking it first. The only way to have a larger slice of the pie is for someone else to have less. It is called zero-sum economics and can create gross misunderstandings of justice and misguided aid. It is another consequence of not making the intrinsic link of business to the creation of general prosperity. While it is true that wealth can be obtained by taking the possessions of others, it is more frequently created by the freedom and creativity of human action. The dramatic increase in wealth since the Industrial Revolution has occurred primarily through the creation of wealth, not by taking it from others. The world did not begin rich and then some became poor because their wealth was taken away. All started poor. The issue will be treated more extensively in chapter 9, "Globalization."

If increasing the general prosperity of society is understood as the result of business activity, then being a businessperson can be seen as having a value other than just being a means for making money. Correspondingly, business as a profession, along with doctors and scientists, is more genuinely grounded. Even more important for our purpose, an intrinsic relation of business and ethics can be more readily understood. While this is a necessary starting point, it is only that.

We have been looking at business activity from the viewpoint of its effects on society. This is instructive and necessary, but it should not overlook a basic point made by A. Sen:

> The freedom to exchange words, or goods, or gifts does not need defensive justification in terms of their favorable but distant effects; they are part of the way human beings in society live and interact with each other (unless stopped by regulation or fiat). The contribution of the market mechanism to economic growth is, of course, important, but this comes only after the direct significance of the freedom to interchange— words, goods, gifts—has been acknowledged . . . The freedom to participate in economic interchange has a basic role in social living.[13]

We have made the paradigm shift from "making money" to "producing goods and services." By now it should be clear that business is not some neutral, free-floating activity disconnected from the substance of human living and human community. If that is the case, then business activity has an intrinsic connection to the social and political life of a people. That issue is beyond the scope of this work. The relative merits of capitalism and socialism need to be explored and debated elsewhere. (A strong and clear defense of a market

---

13. Sen, *Development as Freedom*, 6-7.

economy" was no longer tied to the "real economy." Money became impatient, seeking quick short-term pay-outs rather than long-term investments.

- *1974—ERISA (Employee Retirement Income Security Act) is enacted into law.* Its purpose, noble indeed, was to guarantee that companies would be able to meet their pension obligations by setting aside reserves at the time the obligation is incurred. Huge amounts of money were dumped into the stock market—liquid money looking for the best return on investment. Adding to the rush were 401(k) monies. In effect, it took huge amounts of money out of the hands of business, which formerly paid out pension obligations from current operations and put it into the stock market, where it was controlled by Wall Street investors.

- *The focus shifted quickly to short-term results.* The price of stock becomes the key criterion of success. Deal makers and Wall Street were now in a position to dictate terms. As Carey says, "Mergers and acquisitions were rewarding ways for bankers, lawyers, and executives to make large amounts of money."[17] Interest focused exclusively on shareholder value to the detriment of the other stakeholders listed earlier in chapter 1. Cost cutting became the order of the day. Downsizing is easy to do and improves bottom-line results in the short term. To build a business for the long term is much more complex and demanding. Even if it involves cost cutting, it needs to be done in such a way as to promote the strengths of the organization and to cut excess or waste. The irony of the situation is that it was *the use of workers' money invested in stocks that provided the impetus to cut workers' jobs in order to improve short-term stock gains!* The satisfaction of building and selling products and services gradually changed into the excitement of making money on money. Investing for the long term, patient capital, gave way to short-term quick return—a formula for greed. Practices such as the use of profits to buy back company stock in order to keep the company stock price high rather than using profits for new investment became common. The focus shifts from productivity in goods and services to the value of the stock.

A number of other developments only added to the building momentum.

- *Growth of leveraged speculation.* Carey makes the startling statement that "During the 1990s industry was putting more capital into the stock market in stock buy-backs and mergers than it was taking out in new capital for growth!"[18] In general, he says, "The idea that the stock market is a

17. Carey, *Democratic Capitalism*, 256.
18. Carey, *Democratic Capitalism*, 212.

source of growth capital is exaggerated, for its true mission is to make money on money."[19] Even banks, which traditionally played a conservative role in stabilizing money, have entered the theater of Wall Street speculation. That speculation is further fueled by the fact that it is so highly leveraged. By passing the Commodities Futures Act in 2000, Congress effectively allowed speculators to buy stock futures for ten cents on the dollar. Imagine how much less speculation would result from a requirement to put up 50 percent of the bet by the speculator.[20]

- *Deregulated banking—too big to fail.* The notion that the failure of large financial institutions would create havoc in the marketplace led to a creeping enlargement of government guarantees. In effect, market disciplines are eliminated. Banks no longer need to make loans anchored in a careful analysis of risk and reward since most of the risk has been removed from the equation. Speculation then plays a larger role, and money becomes more volatile. When government guarantees assume the risk of failure, then the market loses its focus on productivity.

- *Derivatives and reinsurance—one of the fastest growing and least understood financial instruments of our time.* In a way, derivatives and reinsurance represent a climax of speculating on speculation. Precisely because they speculate on a bundle of speculative issues, they can be highly arbitrary. Imagine trading in the future cost of currency together with the future value of a company's stock and some future value of its inventory—all unregulated by any governing body. It is a recipe for fraud, for inflated earnings to meet anyone's vested interest, and it comes with the added attraction of not needing to show results for at least several years. In this book, I can only mention this emerging issue. Its study and regulation, including its global implication, is another challenge of our time. Enron is one of the casualties.

This quick glance at financial markets creates more problems than solutions. Many of the issues raised here require a highly sophisticated understanding of economics. Other issues are entirely new, and still others will require further development before clear directions and determinations can be made. Then why bring up the question of ultracapitalism at all? Just let business be business and finance be finance.

Unfortunately, ultracapitalism and the total focus on short-term earnings per share can hold most companies hostage. Instead of Wall Street being at the service of business by providing the capital that drives economic prosper-

---

19. Carey, *Democratic Capitalism*, 213.
20. Carey, *Democratic Capitalism*, 300.

ity, it is the investor and speculator that set the goals for business. Failure to meet expected (by the investor) quarterly earnings by even tenths of a percentage point can send stock crashing, can threaten the viability of the CEO, and even the board of directors. This type of pressure can easily lead to inflated earnings, short-term cost reduction at the expense of long-term growth, and quick profits at the expense of needed capital investment. As a result, a company can lose direction, forget that it is about creating goods and services that promote general prosperity, and focus completely on the price of its stock and earnings per share. Ironically, the desire of each of us for maximum return on investments, be they personal retirement accounts like 401(k)s or IRAs or institutional assets that fund universities and not-for-profit charitable endeavors, fuels the momentum that creates the problem. There are no easy villains. It will take time, deeper understanding of what is really going on, and much wisdom and courage to come to grips with the consequences of ultracapitalism.

In the appendix to Carey's chapter on ultracapitalism, the author proposes ten reforms/corrections that are needed to counter the real threat of this momentum. These ten points of reform are not some simplistic blueprint for corporate integrity, but they certainly are key issues that government, a market economy faced with ultracapitalism, and a democratic citizenship intent on promoting prosperity for the largest number of people must address.

QUESTIONS FOR REFLECTION

1. Read "Natural and Unnatural Methods of Acquiring Goods" in Aristotle's *Politics* 1256b40-1258a27. Discuss both its pertinence and its inadequacy to current economic reality.
2. Do you look for the highest return on your personal investments? Does it not fuel a dangerous tendency identified as ultracapitalism? Make the case for each side.
3. Is there really a viable alternative to a market economy for promoting world prosperity? Discuss.
4. Is much of the current distrust and cynicism directed at business really misdirected? Would it not be better directed at what Carey identifies as ultracapitalism?
5. Does finance have an excessively dominant role in business today? Explain.

SUGGESTIONS FOR FURTHER READING AND STUDY

Carey, Ray. *Democratic Capitalism: The Way to a World of Peace and Plenty.* Bloomington, Ind: AuthorHouse, 2004. A must read for anyone wanting to understand a market economy more deeply. Includes an extensive bibliography.

Drucker, Peter F. *Post-Capitalist Society.* New York: HarperBusiness, 1993. A perceptive look at the future of a market economy. Anything by Drucker is worth reading. Always thoughtful, balanced, and well reasoned.

Jacobs, Jane. *Cities and the Wealth of Nations: Principles of Economic Life.* New York: Vintage Books, 1985. She brings business to the street level, as concrete human interaction.

Kirzner, Israel M. "The Ugly Market." In *The Morality of Capitalism,* ed. Mark W. Hendrickson, 138-51. Irvington-on-Hudson, N.Y.: Foundation for Economic Education, 1996

Kristol, I. *Two Cheers for Capitalism.* New York: Signet Books, 1979. This book first changed the way I looked at business.

Schumpeter, Joseph, *The History of Economic Analysis.* New York: Oxford University Press. 1954. The classical historical reference work.

3

Core Values and Culture

We've met executives from all over the world who aspire to create something bigger and more lasting than themselves—an ongoing institution rooted in a set of timeless core values, that exists for a purpose beyond just making money, and that stands the test of time by virtue of the ability to continually renew itself from within.

James C. Collins and Jerry I. Porras,
Built to Last

CORE VALUES

In chapter 2, we navigated through a critical and foundational shift in understanding the nature of business. Once the primary purpose of business is understood as producing goods and services rather than making money, a whole series of realignments needs to follow. It is not by accident that the book *Built to Last: Successful Habits of Visionary Companies* has become an international bestseller. What the authors, Jim Collins and Jerry Porras, have discovered and been able to substantiate with numerous examples is that the enduring and most successful companies are all driven by a core set of values that permeate the entire operation. Indeed, once the primary focus of a business shifts from making money to producing goods and services, then it must differentiate itself from its competitors by a thorough understanding of what it brings to the marketplace.

Even before Collins and Porras, their insight has been captured in what are considered the three classical business questions:

1. What is our business?
2. Who is our customer?
3. What does our customer consider valuable?

Many a business consultant has made a good living by helping companies answer those questions.

Nor should this realization come as a surprise at this point. Once the paradigm shift from making money to producing goods and services has been made, then core values become a necessary corollary. A business lives or dies on the perceived value of the goods/services it provides.

Try the following exercise:

> Write down a list of retail stores (or different brands of the same product) you are acquainted with.
>
> Then write after each name a few key words that characterize each store for you.
>
> Now reflect on how that characterization affects your own buying habits.

The core value or brand of a company is its single most important asset—its competitive advantage.

Business is spending more and more resources on the issues of competitive advantage and strategic initiatives. Unless a company first clarifies its competitive advantage, that is, the value it brings to a potential customer, it will be unable to evaluate its own performance. The ability to create value not only determines the fate of a business in the marketplace but also determines the internal operations of the company. A department—accounting, marketing, engineering, manufacturing—that is not adding strength/value to the ability to compete will find itself replaced or outsourced. Any individual who does not add value to an operation will be "downsized/right-sized." The whole company must be aligned to producing a value that the market is willing to pay for. In a global economy, those functions operate on a worldwide basis. As China has become, in effect, the manufacturing department of some businesses, so India has become the customer service and information technology departments for others. What drives the process is the need to create a value for which the market is willing to pay. "Making money" is a derivative of that function. Ultimately, and the emphasis is *ultimately*, no amount of coercion or hand-wringing will, or should, change that fact. Obviously, this must be examined much more closely—a task for chapter 9 on globalization. The important point for our consideration now is the realization that at any level of strategic thinking there is a value chain that determines the strength of a company's ability to compete. Value, or the *core value*, of a specific business becomes the critical issue for a company's survival.

The importance of "satisfying the customer," another common mantra of our time, can now be more fully appreciated. A customer is satisfied when there is a strong correlation between price and perceived value. We are also in a better position to understand that often-misunderstood quotation from Adam Smith, "We are fed, not by the benevolence, but by the self-interest of the butcher, baker and candlestick maker." It is self-interest that promotes the businessperson to provide customers with a product they will value, hence, be willing to pay for. In the marketplace, individuals engaged in voluntary exchanges can only promote their own interests by furthering the interests of others. Self-interest is not the same as greed, and profit is not a dirty word.

However, the meaning of that word "profit" needs closer scrutiny. There is an almost spontaneous notion that profits are somehow "added," often with a sense of deviousness, to the cost of goods in such a way as to take advantage of the consumer. In reality, profit represents the *difference* between the cost involved in providing a product or service and the value people place on it.[1] The cost must be below what people are willing to pay. The business that produces goods or provides services that people do not value at the cost required to produce them is not going to make a profit. The cost of a trip into space, for instance, is still higher than the value people, even those able to afford it, place on it. Unless it can change the cost or provide a product that will be valued, business will fail. It is the needs and wants of people that dictate who does and who does not make a profit. Again, we are a long way from looking at the nature of business as primarily "making money." Value is fundamental. Making money is a derivative, though essential, function. If a business is only about making money, then it is, paradoxically, on the way to not making money. This has the familiar ring of the words of Amartya Sen regarding wealth as the "means for having more freedom to lead the kind of lives we have reason to value."[2] We are once again at value and the role of business in the creation of value.

There is an additional advantage in a company's recognition of its core values. The issue is particularly relevant in an international economy. Collins and Porras make an important distinction between core values/enduring purposes and operating practices/business strategies. Core values must never change, while strategies and practices should always be changing in response to a changing world. A company that has a strong sense of its core values will be in a position to change its strategy as needed. Rooted in its prime identity, it will be open to meet differences brought on by changes in history or differences in culture. IBM, for instance, has navigated from adding machines to computer mainframes to PCs and still remains a formidable name in industry. Toyota has found a way to maintain quality manufacturing in various cul-

---

1. Mark W. Hendrickson, ed., *The Morality of Capitalism* (Irvington-on-Hudson, N.Y.: Foundation for Economic Education, 1996), 32-34.

2. Amartya Sen, *Development as Freedom* (New York, Anchor Books, 2000; orig. published, New York: Knopf, 1999), 14.

tures around the world. If a company does not have a clear focus on its core values, it is in danger of either resisting all changes of time and culture or of losing its identity by consistently failing to apply its fundamental values. It does not matter what the country of origin might be for a given company. Visionary companies, whether they originated in the East or in the West, need to be able to preserve their core values and to change cultural practices and strategic goals. Think of how drastically the following companies, recognized as visionary, have changed yet maintained a core identity: IBM (U.S.), Sony (Japan), Motorola (U.S.), Nestle (Europe), 3M (U.S.), FEMSA (Mexico), General Electric (U.S.), Ericsson (Europe), Unilever (Europe), and Disney (U.S.). The task of building core values is not an easy one, but it becomes more critical in a global economy. One need only reflect on how religions and governments have struggled with the same issues for a much longer time, and with mixed results. Consider, for example, the division of fundamentalists, liberals, and conservatives in Christianity, the orthodox, reformed, and conservative wings of Judaism, the liberal, conservative, and independent forms of democracy. All are attempts to deal with the issue of permanent core and changing practice. A clear identification and positive cultivation of core values as opposed to strategy and practice will go a long way in helping to meet the ever-accelerating changes that face the global business community on a daily basis.

What makes sense in theory is being confirmed in empirical studies that demonstrate a correlation between companies with a strong sense of core values and business success. *Fortune* magazine in March 1998 reported that if investors would have invested in its top ten most admired companies and reinvested the dividends, that investment would have produced three times the earnings of an investment in the Standard & Poor's 500 (the typical earnings of the market). In another study conducted by the management consulting firm of Towers Perrin, the market performance of twenty-five companies with strong reputations for public integrity and for being desirable places to work were tracked over a fifteen-year period. These companies—such as Southwest Airlines, Johnson & Johnson, Applied Materials, and Procter & Gamble—delivered a total shareholder return of 43 percent while shareholder return of the S&P 500 performed at 19 percent—less than half. In *Built to Last*, not only is the argument made for the necessity of core values but the actual stock performance of the selected visionary companies shows dramatically superior performance to the market in general.[3] The lesson here is not that good things happen to good people but that there seems to be some

---

3. James C. Collins and Jerry I. Porras, *Built to Last: Successful Habits of Visionary Companies* (New York: HarperBusiness, 1994), 6.

intrinsic relation between business value and business success. A company's reputation and trustworthiness are intangible, but vital, assets that need to be constantly cultivated. They are also very fragile.

Business is coming to the realization that corporate bad behavior costs something. To break the public trust can have serious consequences. Just as cigarette companies have paid the price for deceiving the public about *known* health risks, so pharmaceutical companies in our day are being asked to release not only the positive but also the negative test results of their newest drugs. "Buyer beware" is no longer considered an adequate defense. The world is too complex and corporations too pervasive and powerful to dismiss social responsibility with a glib passing of the buck to the customer. Johnson & Johnson reaffirmed its core values during the Tylenol crisis of 1982 by its quick and total removal of all Tylenol products once a few bottles were found to be tainted. On the other hand, Arthur Anderson, one of the big ten accounting firms with a ninety-year reputation for integrity, was destroyed almost overnight by its perceived ethical compromises with Enron.

Core values, as identified by James Collins and Jerry Porras, have given renewed focus to the basic set of values and beliefs that drive a business. Every company is identified not only by the products or services it provides but also by the unique combination of values and goodwill that "brand" its name. While this goodwill is usually considered a "soft asset," it is given a dollar value and carried on corporate balance sheets. Any buying or selling of businesses always includes financial consideration for the reputation of the company. Try to calculate the value of Coca-Cola, Amazon, Google, or Microsoft without the dominating value of "brand equity." Their "soft assets" (once characterized as "anything in a firm that generates value that you can't drop on your foot") vastly outweigh any hard assets (buildings, equipment, inventory) they carry on their books. The realization of the importance of core values is not lost on the business community. Mission statements are being replaced by corporate value statements. After all, a "mission" can only come from the value that is delivered to the marketplace. "To satisfy the customer" has become the mantra of practically every business enterprise. Unless you can deliver some value in terms of products or services, you are left with the goal of "making money," something that is really a by-product of providing a value. A key element of any company turnaround or major growth initiative is often a return to the basic strengths or values that made the company grow in the first place. That movement might take on the ring of "back to basics" or "what made us great in the first place" to "creating a vision" or "what would our founder have done." It is this unique combination of values and meanings that creates a company's culture. We will return to that idea later in the chapter.

While it might be easy to recognize the key role played by core values in any business, it is not as easy to recognize what the core values are that *actually* drive a company. The question is not about the right values but about the core values. The answer is not what the CEO thinks they should be, but rather what values, in fact, are operative. Core values are self-justifying. They define what a company stands for. How are we to know if proclaimed value statements, mottos, and banners are really more than marketing ploys or inspirational fluff? The following questions can be helpful in discovering the operative values of a company. A list of more than five values probably means that you have not reached deep enough to find the really core ones.

1. *What do the employees believe in?* The question is not about the reputation in the marketplace but the real beliefs of those within the company. And those beliefs are not just the beliefs of the president and officers but the values motivating everyone from the receptionist to the production worker to the sales manager. The values that drive the internal personnel will ultimately determine the value delivered to the customer. These beliefs may not be knowable through some question-and-answer survey but must be discerned in a variety of ways because they may not even be conscious to those who are driven by them.

2. *What is never compromised?* Business is always about compromise, trade-offs, gray areas, and negotiation precisely because it is about the concrete and particular. However, the telltale indicator of core value is the line beyond which there is no more compromise. At what point is quality an absolute? How complete is the product information that is communicated to the customer, especially when it might not all be favorable? Will management lie to its employees? Answers to questions such as these help identify the core values that drive a business.

3. *Where does a company spend money?* "Follow the money" is an old saying that is as true today as ever. Words are cheap, but real core values are discovered when a company spends money. Money is always a limited commodity. What gets priority? Which departments are cut back when cost reduction becomes necessary? What gets shortchanged? Nothing will indicate the hierarchy of values that a company actually lives by more accurately than the flow of money. It sorts out quickly what is really considered important.

4. *How does a company deal with mistakes and defects?* Every company makes mistakes, produces defective product, has accidents. It's the price you pay for trying to do anything at all. How a business deals with its defects is very indicative of its real values. Does the response tend to run along the lines of denial, deception, blame, or flight? A company that acknowledges a problem and takes responsibility for fixing it is grounded in values that go beyond opportunism.

5. *What gives inspiration and guidance to people inside the company?* The tone or climate of a company does not automatically predict business performance because the factors of business success in any given fiscal quarter are notoriously complex. But overall, how people feel about working at a company and about the values that drive them can account for as much as 20 to 30 percent of business performance.[4] The off-the-shelf answer of "increasing shareholder value" will hardly inspire anyone. That is the answer given by a company that has not yet reflected on its core values and purpose. Another way of asking the question is to determine what it is that gives guidance to people who are making decisions in ambiguous situations. How does a customer-service representative handle a tough customer complaint about a less-than-adequate product? How does a manager deal with a successful salesperson who cheats on his expense report? Do engineers solve problems or create "quick fixes"? The core values of a company will be reflected in responses to situations such as these.

6. *What would never change in the company?* If circumstances changed and penalized the company for holding its core values, would it still keep them? If not, then they are not core. A company does not change its core values in response to market changes; rather, it may need to change markets.

Such "value words" as integrity, respect, excellence, cooperation, trust, accountability, and honesty are everywhere. Whether they actually are a source of motivation and inspiration or reason for cynicism cannot always be determined at a first reading. The six questions above are an invitation to look deeper. In any case the significance of the operative core values for the success of a business can hardly be minimized.

Here are some examples of corporate values. They can spur your thinking about other companies you know.

Disney	No cynicism; creativity and imagination; fanatical attention to detail, and the promulgation of wholesome American values
Sony	Elevation of the Japanese national culture and status; being a pioneer; respect and encouragement of individual ability and creativity
Merck	Unequivocal excellence in all aspects of the company; science-based innovation; profit, but profit from work that benefits humanity
IKEA	Innovation; simplicity; looking after the interest of the majority

---

4. Daniel Goleman, Richard Boyatzis, and Annie McKee, *Primal Leadership: Realizing the Power of Emotional Intelligence* (Boston, Mass.: Harvard Business School Press, 2002), 17.

To pursue the exercise further, go to the Web sites of these companies and see how these values are reflected there.

A second component in a company's identity is its *core purpose*, or its reason for being. Like a core value, it does not change, but inspires change. Purpose is never fully realized so progress and change toward that purpose is a continuous imperative. That purpose can be even more difficult to perceive than core value, but it is just as critical. It is not the same as a description of the goods and services the company provides. For example, railroads are not in the business of running trains but of transporting product. More subtly, Sears is not in the "merchandising business" but in the "reliability business" (think guarantees and service); and McDonald's is not in the fast-food business but in the "parent hassle-relief business" (think Happy Meals and playgrounds).[5] Again, here are some examples to get you thinking.

3M	To solve unsolved problems innovatively
Hewlett-Packard	To make technical contributions for the advancement of humanity
Wal-Mart	To improve the standard of living for people who could not otherwise afford the products the company sells
eBay	To create a community of exchange not limited to the geography or resources of the individual

An exercise to help get at the real purpose of an organization is to ask "why" five times. Begin with a description of the company's product and ask, "Why is that important?" After a few whys you should begin to get to the core purpose. Not surprisingly, it will eventually come to making some contribution to the general welfare of society. And that is what can inspire and motivate dedication to the core values of the company. No one, I believe, has pursued the issues of core value and purposes better than Collins and Porras. It is best summarized in chapter 11 of *Built to Last,* "Building the Vision."[6]

There is a sobering side to this reality. The complexity of modern life leaves most of us relying on the expertise of others for sound advice and direction. Whether the expert is the financial analyst, the plumber, mechanic, priest, or doctor, we rely on them in a relationship of trust. Trust becomes the core value. When that trust is broken, the very heart of the "business" is destroyed. It becomes all the more important that the leaders and executives of organizations maintain persistent vigilance and integrity.

---

5. Larry Johnson and Bob Phillips, *Absolute Honesty: Building a Corporate Culture That Values Straight Talk and Rewards Integrity* (New York: AMACOM, American Management Association, 2003), 208-9.

6. Collins and Porras, *Built to Last,* 219-39.

You may be wondering why we have explored the issue of core values and core purposes this extensively. The reason goes back to our original shift in viewing the purpose of business from making money to creating goods and services. Once that first step is taken, then the role of business in society becomes that of increasing general prosperity. Only to the degree that a business can provide some value to society (core values and purposes) can it survive. Making money, or being profitable, will only be a consequence of satisfying, at a reasonable cost, a perceived value to society. And once the primary goal is value rather than money, then morality is not at the fringes but right at the heart of the enterprise.

OUR EMPLOYEES ARE OUR GREATEST ASSET

Recognize the slogan? It's everywhere—on the side of trucks, on Web sites, in practically every corporate annual report. Why such an emphasis in our times? After all, it always took people to make products and deliver services. The slogan is saying something different from the obvious. That difference is instructive. One might like to believe that the difference comes from the fact that our generation is more enlightened and more caring than previous generations. Empirical evidence might be in short supply. More to the point would be to recognize that we are entering a new age where the role of the employee has changed. If, as discussed in chapter 2, the primary asset in an agricultural society is land and the primary asset in a manufacturing society is capital, then the primary asset in an information society is knowledge. Knowledge, finally, flourishes only in people. Accordingly, without any recourse to altruism, it is a simple step to recognize the critical role played specifically by people for contemporary business success. "Our people are our greatest asset" comes less from a moral imperative and more from a business necessity. Are we not back to Adam Smith's insight that we are fed not by benevolence but by self-interest, rightly understood?

The implications of this shift in consciousness are immense. Human activity can be understood on three different levels. There is the first and most obvious level of *behavior*. People speak and act. Activity can be observed and recorded. Conformity to standards can be measured easily. Company rules and codes of conduct are established at this level. If this is the whole story of human activity, then we have the psychology of stimulus-response, reward-punishment, associated most tellingly with B. F. Skinner. Mechanisms for controlling and reinforcing desired behavior can be managed. The strength of such a view is that it is definite, observable, and, some would say, most accurate, since what one says and what one does may be two different things. This first level of behavior was well suited to the innovations of the Industrial Revolution. People tended the machines that allowed for immense progress in the creation of wealth. At that time there was one dominant model for the organization of peoples, whether in government, as those who rule and those who are subject to rule, or in the military, as the one who orders and the one who obeys. The same model was also common in religious associations. The model still prevails in the military as "command and control." We can call this type of observable behavior *Level One*.[7] It was the common model of business well into the second half of the twentieth century. It spawned a whole generation of time-and-motion engineers who measured every movement needed to perform a specific task on an assembly line. It also tended to see the people performing the tasks as necessary costs. To the degree that the same tasks could be performed by fewer people, to that extent one could obtain a competitive advantage in the marketplace.

At a second level, people not only act but also *think*. We can see what a person does but not what she thinks. Since thought is not observable, it is more difficult to measure. However, thought is conscious and so can be shared in total or in part depending on a person's willingness to share. Although thought cannot be seen, it does have a strong impact on *Level One* observable behavior. For that reason, business tries to align a person's thinking with company objectives. On this level a company manages through systems and structures. The design of systems, whether production lines or process flows, was the task of management. The intelligible ordering of activity to specific objectives has been a key management responsibility since the Industrial Revolution. Bureaucracy, both in its strengths and its weaknesses, has been its fruit. The alignment of systems and procedures throughout an organization to specific objectives is one of the factors that has contributed to the flourishing of large corporations. This second level of human activity, which encompasses conscious but not observable thought, is *Level Two*. It has its limits, however. Once systems are established, they tend to reduce the person once again to defined behaviors, even if more sophisticated than the repetitions of the production lines. Accountability gets pushed further and further up the line. More and more systems are put in place to eliminate errors and assure desired outcomes. Only an elite few do the thinking and assume responsibility for results. But countermovements started to appear. They began to show themselves through such realizations as "the person closest to an activity is the expert in that activity, both to recognize problems as well as provide solutions," and "quality cannot be inspected into a product but must be built in."

---

7. James G. Clawson, *Level Three Leadership: Getting Below the Surface* (Upper Saddle River, N.J.: Prentice Hall, 1999), 2-14.

There is also the added complexity of contemporary business activity that makes it impossible for any one person to have all the knowledge necessary to make informed decisions. The answer is not just bigger computers, able to crunch more numbers, but a team of persons who share common meanings and values.

This realization leads us to a third level of activity, one that is the hardest to get hold of. We not only act and think, but also respond, at a level strongly associated with feelings. Like thought, that level is not observable, but, unlike thought, much of it is not necessarily conscious. It is a level that begins before birth and develops over a lifetime. It is the basis of our values, assumptions, beliefs, and expectations. It determines what we hold dear, what is important, what is not negotiable. Our values and expectations are, by their nature, highly emotionally charged and anchored in personal relationships that begin in the family, find development in personal friendships, and most often end in founding families of our own. All of our personal life experiences and relationships contribute to the development of this level of activity. While we can take courses and workshops to deepen our thinking and learn new ideas (*Level Two*), courses or books (not even books on ethics and business!) will change our values. Over a lifetime we can become more aware of their motivating power, discover their sources, broaden their reach, nuance their application, but never surpass them. Perhaps, on rare occasions, we might actually "fall in love," which will provide a new basis for our activity. In business, it is the difference between the manager (*Level Two*) and the leader. We will simply call this *Level Three*.

Another way of identifying the three levels would be to speak of the *body* (observable activity), the *mind* (unobservable conscious thought), and the *heart* (unobservable and often-unconscious source of our values). A schematic of the threefold distinction in human activity might look like this.

Level One	observable acts	body	rules/regulations
Level Two	nonobservable thought	mind	systems/structures
Level Three	values/beliefs	heart	core values/vision

Perhaps we can now better appreciate the wisdom embodied in the slogan "Employees are our greatest asset." Level One activity simply requires conforming activity. One person is as good as the next as long as he carries out the prescribed behavior. However, as we move deeper into the Information Age, knowledge becomes king. Information becomes more complex; systems need to develop. Structures must keep pace, and the complex system is driven by the active engagement of peoples' minds. Learning, adapting, creating, and teamwork become critical elements of any successful business. This realization has probably been captured best in Peter Senge's simple but powerful term, the *learning organization*.[8] Obviously the value of the individual person increases exponentially in this environment.

However, if the real business story today is about delivering value, as we argued in the first part of this chapter, then the role of the individual becomes even more significant. Since only persons have values, only persons can deliver values. People within an organization cannot deliver the values of an organization unless they are attuned to those values. Since values are the result of one's lifetime of experience, they cannot be learned in some straightforward fashion, as in learning a new computer program. By the same token, there can be no grounding of values without considering the moral base of what a person holds to be right or wrong, important or insignificant. By all accounts, the hiring, promoting, and dismissing of personnel become key elements in a company's success. It is why visionary companies will always try to do most of their promoting from within. In this way the company is assured that the values that drive it are embodied in those destined for greater responsibility. Most skills can be taught; basic values are nurtured.

Just as a person's values develop only within the emotionally charged fields of family, friends, and culture, so the sustaining and further growth of values in a business environment will grow only within the culture of that business organization. Little wonder that business culture has become the focus of so much attention. We are not, as we might sometimes like to imagine, autonomous, self-sustaining, and self-defining individuals, able to think entirely for ourselves and determine who we are. We are essentially social creatures, no matter how eccentric, who were born out of the relationship of a man and a woman, nurtured in a society, and sustained by mutual interests. By the same token, a business organization is more than a collection of individuals. No matter how contorted its internal politics or how controlling the dominance of huge egos, it is always something more than a group of people who happen to be contractually related to the company. We are, or must become, a community of shared values if we are to succeed. Building a company culture that is sustained by common meaning and shared values becomes one of the most critical issues of business leadership today.

It is this understanding that grounds our opening quote. Succinctly, the first creation of every business is not its product or service but the community of people who deliver it. Early on in their investigation of great companies, Collins and Porras came upon a startling insight:

---

8. Clawson, *Level Three Leadership*, 10.

We had to reject the great idea or brilliant strategy explanation of corporate success and consider a new view. We had to put on a different
lens and look at the world backward. We had to *shift from seeing the company as a vehicle for the products to seeing the products as a vehicle for the
company.*[9]

Products will change; manufacturing methods can improve; marketing strategies are always subject to revisions. What does not change is the group of
people deeply rooted in shared meanings and values, that is, a culture that
becomes the source for an ever-changing array of new products and innovations. Demotivated or disgruntled employees will not be able to sustain core
values for very long. The "hard assets" of delivered products and services and
the "soft assets" of employee morale and commitment are really two sides of
one and the same "successful business." It is that realization that prompted
Bill Hewlett, cofounder of Hewlett-Packard, to say,

As I look back on my life's work, I am probably most proud of having
helped to create a company that by virtue of its values, practices and success has had a tremendous impact on the way companies are managed
around the world. I'm particularly proud that I'm leaving behind an
ongoing organization that can live on as a role model long after I'm
gone.[10]

This critical function of building the community of shared meanings and values is also recognized in the notion of *alignment.* It is explored most thoroughly and convincingly in the recent publication of *Good Work*, appropriately
subtitled *When Excellence and Ethics Meet.* The book begins with a realization
first identified by Mihaly Csikszentmihalyi as "flow experiences."[11] In flow, a
person feels in total harmony; what is difficult becomes easy; and there is a
sense of being totally involved in a seemingly effortless performance. Mihaly
claims, surprisingly enough, that flow experiences "occur more often on the
job than in leisure time."[12] The reason is what he, and others, call alignment.
It occurs when there is the alignment of (1) the responsible exercise of the
deeply held values of an individual; in harmony with (2) the core values of the
company; contributing to (3) a value to society. Let's identify what might be
the flow experience of

---

    9. Collins and Porras, *Built to Last*, 28 (emphasis in original).
    10. Douglas K. Smith, *On Value and Values: Thinking Differently about We in an Age of Me* (Upper
Saddle River, N.J.: Financial Times Prentice Hall, 2004), 26.
    11. Howard Gardner, Mihaly Csikszentmihalyi, and William Damon, *Good Work: When Excellence
and Ethics Meet* (New York: Basic Books, 2001), 5.
    12. Gardner, Csikszentmihalyi, and Damon, *Good Work*, 5.

1. salesperson:
   a. person with a gift for connecting with others and initiating new relationships . . .
   b. and a company that makes quality air conditioners at a fair price . . .
   c. that can provide the climate control to energize people for other types of activity.
2. journalist:
   a. person with a nose and interest at getting to the facts . . .
   b. with a journal that has a reputation for integrity . . .
   c. that promotes the democratic process within a community
3. yourself? (try it in terms of your own profession or aspiration):
   a. deeply held personal values
   b. values of the company/association
   c. contribution to society.

If any of the three levels is seriously out of alignment, then the type of flow or harmony necessary for deep satisfaction and superior performance is compromised. Of course, no person will have all of these factors in complete alignment except maybe for some favored moments in a career. By the same token, the more we can attempt to bring these three elements together, the more we will be in a position to experience what has been identified as "flow."

Once again there is the realization that what a company produces will flow from what the company is. And "what the company is" is members sharing deeply held and clearly articulated meanings and values. A number of consequences should be coming clear:

For the individual: leave a company that does not have the same basic values as you do or else it will only lead to deep frustration in which the only relief is taking home a paycheck and waiting for the weekend.

For the company: in hiring personnel, more care must be given to assuring proper values than appropriate skills, and people without the company's values must be removed.

These are tough words for both, but they are the basic condition for building a great company and finding genuine satisfaction in work.

When Peter Drucker, the guru and father of management theory, died in 2006, there was an explosion of eulogies praising his contributions to business management. Some of his most important lessons might make a fitting conclusion to this part of the chapter.

• Management is about human beings. Its task is to make people capable of joint performance, to make their strengths effective and their weaknesses irrelevant.

- Because management deals with the integration of people in a common venture, it is deeply embedded in culture. What managers do in Germany, in the United Kingdom, in the United States, in Japan, or in Brazil is exactly the same. How they do it may be quite different.
- Every enterprise is a learning and teaching institution. Training and development must be built into it on all levels; training and development never stop.
- Profitability is not the purpose of, but a limiting factor on, business enterprise and business activity. Profit is not the explanation, cause, or rationale of business behavior and business decisions, but rather the test of their validity.
- True marketing starts out . . . with the customer, his demographics, his realities, his needs, his values. It does not ask, What do we want to sell? It asks, What does the customer want to buy?[13]

CORPORATE SOCIAL RESPONSIBILITY

There is no way of talking about corporate values without addressing a whole series of issues, causes, and concerns that find a home under the general rubric of corporate social responsibility, often referred to simply as CSR. It is a term that is praised by some, condemned by others, and often manipulated by anyone with an axe to grind. Let us begin with the basics. Fundamentally, every progressive and socially responsible organization should strive to achieve three goals: (1) to serve society with specified services or products; (2) to operate in an economically sustainable manner; (3) to achieve these results while rigorously adhering to a defined set of ethical principles and shared values.

The goal of meeting a need in society should be a central condition for every business and should be a fundamental condition for legal incorporation.[14] "Trafficking in children" or "*mere* shareholder value," for instance, are not adequate grounds for a state to grant legitimacy to a business as a corporation. Having said that, is it really true that business has other social responsibilities? Is it not enough for business to do what it has proven it does best, namely, increase general prosperity? Is not the creation of wealth and jobs adequate justification for the existence of business? Of course, if business is viewed as immoral or amoral, then there is a need not only for justification but also redemption! And when business tries to justify itself by pointing to

---

13. Peter Drucker, *The Essential Drucker* (New York: HarperCollins, 2001).

14. Dennis W. Bakke, *Joy at Work: A Revolutionary Approach to Fun on the Job* (Seattle, Wash.: P V G, 2005), 152.

the money it donates to charities or to the cultural events it sponsors, then it only contributes to the false assumptions and expectations of a mistaken premise. And is it really an act of charity to give away other people's (the shareholders') money especially when they have no control over the process? A recent article in the *Wall Street Journal* headlined a debate on the issue with the words "Corporate Social Responsibility: Good Citizenship or Investor Rip-off?" There is a real danger in asking any organization to do too much. If anyone is responsible for everything, then does anything really get done? Is it not a hallmark of civilization to create specialized institutions each of which does some things very well? Does not the creation of wealth allow individuals in their various roles the opportunity to advance the values they care about? In some ways we are back to the shareholder vs. stakeholder debate.

While recognizing that the primary purpose of business is to create wealth in a legally responsible way, there remains a general sense that business does have a further responsibility that is recognized by the emergence of the expression "corporate social responsibility." Why is that a new issue of our day? I believe it has to do with the very size of the modern corporation. The corporation has become as large and powerful as nations/states and wealthier than many. Corporations have played a vital role in determining our way of life: from what we eat and wear to where we live and how we play. They have drawn on resources around the globe and brought them to our doorsteps. They have harnessed the energy, talent, and resourcefulness of the best and brightest of us. Is there any wonder, then, that we expect more from them? Just what that "more" is, can and must remain open to legitimate debate.

One aspect of that "more" is the fact that people today evaluate not only the particular goods and services of a company but also the company *behind* the product. A positive social profile is considered not only a marketing advantage but also a *competitive* advantage. There is a general recognition that social responsibility protects reputation and promotes brand value. There is much greater acceptance of the notion that it is not only possible or desirable but actually profitable to build social consciousness directly into the core of the enterprise. The positive impact of Johnson & Johnson voluntarily recalling all Tylenol products at the first realization of a tainted product was not lost on the business community. On the other hand, the negative reaction to Wal-Mart's perceived minimal pay to its employees or Nike's loss of marketing position as a result of the accusation of building shoes with child labor was also a wake-up call to business.

Conventional business wisdom assigned the responsibility for making money to business and the responsibility for social and environmental consequences to governmental and not-for-profit agencies. While business is still looked to for the value of constantly driving down cost and reducing prices, there is a growing consensus that business is also responsible for other values, such as the preservation of the environment, the safety of its products, the health of the consumers, the well-being of its workers, the future impact of its activities. This new and growing consciousness is what is understood by corporate social responsibility. What is particularly new about this emerging consciousness is that "socially responsible" is the tag not only for individual products but for the entire company that produces the products.

A 1999 Millennium Poll conducted by Environics International (which interviewed 25,000 citizens across six continents) indicated:

- In forming impressions of companies, people around the world focus on corporate citizenship ahead of brand reputation or financial factors.
- Two out of three citizens want companies to go beyond their historical role of making a profit, paying taxes, employing people, and obeying all laws. They want companies to contribute to broader societal goals as well.
- More than one in five consumers reported either rewarding or punishing companies in the past year according to their social performance and as many again would consider doing so in the future.[15]

A word of caution is in order. While there is no doubt that a new awareness of interdependencies must lead corporations to responsibilities that go beyond a strict "production of goods and services," we cannot lose sight of the fact that business cannot do everything. We are back to the argument in chapter 1. Taking account of stakeholders is the first act of social responsibility—being fair to the claims of customers, suppliers, employees, managers, local communities, and shareholders. Business's ability to increase general prosperity is its reason for being and its justification. It should not try to do the work of government, just as government should not try to do the work of business. A too-cozy relationship between the two ought to arouse suspicion on both sides. Just as governments can use the mantra of social responsibility to exercise excessive control over business operations, so businesses can use large financial contributions, under the guise of social responsibility, to unduly influence government.[16] The question is one of balance. Corporate social responsibility is here to stay. It represents an advance in our understanding of our relationship to the earth. The fact that courses on the various aspects of social responsibility are now offered in the country's leading business schools is another indication of how significant this dimension has become. While everyone has

---

15. Jeffrey Hollender and Stephen Fenichell, *What Matters Most: How a Small Group of Pioneers Is Teaching Social Responsibility to Big Business and Why Big Business Is Listening* (New York: Basic Books, 2004), 47.

16. "Globalisation and its critics: A survey of globalisation," *The Economist* (September 29, 2001) offers a healthy suspicion on both sides.

her own ideas of what constitutes a socially responsible company, an initial definition might go like this:

> The term generally refers to an ongoing commitment by business to behave ethically and to contribute to economic development when demonstrating respect for people, communities, society at large, and the environment. In short, CSR marries the concepts of global citizenship with environmental stewardship and sustainable development.[17]

Whatever else CSR might eventually include, its focus in our times is on those two key issues of "environmental stewardship" and "sustainable development." We must examine each of them.

Sustainable Development

Naysayers and business antagonists are quick to bewail the apparently irreconcilable conflict between the imperatives of economic growth and environmental and social protection. They point alarmingly to the fact that the industrialized nations consume 80 percent of the resources while representing only 40 percent of the population. Their solution tends to run along the lines of halting growth in developed countries or massively redistributing the wealth of the world. The solution suffers from all the misconceptions of business typically espoused by social engineers. To adopt a no-growth economic policy for a world experiencing a population explosion would result in full-scale economic and social disaster. The problems of poverty and underdevelopment demand a new era of growth in which developing countries play a larger role and reap larger benefits.

However, this does not mean that there is no problem. The real issue does involve a revised model for global economic development that might be called "sustainable." Sustainable development could be defined briefly as "seeking to meet the needs and aspirations of the present without compromising the ability to meet those of the future." This is still a tall order, but it has the advantage of moving the issue forward rather than pulling backward. It still gives plenty of room for the apocalyptic heralds of doom who remind us (not without some evidence) that we cannot continue to extract and wastefully consume our limited, nonrenewable resources, that toxic chemicals cannot continue to be manufactured and dumped into the environment without serious consequences. Simply to continue the present course is to impose burdens on future generations that could become unsustainable. While the business

---

17. Hollender and Fenichell, *What Matters Most*, 29.

model of innovation, growth, prosperity, and progress is not only part of the problem but also a key to its solution, it is, in itself, too simplistic to meet the demands of sustainability. And to renounce sustainability is to renounce all concern for the future and future generations. This an issue *now*. To address the issue adequately demands the further notion of "environmental stewardship," often referred to as *externalities*.

Environmental Stewardship

"Externalities" is a term that has come into use as a result of a new awareness of environmental consequences. It refers to all the consequences of producing goods and services that are not directly realized in the product itself. Industrial processes leave in their wake a series of consequences that operators externalize in the sense that they disregard, discard, or discharge into the environment. Billowing black smoke, mountains laid bare by strip mining, mercury discharged into rivers and lakes, used car oil, atomic waste, discarded TVs and computers—all are the result of our accepted standard of prosperity and progress. They are all the consequence of a way of life that we take for granted.

What is new is our awareness of the long-term impact of these externalities. It is instructive that advertising once gloried in these images as indicators of progress and vitality. Drawings done at the end of the nineteenth century would actually exaggerate the smoke coming from huge smokestacks in order to reinforce the notion that a given location was a desirable place to be! Smoke pouring out of the stack of a steel mill or a train engine was a sign of economic vigor and human achievement.

Business used to be able to walk away from its externalities with the proud realization that it had produced a wide range of desirable products, provided good-paying jobs, increased the standard of living, and made a profit for its shareholders. Others—most often governments—were left with the responsibility of cleaning up the environment, if the matter was considered at all. Today the issue of responsibility for the externalities of any given business can no longer be ignored. Business can no longer dump the environmental and social costs of production onto those communities who are least represented by the market, that is, the poor and disenfranchised. Bill Moyers in one of his PBS specials[18] showed how a small city called Guiyu ("Gwee-you"), bordering on Hong Kong, developed its entire economy around recycling computers from the United States. The residents would grill motherboards over open charcoal fires to extract the chips and trace amounts of gold and other metals.

---

18. Hollender and Fenichell, *What Matters Most*, 131.

Without protective gear, they could be seen melting the carcinogenic PVC off the computer's copper cables, which created dense clouds of black, toxic smoke. This one-time farming community on the Lianjiang River is now covered with black ash residue. That river, which provides drinking water for the villages lining its bank, now contains levels of lead, cadmium, zinc, and chromium 190 times higher than the threshold set by the World Health Organization for drinking water. Today the residents of Guiyu drink water that is shipped in from a town that is thirty kilometers away. Do the people want to stop their activity and go back to their pastoral farming? No, they often do the burning at night to reduce detection, and camera crews were begged to go away and even threatened bodily.

The point is not to use these stories to bash business but to realize that the cost of the externalities of business cannot simply be passed on to the government or to an unsuspecting community or to future generations. The cost of goods needs to be tracked through the whole process of production from its origin in any part of the world to its final disposal as waste. This is being more commonly referred to as the complete "value-chain," which is recognized in a move toward full-cost accounting for externalities. Proponents define this full-cost accounting in fairly comprehensive terms:

> The price of goods ought to reflect *all* of the costs—financial, environmental, and social—involved in making them, using them, disposing of them or recycling them. The prices of services ought also to reflect their full cost. That way the market reflects environmental and social as well as financial realities. It reflects scarcities. It requires less government tinkering. Leadership companies would be happy with full-cost pricing because, being cleaner and more efficient than other companies, they would be producing goods and services for less.[19]

Whether these real costs are captured through some form of tax on all amounts of pollution and waste (which can then be reduced by lowering those amounts, as exemplified in a proposed carbon tax) or including a set disposal fee in the purchase price of a computer, for example (which can then lead to new profitable recycling industries), is a matter for further discussion. What is becoming clearer and more compelling is the realization that companies can actually become more efficient and effective by taking more responsibility for their entire value chain. Certainly the current government practice of regulation, surveillance, and fines is not adequate. Government effort might better be used to create the regulations that would insure a level playing field

---

19. Hollender and Fenichell, *What Matters Most*, 89, 91-92.

for all, and then allowing the creativity of business to figure out how best to develop the effective means.

Nor is some form of full-cost accounting wishful thinking. Hewlett-Packard, for instance, has already built two massive product-recycling units. The CEOs of DuPont and Royal Dutch Shell have come out in favor of companies paying for externalized costs. This is definitely an issue that is here to stay. More and more companies are including some form of environmental awareness in their value statements to the effect that "protecting the environment" is a conscious value of the company. In fact, companies with strong environmental values actually attract some of the best and brightest candidates for jobs. It goes back to the realization that the harmony found in alignment includes the desire to produce something that is socially beneficial.

CONCLUSION

We have come to the end of a rather involved and closely reasoned chapter. Its purpose is to set the framework for understanding what is required for business to be successful in our times. In chapter 2 we made the fundamental transition of understanding the nature of business as a process of producing goods and services that increases general prosperity. In this chapter we have tried to spell out the implications of that shift in understanding. It has taken us along the following path:

- If business is about producing goods and services, then the value of a particular product is key to business success.
- Successful businesses are driven by core values that support and permeate every aspect of the business.
- The identification of the core values and purposes of a business is something deeper than a description of its particular product and provides a base for meeting changes in time and culture.
- Profit is the difference between the cost of making a product and the value attributed to it by what the market is willing to pay.
- The meanings and values of a company are first embodied in its members and become the company's culture. Only then does it issue in a defined product.
- Persons are the critical difference in a world where knowledge and values are the competitive advantage.
- Corporate social responsibility is the recognition of the long-term consequences of business activity, especially in the areas of sustainable development and environmental stewardship.

QUESTIONS FOR REFLECTION

1. Take your own company, or one you admire, and identify its core values and its business purpose.
2. Identify your own core values, and examine how they align with the values of your company. Where are the misalignments? What can you do about it?
3. Make your own list of (a) abilities that cannot be taught; (b) abilities that can be taught to some degree with difficulty; (c) abilities that are relatively easy to teach. If this is a group exercise, each person should first put the list together privately and then share and discuss findings with the group.
4. Eighty-three percent of executives polled by an executive search agency rated a company's record of business ethics "very important when deciding to accept a job offer."[20] Would you, and Why?

SUGGESTIONS FOR FURTHER READING AND STUDY

Albion, Mark S. *True to Yourself: Leading a Values-Based Business*. San Francisco: Berrett-Koehler, 2006. Examines the impact of environmentally friendly businesses on its employees.

Barkey, Michael B., ed. *Environmental Stewardship in the Judeo-Christian Tradition: Jewish, Catholic, and Protestant Wisdom on the Environment* (Grand Rapids, Mich.: Acton Institute for the Study of Religion and Liberty, 2000). A biblical study on environmental issues from a free-market perspective.

Collins, James C., and Jerry I. Porras. *Built to Last: Successful Habits of Visionary Companies*. New York: HarperBusiness, 1994. If you have time for only one book, this is the one to read.

Drucker, Peter F. *Management Challenges for the 21ˢᵗ Century*. New York: HarperBusiness, 1999. A look ahead at the challenges facing business in an information-based economy.

"The Good Company." In *The Economist*, January 22, 2005, 3-22. A salutary corrective to crusaders with an antimarket agenda using corporate social responsibility as a tool to promote that agenda.

Hollender, Jeffrey, and Stephen Fenichell. *What Matters Most: How a Small Group of Pioneers Is Teaching Social Responsibility to Big Business and Why Big Business Is Listening*. New York: Basic Books, 2004. A good study of how some small companies are putting the call to social responsibility into action. Also contains a wealth of bibliographical materials as well as lists of agencies and organizations working for corporate social responsibility.

---

20. *Human Resources Magazine*, November 2004, 19.

4

Leadership and Ethics

In order to collect the people,
a leader must first collect himself.
I Ching (1500 B.C.)

In chapter 3 we examined the role that value and value creation play in the successful functioning of business. The effort and discernment required for a company to identify its core values is not an exercise in the obvious. Even more demanding is the subsequent task of implementing those values throughout every aspect of the business. The process of value creation is primarily the work of people, and so we ended the chapter with the conclusion that the first creation of any business is not a product but a community of meaning and value that is capable of delivering a product that is valued in the marketplace.

If the last chapter was an exercise in determining the core values of the business, then this chapter will be an exercise in discovering one's own core values. A second step will then try to bring those personal values into an enriching alignment with the values of the business through a discussion of the meaning of leadership. This is another way of approaching the wisdom contained in the opening quotation from the I Ching. For to "first collect himself" requires a person to pull together the dynamics that create one's personal identity, and to "collect the people" is to exercise a leadership that flows from that identity. Not only are the two integrally related but they are also both morally grounded.

PERSONAL IDENTITY

The issue begins with the question of one's own identity, not in the abstract, but in the specific sense of what's important to me, what matters, where do I stand as a person, what do I really care about, what do I value. If I have no word or deed that is my own, then I remain in the classical state of the drifter.

My word is what others happen to be saying; my deed is what others happen to be doing. My only purpose is to get along, summed up in the adage "go along to get along." While such a stance is an important stage of childhood socialization, it is not an adequate response of moral maturity. The transition to recognizing and accepting responsibility for my words and my deeds is a key moment in each person's development. And once it is reached, it is never surpassed. In fact, it becomes the permanent base for an ever-widening horizon of finding my word and my deed. "Eat, drink, and be merry, for tomorrow you die" has the hollow ring of life totally captured by the moment, without further identity or purpose.

The process of finding *my* word and *my* deed is really a process of finding my own identity and my power. It begins when the child grabs hold of the spoon with which she is being fed and says, "Let *me* do it!" The drifter, on the other hand, has no power of his own. All the power is in the words and deeds of others. What others are saying, what others are doing remains the source of motivation. All personal power and identity are turned over to others. Unfortunately, if I don't lead myself, there will be no lack of others willing to take over! At best, my ethics would be an ethics of conformity, or, minimally, "what is legal and what is illegal." Yet, I can only find my word and my deed when I discover what is important to me, what I find to be worthwhile, what has value, what is really me. This is not the same as saying that I create my own values out of nothing. It is, first of all, a matter of *discovering* the values that are actually operative in my life. That process is the task of a lifetime. It does, however, have some defining moments and stages. There are many ways of coming to a deeper understanding of who I am and how to deepen that identity. All sorts of exercises have been employed to aid in that discovery and assimilation. They range from religious ascetical practices to psychological counseling to secluded retreats and workshops to heartfelt conversations with good friends. A simple exercise that can be helpful in getting started consists of three stages: (1) discover what matters; (2) find your voice; and (3) connect with others.[1] It is presented here not as a technique to be learned but as an exercise to be performed. It is about you!

Discovering What Matters

Just as companies have an established body of core values that drive their success, so an individual is driven by the unique composite of values that makes

---

1. I am indebted to the consulting firm of BlessingWhite for the general framework of this exercise, which was also presented by Christopher Rice, "Leading Out Loud," *Leader to Leader* (Fall 2001). BlessingWhite North America, 23 Orchard Road, Skillman, NJ 08558-2609.

the person who he is. There is a big difference, however, between the clearly definable, deliberately chosen core values that identify a company and the lifetime quest of every individual to answer the question, What is my life about? Or, to rephrase the question, What concerns me, interests me, what captures my imagination, my leisure thinking moments, my dreams? What causes me to smile spontaneously, what increases my pulse, causes me to speak more animatedly? What motivates me to expend tremendous energy, mental and physical?

The growing awareness of who we are is a lifetime development. It reaches into the depths of our being, our center or, as T. S. Eliot calls it, "the still point of the turning world."[2] It is further complicated by the fact that it is impossible to experience all of life in any one moment, even though there are moments more defining than others. We discover ourselves not just by reflection and introspection but also by how we act and react to the world in which we live. As a result, there are many ways of gaining greater self-awareness. What is without question is that growth in self-awareness is critical to both moral identity and leadership.

This process begins by connecting with the dreams that release one's passion, energy, and excitement about life. It involves getting beyond the "oughts" of our life. That is hard work because the habits of our thoughts and feelings have built heavily traveled, highly reinforced neural circuitry in the brain. Exercises to release our dreams and our aspirations for the future can help. Focusing on a vision of ourselves in the future can get us beyond some of the inevitable obstacles of the present. The "iron cage"[3] in which we are all trapped is largely unexamined. Over the course of a busy life we assume the expectations of others or are seduced by accepted ideas of power, fame, or success. You know you have begun to move beyond that to the core of your self when you suddenly feel passionate about the possibilities that your life holds.

To gain a sense of what is involved in coming to this greater self-awareness, we will pursue one exercise that not only turns us inward in introspection but also includes the history of our personal life. First, think of your life in the following time segments: (a) preteen years; (b) teen years; (c) college years; (d) twenties; (e) thirties; (f) forties and fifties.

Now, reflect for at least a few minutes on each of these periods. Try to imagine that time again. Do not shift back and forth from one period to the next. What events or experiences do you remember vividly from that period,

---

2. Carole S. Napolitano and Lida J. Henderson, *The Leadership Odyssey: A Self-Development Guide to New Skills for New Times* (San Francisco: Jossey-Bass, 1998), 57.

3. Daniel Goleman, Richard Boyatzis, and Annie McKee, *Primal Leadership: Realizing the Power of Emotional Intelligence* (Boston: Harvard Business School Press, 2002), 118.

even if they seem insignificant? In particular, think of incidents when you formed your own values and principles. How did you *feel* about yourself at that time? When did you act differently than expected? Are there incidents that you did not initiate but which left a profound impression on you? Jot them down and only then go to the next period.

After you have gone through each period, look over what you have written down. Is there any theme that carries through? Is there some thread that intertwines and connects the incidents? What are the defining moments of your life as you look back? Can you see some connection between what is important to you now and the key incidents of your life as you have defined them? Any such analysis will be accompanied with strong feelings if you have indeed fixed on key experiences. What were the dominant emotions connected with each incident? Give yourself a reality check by talking over your findings with a group or a friend and getting some feedback.

In some ways an exercise like the above is never completed. It can provide the agenda of a lifetime. It calls for ongoing reflection, which is shunned by the drifter. On the other hand, this reflection can be accomplished in various ways. What is indispensable is the need to tap into one's center, one's dreams, hopes and passions if life is to be lived with integrity and authenticity. The popularity of works such as Daniel Goleman's *Emotional Intelligence* and *Primal Leadership* as well as the bestselling works in business of Warren Bennis such as *On Becoming a Leader* and *Learning to Lead* is a further indication of the critical nature of self-awareness for leadership. An exercise from Bennis's book can be found in the exercises at the end of this chapter.

From another point of view, there is a recently published book with the title *What Would Buddha Do at Work?*[4] Its basic message is that dealing with the inevitable frustrations at work always means dealing with who you are and what you desire deep inside. Much in Eastern religious practice is aimed at helping people reach their center, where the pushes and pulls of the moment do not determine one's actions. Jagdish Parikh, a Harvard MBA graduate, returned to Bombay where he became the successful director of the Lemuir Group of companies. At the same time he suffered physiological and psychological effects of stress. Was there not a way to be successful and happy at the same time, he wondered? There are hundreds of books telling people how to become leaders. All sorts of skills and role models are proposed for emulation. But Parikh's fundamental realization came to the same recognition proposed in the quote from the *I Ching* that opens this chapter. "Unless one knows how to lead oneself, it would be presumptuous to lead others," he concluded.

---

4. Franz Metcalf and B. J. Gallagher Hateley, *What Would Buddha Do at Work? 101 Answers to Workplace Dilemmas.* (Berkeley, Calif.: Seastone, 2001).

Operating out of continuous stress can act as rocket fuel for a short time but will end in burnout. And operating out of fear of losing is just as self-defeating. We must move from the fear of losing into the "joy of doing." "Detached involvement" is a fundamental Eastern concept. Here are some other comments from a talk Parikh gave at Harvard on April 19, 2006.[5]

> If you don't know how to lead yourself, someone else will.

> It is important to get to know one's own inner dynamics deeply "in order to achieve sustainable peak performance."

> Leadership is not a quality, strategy, or tactic, in my opinion. It's a way of life, a way of being.

> In formal education we learn nothing about feelings, but we exist at a feeling level. We cannot change just by wishing. We must discover ourselves.

There is certainly something both elusive and yet universally significant in this first requirement of "discovering what matters." Prayer, as practiced in any of the religious traditions, can have this same centering effect, especially for persons who pray on a regular basis. What is clear, however, is that unless a person steps aside and takes deliberate time for reflection and quiet on a regular basis, there will be little progress in identifying what is important and even less in allowing that core identity to take ever-deeper hold. We need to find a way to get beyond everyday tasks and responsibilities. If we wait till we have time, we will never have time.

Another way of looking at this issue is to ask, "Why would anyone want to be led by me?" It may seem like a strange question at first. But unless you have an authorized position of power, such as "boss," "parent," or "teacher," your power can come only from something within you—a point of view about yourself and the world. And the one thing about a point of view is that you cannot borrow someone else's. You can learn management techniques, systems, information, engineering, accounting, etc., but you can't learn a point of view, a vision, or a new self. The best you can do is to discover and then develop your own. In a recent work by Bennis and Robert Thomas, *Geeks and Geezers*, with the instructive subtitle *How Era, Values, and Defining Moments Shape Leaders*,[6] the authors conducted extensive interviews with "geezers,"

---

5. "The Zen of Management Maintenance: Leadership Starts with Self-Discovery," in *Working Knowledge*, ed. Martha Lagace (e-mail newsletter of Harvard Business School, May 9, 2005. http://hbswk.hbs.edu/forms/newsletter.html).
6. Warren G. Bennis and Robert J. Thomas, *Geeks and Geezers: How Era, Values and Defining Moments Shape Leaders* (Boston: Harvard Business School, 2002).

defined as those whose formative years occurred between 1945 and 1954, a period shaped largely by World War II, and with "geeks," who are defined as coming of age between 1991 and 2000, a period largely shaped by the "virtual, visual, and digital." They conducted forty-three extensive interviews with business leaders from each of the two eras and found more similarities than differences. However, what was most telling, I believe, is that every leader, regardless of age, had undergone at least one intense, transformational experience—what the authors call a "crucible" experience. These are experiences in which the person has had to risk, to take the unpopular stand, to see things differently, and to put everything on the line for the sake of those convictions. They are really spiritual experiences because they involve personal transformation. They call for a kind of self-surrender, not in the sense of the dissolution of the self or the surrender of personal moral autonomy, but in the surrender of the illusion of absolute autonomy. They de-center the ego and open the person to a higher principle, power, being. These crucible experiences can make or break, refine or incinerate a person. They are profoundly isolating experiences. What they do is force a person to come to grips with one's own center, take one out of one's self-defined world to what is really important and what really matters. How one responds sets the stage for all that follows; it defines a "point of view" that is truly one's own, not borrowed or simply learned from a book, even from a book about leadership and ethics! Every leader, as every moral person, will face situations of loneliness and vulnerability to attack, whether justified or not. Only commitment based on deep self-awareness will see the person through. Unless a business leader has faced some type of crucible or transformational experience that moves a person to a higher level of value, the only recourse is to focus exclusively on the material *goal* of making money.[7] Even qualities such as courage or risk taking, if they are not just foolhardy excesses, depend on how well a person is realistically anchored in a personal point of view.

Another approach to the issue of discovering what matters, especially for someone younger, is to ask, What does success look like to me? and Will I recognize it when it comes? If we don't try to answer that question early in life, and perhaps often, it will easily become a regretful lament in later life. Consider both work and nonwork values and goals. How do you integrate core values, work, dreams, personal and family priorities, finances, friendships, fun, interests, location, health, society?[8] Deal early with your desire for balance.

---

7. For a more sophisticated and robust understanding of spirituality and spiritual leadership in business organizational structure, see Margaret Benefiel, "The Second Half of the Journey: Spiritual Leadership for Organizational Transformation," *The Leadership Quarterly* 16 (2005): 723-47.

8. "Not sure how to devise your own life plan?" in *Inc.* (February 2004): 70.

Without a point of view nothing else will ultimately matter. People who are interested in going into business for themselves tend to ask themselves the following questions, in this order:

1. Where do I get the money—and how much do I need?
2. How do I come up with the right idea?
3. Do I buy a business or start one?
4. How do I get started?
5. What do I want out of life?

Norm Brodsky, an *Inc.* magazine columnist, points out clearly that it is the last question that must be asked first, along with the question, What do I like to do? Again, the issue is one of self-awareness. Who we are precedes what we do, just as a community of value precedes products and services of value.

Find Your Voice

While growth in self-awareness is foundational, it is only a beginning. Left to itself it can become narcissistic navel-gazing, as detrimental to development as frenzied activity without reflection. We all have at least some vague sense of ourselves, but it remains undeveloped because it is kept very private. After all, is not our self-awareness a very personal matter? Yes, it is personal, but not private. For self-awareness to grow it must come to expression. The transition from a drifter to a moral person involves finding *my* word and *my* deed. Take a moment to reflect on your words and deeds from yesterday. Were they internally driven? Once you become aware of what matters to you, you then become compelled to speak and to act out of that conviction. If you find that you never speak out against the flow, then you can be certain that you have not found your own center. There is no such thing as a safe risk! Courage comes from finding out what matters to you and then speaking and acting from that source. Another way of looking at the same thing is to observe what it is you *do* speak up about.

Merely ranting and raving are not the same as finding your voice. Neither is an incessant flow of self-congratulations and self-aggrandizements. The only thing they demonstrate is the discovery of an ego centered on the self. Finding your voice asks if you can express a *difficult* truth. What are you willing to risk to speak honestly? If you are unwilling to risk much, then you have not found your voice. There is always risk when speaking a difficult truth. Many everyday situations challenge us by questioning how much of a risk we are willing to take to find our voice: to jeopardize your position by saying something your boss doesn't want to hear; possibly to alienate a friend for the sake of the truth; to risk appearing foolish by speaking up against an idea/project that everyone else is buying into; to defend someone who is being bad-mouthed by everyone else or to question someone who is admired by all; to report an unethical practice that seems to be successful. Failure to speak out is to retreat to the performance of the drifter—"go along to get along." Perhaps the greatest enemy to courage is "group think," a sure sign that a person has not found her own word and deed.

But "getting along," you might counter, is not a vice. Harmony can be a virtue. In fact, teamwork is prized as elemental for successful business. There is a fine line between the crusader who is always pointing out what is less than perfect and the drifter who never finds his voice. How can someone know for sure which is at work? The "for sure" can come only from the person himself. But a practical test might be to reflect on whether you *always* come up with some good reason for not speaking the difficult truth. At that point "harmony" begins to sound like rationalization. Who you are and what matters to you do indeed become the final arbiters. As you become more in touch with your own word and deed, you will find yourself taking more initiative and more risks in speaking out and taking action. There is a snowball effect. As you begin speaking out, you will find yourself more in touch with what matters to you; and as you discover more of your own identity, you will also find more of your word and deed.

Connect with Your Listeners

Empathy sounds like a strange word to use in a business environment. After all, business is about the bottom line. What are the facts? Yet empathy, or the ability to connect with your listener, be it employee, customer, or supplier, is critical to business. Indeed "connecting with your listeners" is really the third stage of full self-awareness, or discovering what matters. If your sense of self does not resonate emotionally, then it is a partial self at best. Emotions, after all, are the best indicators of the operative values in our lives.

To speak of empathy, however, is not to speak of some kind of "I'm okay—you're okay" sentimentality. It doesn't mean trying to adopt someone else's feelings or trying to please everyone. It is more than just being friendly. It *does* mean to be aware of not only what others are thinking but also feeling, and to recognize that those feelings are at the heart of their identity as they are of yours. It is to find a way of reaching others and speaking to their concerns. To try to relate to people and not be aware of their feelings is to miss the mark completely or to come across as uncaring and manipulative. On the other hand, the empathetic person recognizes the needs of others, is approachable, and carefully picks up on what truly concerns the other.

The person with a true sense of self speaks not just to the mind but also to the heart. To speak only from the mind may help someone understand a program. Wonderful Power Point outlines can detail every step of the process so that no one can doubt the clarity of the change being called for. But by itself, the question remains, "Will anyone care enough to really commit to it?" The only force left to move the heart is the power of coercion, a poor substitute for engaging the whole person and achieving "buy in."

Yet, to speak only to the heart does connect emotionally to the listener. Everyone "feels good." The flow of energy is almost palpable. Everyone cares about change, but all are confused about what to do. It takes only a little time until everything settles back to "normal." This is the particular danger of the motivational speaker or the boss who constantly explodes. There is much heat but little light.

The harmony of mind and heart is a critical indication of the person who has found what matters to her. The connection to the mind and the heart of the listener is directly from the same center in the speaker. People will stop and listen. They sense that what is being said comes not just from a knee-jerk emotional outburst or from a "talking head" that does not know pain and sweat and doubt. There is a deeper connection of person to person. If a CEO is giving everyone an unexpected holiday, no one cares much about how it is said. However, if the CEO is announcing a layoff or trying to create a vision of hope for the company, then what and how something is said become critical. I have witnessed more than once how a CEO gets a reputation for being cold and calculating because of a necessary layoff, when I personally know the anguish and doubt that preceded the decision. The inability of the person to connect with both the head (the economic rationale) and the heart (the personal upheaval and pain) results in the inability to "connect with the listener"—the final outcome of not being deeply in touch with what really matters. Only what resonates in the leader can resonate in the follower. And the continual exercise of reflecting on what is important, finding your voice, and connecting with others will only deepen your sense of personal identity and form the center from which will flow both your morality and your ability to lead. Here are the building blocks required for real connectedness, as described by Dr. Henry Cloud in his outstanding book *Integrity: The Courage to Meet the Demands of Reality*:[9]

---

9. Henry Cloud, *Integrity: The Courage to Meet the Demands of Reality* (New York: HarperCollins, 2006), 58-60.

1. You need the ability to feel and be what is referred to as softhearted. It means you must first be in touch with your own emotions.
2. You must have good boundaries. You realize that their feelings are not yours. If you lose yourself in another person's feelings, you can usually not be very helpful. This requires balance. You feel for the other person but still know it is not *your* experience.
3. You need to listen in a way that communicates understanding. True listening and understanding occur only when *the other person understands that you understand.*

> For now try this on for size. As CEO you have come to the conclusion that a layoff is necessary. Write a script or make a presentation announcing the decision—keeping in mind what has been said here about connecting with the listener, as well as the danger of simply manipulating the feelings of others.

A similar realization is at the heart of Daniel Goleman's bestseller, *Emotional Intelligence.* Our emotional harmony, in short, reveals to us an understanding of ourselves that is richer, deeper, more powerful than any merely reflex understanding we might have of ourselves. In fact, there is substantial evidence that neither academic talent nor IQ are good predictors of on-the-job productivity. For example, when outstanding performers at Bell Labs—certainly a prestigious assembly of highly motivated, intelligent, and creative people—were examined for the secret of their success, one of the most important characteristics turned out to be their rapport with a network of key people. What they had mastered included "effectively coordinating their efforts in teamwork; being leaders in building consensus; being able to see things from the perspective of others, . . . persuasiveness; and promoting cooperation while avoiding conflicts."[10]

There is an interesting parallel here with a Chinese awareness called *guanxi,* the networks of mutually beneficial relationships essential to success. It is an awareness that there is no such thing as a purely business relationship. Rather, "you must blend formal relationships with personal ones, often on different levels. And even as you take, you must also give back."[11] My guess is

---

10. Daniel Goleman, *Emotional Intelligence* (New York: Bantam Books, 1995), 163.

11. For an interesting glimpse at Kai-Fu Lee, considered a technologist and self-help guru who has become a celebrity on Chinese university campuses, see Robert Buderi, "The Talent Magnet," *Fast Company* (June 2006): 80-84. Lee's book *Be Your Personal Best* is rooted in his attempt to incorporate the values of the West and East.

that every culture has some sense of this fact, whether it has a specific word for it or not. What we have tried to identify in the first part of this chapter is an attempt to get at the same thing. Lee's book describes "three concentric circles—representing value, attitude, and action—around which people should evaluate, plan, and live their lives."[12]

LEADERSHIP

What are the images that come to mind when you hear the word "leader"—CEO, general, president, boss, bishop, someone riding on horseback at the head of the troops? Do the images not turn spontaneously to some person in authority with a clearly defined status, role, and power? This is neat and clean—and conveniently takes most of us off the hook. Leadership in this scenario is always about "them"— management, president, board of directors, government. It is the classical "command-and-control" model that many of us have internalized at the same time that we rebel against it. If leadership is about "collecting the people," of bringing together the energy, talent, and values of each person toward the common values that the business brings to market, then leadership is more than management, and power is more than coercion. You can manage money and systems, but people must be led, unless, of course, you are only talking about controlling external behavior. In chapter 3 we have seen how business is first of all about creating a community of values. Values reside only in people. Those values, as we have seen earlier in this chapter, can be discovered, developed, enlarged, but they cannot be controlled or changed by regulating external behavior. However, once we have discovered and deepened what is important to us and found our point of view, we have by that fact found our own power. It is this power that is the basis of our leadership. Once we recognize that the power of authority is only one kind of power, we are in a position to explore all the different types of leadership that "collect the people." Of course, we will then also have to assume responsibility for our own power and the leadership that it implies. We all have the power to influence other people, and that sense of self, of my point of view, is the base of my power and leadership.

The following list of eleven sources of power is meant primarily as an exercise in identification. There may be more or they might be distinguished differently, but they do need to be recognized if we are to assume responsibility for leadership.

---

12. In Buderi, "The Talent Magnet," 80-84.

———— 1. *Physical force.* This is the most immediate, naked, and direct use of power. While it can play some role in the parent-child relationship, it is also present in the adult in the form of physical threat, fear for one's safety, or concern for one's property. If there is any significant degree of this type of power operative in a business, then not much else will matter.

———— 2. *Coercion.* This type of power is connected with people in authority and is what we usually associate with leadership and power. It comes from a recognized position that is the basis for granting tangible rewards for compliance or punishment for noncompliance. It is the form of power associated with the boss, the general, the manager. It is the power of those "in control" within a command-and-control model. Budgets and approvals, hiring, firing, promoting, salary increases are common business expressions of the power of coercion. There are times when this exercise is critical in business. It sets clear lines. It can create direction in an emergency. It is required when limits need to be set for a difficult person. However, if it becomes the most commonly operative power in a business, then there are other problems. Threats and fear will not bring out the best in people over the long haul.

———— 3. *Vision.* "Where there is no vision, the people perish" gives some indication of how important this power can be. People are willing to endure much if there is a future, a hope, something to look forward to. People need meaning not only in their personal lives but also in their work. If you have ever seen persons doing work that they consider meaningless, you will understand how crucial this aspect is. All of us have been engaged at times in work that is more meaningful than at other times. Consider how different your energy, interest, and commitment were to the meaningful work. After all, is *importance* not in direct proportion to the meaningfulness of a task? The person who can reach the mind and heart of others with a meaning they can identify with has perhaps the most power of all. Usually the person with the highest position of authority should be the one who articulates the vision or meaning. Others, however, may be able to communicate the vision more convincingly. There is also another dimension to meaningfulness beyond the larger meaning of a company's purpose and mission. It is the meaning that a person finds in the specific function he performs within the larger organization. The one who can help another find that specific meaning within the larger activity of the whole company shares an important function of leadership. A necessary caveat: vision is not the same as wishful thinking or fantasy. For a vision to be credible, it needs to be intelligible and rooted in truth. Much of what has been said about core values and personal identity is pertinent here. The focus of ultracapitalism on exclusively financial results has distracted many from the key leadership role of the creators and communicators of meaning—a meaning, as we have discussed previously, that does not begin or end with quarterly earnings.

_____ 4. *Identification.* This is the power exercised by the people who are admired or looked up to not because they can reward or punish but because they have a quality of life, a vision or character that others find meaningful in some way. While not always recognized as a source of power, these persons can have a huge influence on others. A telling question in a business is to ask who is admired and respected, and, even more telling, to find out why. It will tell you much about the company and its values, much more than a value or mission statement.

_____ 5. *Expertise.* This is the power that comes from knowledge. In an age when knowledge is king, the power of the expert is critical. The engineer, the accountant, the teacher, the inventory analyst, the IT professional—all have immense power over an entire operation, although they probably have none of the power associated with the coercive power of authority. In fact, these persons often have more real power than managers, although the manager has all the trappings of power. A number of aberrations can easily set in. The expert can belittle the power of the manager and set up a negative power struggle without ever accepting responsibility for the power inherent in his expertise. On the other hand, the expert can be promoted to manager in recognition of his power, with the result that the effective expertise is lost and a poor manager is gained. There is a real need to develop career paths for experts who recognize the leadership power they have without making them managers. By the same token, the knowledge experts need to acknowledge and assume responsibility for the real power and leadership they do have.

_____ 6. *Group norms.* This power is based in the group ethos, culture, and tradition. It is reflected in "the way we do things around here." While this power really resides in the group as a whole, it is exercised by those who, in one way or another, are the enforcers of the group norms. And that could be anyone from an administrative assistant who controls whom and what the boss sees, to the customer service rep who responds to a customer issue, to the human resource and accounting departments' enforcing company policy. Seniority can easily be the carrier of this power, which can range from the extremely subtle exclusion from the in-group to the blatantly "in-your-face" confrontation. Like all forms of power, its exercise can be ambiguous. For a company deeply rooted in core values, this is a power for maintaining and developing those values. For a company, department, or individual that doesn't like change, it becomes a club to ward off innovation and development.

_____ 7. *Access.* This is the power of relationship and reference—who has access to whom. While this includes the sense of personal access, its real power is in the deeper sense of who really *listens* to whom. In any given organization, to recognize who really has the ear of those in authority is to understand one of the most profound sources of power in that organization. These individuals can make or break another person or project. Who those individuals are cannot be determined by position or title on an organizational chart. They must be discerned in each organization. In any case, it is a sure bet that some people with this type of power are linked to the persons with positions of authority. It is the role of confidant and advisor when the person in authority is unsure of himself. That person also becomes the door to allow new initiatives or possible correctives to get the attention of the decision makers.

_____ 8. *Persuasion.* This is captured in the phrase "the power of persuasion." There is no doubt that it is a genuine source of power. Beyond the power inherent in the merits of the situation, it adds a further dimension of appeal that is convincing. Sometimes it might be a knack for strategic timing or an ability to connect emotionally, but it is real. Some people, and not others, are recognized for their power of persuasion. For some, it might be most effective on a one-to-one basis, and for others it becomes most apparent in a group situation. Its strength lies in its ability to mobilize and energize others. Its danger is that it can also lead people astray. It is a power independent of the merits of the idea or correctness of the direction being presented.

_____ 9. *Empowerment.* This buzzword of business contains a deep sense of power. It does not mean handing over power to another nor is it simply sharing one's own power. It is, in its best form, the *creating* of power. It is to help another find, and then support, the power within that person. It is born of the discovery of talent and ability and then nurtured by trust and encouragement. The person who can empower others truly is a source of power.

_____ 10. *Manipulation.* If power is the ability to influence others, then manipulation must also be reckoned with as a power. The problem with this form of power is not that others do what you want them to do, but with their being unaware of the consequences of what they are doing. That it works at least some of the time is attested to by the fact that most organizations have at least one manipulator or "politician," as this person is often termed. This form of power is high risk and usually deadly in the long run because, by its nature, it destroys genuine freedom and the search for the truth. It undermines real collaboration and teamwork. The power of manipulation must be confronted directly and decisively or it will feed a level of distrust throughout the organization. And the situation goes downhill from there if the manipulation is perceived as working.

_____ 11. *Negativity.* This is an extremely corrosive form of power. It can worm its way through an entire organization without even being recognized. It can take many forms, from not doing and not speaking to always complaining and always finding obstacles. A distinction needs to be made, however. There are complaints that originate from real caring about the organization. That type of complainer can sometimes be turned around by giving her authority to make needed changes. Remember that if no one ever complains, then one needs to worry if anyone really cares enough about anything. This type of complaint must be recognized as different from the ones that come from a negative attitude. Unfortunately, it is almost impossible to change a truly negative attitude. The person usually needs to be removed from the group. While most people can recognize the signs of a negative attitude, what they often overlook is that it is indeed a form of *power* over others.

> At this point, take the above list of types of power and rank them, from highest to lowest, as you exercise them in your work world or your personal life. Do the same for the actual exercise of power as you experience it at your business. It is probably most helpful to start with the top three most influential and the bottom three least influential and then fill in the rest. Another exercise might be to have someone who knows you well fill it in as they see you.

The point of this exercise is not to see how you might compare to some hypothetical model of the "correct order" for an effective leader. Other than the last two forms of power, the others are all legitimate and effective forms of leadership. The point here is threefold. First, there should be the realization that power and leadership are not restricted to just one type. Not only are there quite different styles of leadership, but also most of us operate out of more than one of them. In fact, the most effective leaders probably use a combination of several different styles depending on the circumstances and their ability. Second, the recognition of the types of power and leadership can lead us to the important realization that we all have power of some kind and therefore exercise some type of leadership. It is critical for each of us to recognize and to appropriate our own power so that we can grow in its exercise. As long as we can pass off leadership as belonging to those in "positions of power," usually meaning coercive power, then we can remain the drifter who takes no responsibility for our word and our deed. Third, in a healthy company, all of these forms of leadership (apart from manipulation and negativity) should be vibrant and alive, with everyone exercising some form of leadership. This realization did not go unnoticed when business executives from Fortune 1000 companies were asked by the Johnson School of Management at Cornell University, "What characteristics will business leaders need for success a decade from now?" The top two answers were *team building* and *compassion*.[13]

---

13. Marlene Caroselli, *The Business Ethics Activity Book: 50 Exercises for Promoting Integrity at Work* (New York: AMACOM, American Management Association, 2003), 103.

This critical function of building the community of shared meanings and values is one of the great joys and achievements of any business. Leadership is the art of being able to "collect the people" in developing a community of persons who find their own deep values actualized in their work. Is it any wonder that what people miss most when they retire or leave a company are the people with whom they have shared common meanings and values?

A final reflection from a group of business management consultants can bring this chapter to an end. Creativity is

. . . a search for two fundamental questions:
1. Who is my self?
2. What is my work?
. . . you can't know what or how you want to create until you know who you are and what you hope to do with your life . . . creativity exists within everyone, and that when people can't tap into their creativity it's because of an internal "voice of judgment" which is often heavily influenced by society, employers and parents.

People will be most creative when they feel motivated by the work itself. When people are engaged because of their own natural interest and satisfaction in their work, they will be challenged to be creative through their own intrinsic motivation. External pressures or rewards are never as effective as internal motivation. In order to tap into that resource, people must be matched to jobs that tap into underlying values that motivate and excite them.[14]

QUESTIONS FOR REFLECTION

1. What was the best and the worst day at work during the last three months? Why? Does it tell me anything about my own deeper values?
2. If my job leaves me working just for a paycheck and waiting for the weekend, what can I do to change myself or my situation?
3. An exercise in leadership development from Warren Bennis and Joan Goldsmith, *Learning to Lead.*[15]
   A. Given my goals for reinventing myself as a leader, what are the qualities that I bring that will enable me to be successful?
   B. What are the elements of my style, personality, and skills that will make learning to be a leader more difficult? What is it about me that tends to get in the way of being a successful leader?

---

14. "Creating a Climate for Innovation," *Wolf Management, Consultants Coaching Matters* 3, no. 6.
15. Warren Bennis and Joan Goldsmith, *Learning to Lead: A Workbook on Becoming a Leader* (Reading, Mass.: Perseus Books, 1997).

C. Remember a time in recent years when you learned a new skill, played a new role, or took on a new physical challenge. What talents did you draw upon? What was it about your thoughts, feelings, and actions that allowed you to be successful? What stood in your way?

D. How did you undermine yourself, devalue yourself, or misjudge yourself? What did you draw upon to overcome the odds and succeed?

4. Explore within yourself the three phases of leadership ("discover what matters"; "find your voice"; "connect with your listeners"). This can be done very effectively in a group, particularly if you are known by the group and can get feedback.

5. Name three people who walked through your dreams as heroes from the past and three leaders whom you respect from your current life. What difference have they made? What qualities do they bring?

SUGGESTIONS FOR FURTHER READING AND STUDY

Benefiel, Margaret. *Soul at Work: Spiritual Leadership in Organizations.* New York: Seabury Books, 2005. Addresses the spiritual dimension at work in organizations, with good illustrations of companies that live it.

Bennis, Warren, and Joan Goldsmith. *Learning to Lead: A Workbook on Becoming a Leader.* Reading, Mass.: Perseus Books, 1997. A book of exercises for developing business leadership. Anything by Bennis is worth reading. He can be considered the guru on leadership.

Cloud, Henry. *Integrity: The Courage to Meet the Demands of Reality.* New York: HarperCollins, 2006. A solid, no-nonsense psychological analysis of the qualities needed for business success.

Goleman, Daniel. *Emotional Intelligence.* New York: Bantam Books, 1995. An excellent summary of the role of emotions in human living.

Goleman, Daniel, Richard Boyatzis, and Annie McKee, *Primal Leadership: Realizing the Power of Emotional Intelligence.* Boston: Harvard Business School Press, 2002. The application of emotional intelligence to leadership, especially business leadership.

Greenleaf, Robert K. *Servant Leadership: A Journey into the Nature of Legitimate Power and Greatness.* New York: Paulist Press, 1977. A wise exploration of the nature of legitimate power and greatness.

Napolitano, Carole S., and Lida J. Henderson. *The Leadership Odyssey: A Self-Development Guide to New Skills for New Times.* San Francisco: Jossey-Bass, 1998. The book presents an exercise in leadership awareness through 360-degree feedback that is very effective but rather complex. It can be pared down without losing its power.

5

Personal Integrity

Money motivates
neither the best people nor the best in people.
It can move the body and influence the mind
But it cannot touch the heart or move the spirit.
That is reserved for
belief, principle and morality.

Dee Hock, CEO of Visa

In chapter 4 we explored the critical function of discovering our own identity, not in terms of what job we have or how much money we make but by identifying and owning what drives us, what is important to us, and what we really value. Only in this way will we tap into our own power. And it is that power that is the basis for the various forms of leadership that we are all called to exercise. In this chapter we need to explore more closely the relationship of that sense of personal power to what we generally call "belief, principle, and morality."

ETHICS: COMPLIANCE OR ACHIEVEMENT?

The Ethics of Compliance

Just as there is a spontaneous inclination to see business as a free-for-all restrained by external laws, so there is a natural inclination to associate ethics with external restrictions that limit our freedom. Nor should this be surprising. It is only natural to think of ethics or morality as something handed down. After all, is not our first encounter with morality the commands of our parents telling us "do this" or "don't do that"? Have not our first "sins" been those of "disobeying our parents"? Our first contact with morality comes as constraint from outside ourselves. Did not Moses bring down the commandments, hnaded down from God, from the mountaintop? Not only is ethics handed down, but it is also something handed down by a recognized authority that has the power to punish. It's only a small step, then, to see morality in terms of prohibitions and constraints. Ethics then becomes a question of compliance, if no longer to our parents or to God, then to our bosses, our peers, society's expectations, the law.

There is a broader dimension to this scenario. The United States is a nation founded on rights and law. Personal morality was a matter left to individual conscience formed in the nurturing communities of families, neighborhoods, and religions. However, there has been a growing tendency to distrust the power of personal morality and decency in favor of an ever-more-comprehensive web of law to control larger and larger sectors of human behavior. The ability of children to sue parents for neglect of one kind or another is just an extreme example. But as personal behavior becomes increasingly defined by legality, so the move to equating the legal with the moral becomes an easy, even unconscious, transition.

Business, then, can easily fall into the same cycle. Its ethics becomes compliance with the law. And government is more than happy to oblige, as evidenced in the incessant flow of new regulations concerning hiring and firing, taxing and filing, trading and polluting. This is not meant as a denunciation of laws or a simple-minded abandonment of their necessary role in society. After all, most legislation arose from abusive situations that demanded change. The areas of business law and regulatory compliance are necessary aspects of responsible business. Law, as legislated by elected politicians, does represent the will of the community. The corporation is itself a legal entity, and so is responsible to the legal authority that brings it into existence. True as this is, corporate law is *not* business ethics. Corporate law is the domain of a host of lawyers and politicians who sort out the limits of the legal and the illegal. While complying with the law is certainly a first, and usually necessary, step toward justice and morality, we are also aware that legal is, at best, only a crude approximation of justice. The law can be manipulated. There is first of all the issue of who controls or influences the politicians and lawmakers. Who gets heard and who doesn't? What type of issues will be declared legal or illegal? Then there is the question of who has access to the legal system, who gets caught, who can hire the best lawyers, and who has the deepest pockets. These factors can be more decisive in determining outcomes than the merits of the case. In addition, as Aristotle says, law by its nature is always a generalization. There is always one more judgment needed to determine which law fits which particular situation. When business ethics is reduced to legal compliance, then the very meaning of ethics is lost. At best, one can speak of an ethics of compliance. It is the immature morality of a child whose morality consists largely in doing what he is being told to do. If we see business as "free enterprise" and ethics as "constraint," then we are back to our initial dilemma, and both business and ethics are impoverished.[1]

In a global economy, the issue also has broader implications that will have to be addressed further in chapter 9 on globalization. If the challenge of the United States is to move beyond equating the moral with the legal, other cultures may face a quite different problem of equating morality with the commonly accepted ethos of the culture. Both situations call for a different perspective on the meaning of morality, in personal living as well as in business transactions. I will call this an ethics of achievement. It will form the basis of this chapter.[2]

The Ethics of Achievement

In order to focus clearly on the nature of personal morality, it may be helpful to separate it from its distortions. The deeper anything is rooted in the human person, the more potential it has both for a rich variety of expression and for every form of distortion and perversion. Happiness, love, marriage, religion, success—all have thousands of meaningful expressions as well as their corresponding aberrations. On the other hand, something more immediate, such as strong muscles or good abs, is fairly straightforward and easily defined. Obviously, a person's morals lie at the heart of who a person is. A first approximation, then, would be to clearly distinguish morals from some of its perversions.

First, a moral person is not "perfect." Indeed, those who measure morality in terms of being flawless or without fault suffer from an underlying sickness: a poor sense of themselves. At a deep, perhaps unacknowledged, level they yearn for an acceptance and approval that they really feel they don't deserve. The way to that Holy Grail of acceptance is to do everything right, to be all good, not to make mistakes. As Dr. Henry Cloud says, "They thrive on praise and being admired as a medicine to the underlying vulnerability in their souls."[3] After all, someone who is perfect, or almost so, must be accepted. They fail to realize that *"There will never be enough accolades to overcome bad feelings about the self."*[4] The real cure involves finding love and acceptance also in one's

---

[1] Robert C. Solomon, *A Better Way to Think about Business: How Personal Integrity Leads to Corporate Success* (New York: Oxford University Press, 1999), xv.

[2] This material draws heavily on Bernard Lonergan's writings, and the work of J. Michael Stebbins, director of the Gonzaga Institute of Ethics, Gonzaga University, Spokane, Washington.

[3] Henry Cloud, *Integrity: The Courage to Meet the Demands of Reality* (New York: HarperCollins, 2006), 188.

[4] Cloud, *Integrity*, 189 (emphasis in original).

weakness and failure. In other words, love must be found in who we are rather than in what we do. Easier said than done. The challenge is lifelong, but it is important to seek a solution in the right direction.

The failure to move in that direction usually leads to alternative options, both of which result in real immorality and are detrimental to business. Since no one really lives without fault, one solution moves in the direction of covering up mistakes, always finding someone or something else to blame. The other option leads down the path of nonperformance. Don't risk anything because you might fail. Don't try something new or different because you may not know what to say or how to act. Don't exercise any leadership because you may become too visible and vulnerable. It is so easy to criticize bosses and leaders. One reason, I believe, is because people who take on responsibility become very *visible*. As such, not only the strengths that brought them to the position but also their weaknesses and limitations become manifest for public scrutiny. It's so easy, then, to wonder how someone so imperfect could be considered a moral leader! It is even easier to shun your own responsibility for leadership under the pretext that you aren't good enough—meaning you are not perfect. Unfortunately, the person who is always after the pursuit of achieving the "ideal self" will be set up for a lifetime of excuses, blame, and nonperformance. The best one can do (the most moral!) is "to give up being perfect or ideal and, instead, embrace ownership of the results, go through the pain to improve, and enjoy the benefits."[5] In contradistinction to being fearful about not being able to do something perfect, Chesterton said wisely, "What's worth doing, is worth doing badly."

Second, a moral person is not just "nice." This is perhaps one of the most common assumptions and distortions of what constitutes, if not the leader, then surely the moral person. "Nice" is a very ambiguous term at best. We use it in such flattering senses as a "nice touch" or what you did for someone was really a "nice thing." At the same time we carry around spontaneous images of the "nice guy" being a wimp who is really afraid of confrontation, anger, or anything that will disturb the situation, as in "nice guys finish last." "Being nice" is not a virtue. In fact, it can often mask hypocrisy and superficiality. It can be very manipulative when it becomes an attempt to get people to "like me." It can neglect to offer corrective feedback because of excessive worry about getting along with people or fear of getting too deeply involved with others. Unfortunately, Jesus Christ is often portrayed as "nice." One need only be reminded that nice guys don't get killed. Considerateness and kindness and caring are virtues that are quite different realities from "being nice."

---

[5] Cloud, *Integrity*, 190.

Third, a moral person is not just "principled." Persons who claim to be principled have usually picked their own principles. After all, are not racists also "principled"? There is certainly something of value in being principled. That value lies along the lines of consistency, determination, steadfastness. Surely these are worthwhile qualities. But they are not absolutes, nor do they constitute the moral person. The downside of these same qualities is rigidity, stubbornness, and closed-mindedness. There can be a very fine line in any given action or judgment between being principled and being stubborn. How do you know which is at work? Certainly not by some other "principle." It's too easy to paint the moral person as someone on high who holds forth from his pulpit of principle. In this case, principles easily become effective weapons to beat up on other people. The real answer to the nature of morality lies at some deeper and more complex personal level.

Fourth, a moral person is not just "spontaneous" or "natural." Our age has become so complex, both in the exterior world of planning, managing, designing, forecasting, and in the interior world of psychological analysis and introspection that we yearn for a supposedly less-calculating, or some might say less-devious, response to the situations of our life. If only we could just be more spontaneous in our words and deeds, we would be more honest and, consequently, more moral in our responses. After all, do not the Gospels call for us to be "like children"? However, what is cute in the child is an embarrassment or even immoral in the adult. It is only cute in the child before the child reaches the age of reason or the age when the child starts to become a moral being. To ask Grandpa "why his teeth are so yellow" comes from a natural curiosity and openness that is admirable in the child not yet sensitive to the larger world of aging, image, and manners. The response is only more spontaneous, not more moral. Yet there is something of value in being aware of our natural and spontaneous reactions, as we shall see.

Fifth, being a moral person is not just a matter of being "altruistic." Surely to be altruistic, to be focused on the other rather than on oneself, must be some indication of real moral achievement. The problem comes from setting up a polarity between self-interest and the interest of others. They are not two ends of a continuum. When Adam Smith (who was a moral philosopher, not an economist as such!) wrote in *Wealth of Nations* that business would prosper most profoundly through the principle of self-interest, his meaning of self-interest is far different from the "greed-is-good" caricature that is often paraded as his meaning. Smith insisted that what people really want is respect and approval. If that is the case, then to care about others and what they want also comes from one's deepest sense of self-interest. Whenever an individual or a business sets up a dichotomy between self-interest and the interest of others, there is some serious problem at work. Self-interest becomes a short-term, "who-really-profits" type of thinking as opposed to genuine self-inter-est, which sees a relationship between acting in one's own best interest and acting in a way that is socially productive.[6] Self-sacrifice and altruism, while helpful categories in some contexts, can easily be misleading in our discussion at this point.

Sixth, being moral is more than "being human." While to call someone "a real human being" is high praise, it is also a very ambiguous term. On the one hand, we extol the human as the capacity for greatness in thought, feeling, or achievement. On the other hand, we excuse the folly and frailties of ourselves and others as "it's only human." In other words, while we seem to instinctively know the difference between the two uses of the word, it really is not very helpful in trying to define what it is that makes us moral human being.

INTEGRITY/AUTHENTICITY

Having reflected on a wide range of common misunderstandings of morality, we should be in a better position to explore further what specifically consti-tutes the moral person. "Human" comes close, but it is still too ambiguous. I am suggesting that the words "integrity" or "authenticity" might be more helpful. I have yet to see a discussion of leadership that does not give highest priority to that quality. The following sequence of qualities, outlined by Dee Hock,[7] puts the issue squarely at the heart of any consideration for hiring or promoting:

1. integrity
2. motivation — dangerous without integrity
3. capacity — impotent without motivation
4. understanding — limited without capacity
5. knowledge — meaningless without understanding
6. experience — blind without knowledge

Put in other words, without integrity all other outstanding qualities are put in jeopardy. We are once again faced with the issue of just what do we mean by integrity or authenticity. We usually have a fairly good sense of recognizing it when we see it in action over a period of time, but we're just not sure what it is, even though we recognize it as fundamental to human living. Another dif-ficulty is that it does not look the same in every person that has it, nor in the same person at different stages of life. It is so elusive because it does not refer

---

[6] Solomon, *A Better Way to Think about Business*, 32-34.
[7] In Solomon, *A Better Way to Think about Business*, xv.

to a specific virtue, such as courage or kindness, but to the unity or the relationship of all virtues to one another. Integrity comes from the root word for "whole." It refers to the wholeness of the person, to the totality of character, to the unity of the self. Other qualities that we associate with integrity include a sense of what endures through change and a sense of something that is never a permanent achievement but an ever-present challenge.

That still leaves the term, though used by all, vague at best and arbitrary at worst. On what basis is one person considered authentic and another is not? Or even, how do I strive for authenticity in my own life? What should be clear by now is that it is something that comes from within the person. As discussed above, an ethics that remains outside the self, whether that be handed down from family, friends, law, social expectations, even God, will always remain at best an ethics of compliance. While law can and, at its best, does reflect the general wisdom of tradition and the community at large, it does not create morality. As such, it will be viewed as a constraint that set enforceable limits on behavior. Our current obsession with passing more and more laws and engaging more and more lawyers does not represent an advance in morality. The very fact that more and more aspects of life in society are being regulated by law indicates, I believe, a deterioration of morality, which comes from within and is really unenforceable from without. The encroachment of law into ethics leads to a further equating of law and ethics which only further fuels the vicious cycle.[8]

If, to ground an ethics, we start from within the person, then we need to examine our own consciousness. The human spirit is not like an open port on a computer into which an ethical code is inserted. Nor is the mind an empty bucket into which information and learning are poured. Rather, there is an innate dynamic to the human spirit that constantly moves us beyond the present moment. It moves us forward by what Aristotle already had identified as a sense of wonder and which others identify as "the question."[9] It is the question that reveals an innate dynamism, that leads us on, that grounds the moral sense of the "ought" or "should" rising up within us, and that ultimately leads us to consciousness as conscience. It is the dynamics of our own consciousness that constantly calls for the "more" from us, that doesn't allow us to settle for anything but our best. The uneasiness of conscience lets us know that, despite

---

[8] Rushworth M. Kidder, *How Good People Make Tough Choices: Resolving the Dilemmas of Ethical Living* (New York: Fireside, 1995), 68-69.

[9] The works of Bernard Lonergan give a comprehensive, philosophically and theologically grounded account of the innate dynamism of the human spirit. See Margaret Benefiel, "The Second Half of the Journey: Spiritual Leadership for Organizational Transformation," *The Leadership Quarterly* 16 (2005): 723-47, who proposes a conceptual framework for spiritual leadership of organizational transformation using Lonergan's levels of consciousness.

any apparent well-being or complacency, we are being urged to move on. Without the question there is no learning, only memory. The question is the leading edge of my intending more than the present moment contains. My question is probably different from your question, and my questions today are not the same ones I had twenty years ago, but the process of questioning remains the same. It is this dynamic of constantly intending more than the present moment contains that not only grounds our own individual development but continues to drive the progress of the human race.

This intentional dynamic of the human spirit grounds an ethics of *achievement,* as opposed to an ethics of *compliance.* An ethics of compliance basically forbids us from doing things while an ethics of achievement demands our engagement. A person or a business becomes moral not by "not doing things" but by doing things rightly. An ethics of achievement calls out the best in us: have courage, be creative, find a way. This dynamic of the human spirit engages us fundamentally in four different types of operations that ground four basic moral imperatives. Each operation has distinctive and normative characteristics that must be examined in detail if we are going to stay true to our own dynamic. Let us examine them briefly.

Pay Attention

At the most fundamental level, our questioning takes us to data. What are the facts? They are the familiar questions of the reporter or of a good storyteller: Who? Where? When? What? Data is not only the data of the world about us that we sense through seeing, listening, feeling, but also the data of the world within: the awareness of the emotions that rise up, the images that come to mind, the sensations that attract us as well as the fears that repulse us.

Pay attention, be open to all that is relevant, whether agreeable or disagreeable. Do not exclude anything or anyone on the basis that it will conflict with my own view or my own purpose. Pay attention. It sounds so simple and basic yet is extremely difficult to follow all the way. There are many concerns that pull us in other directions. If we are in a hurry, we don't take the time to gather all the facts. We take another's word too easily. We don't get firsthand information. If we are under pressure to produce, we don't listen to dissenting voices or conflicting data. If we are tired or lazy, we want simple solutions without the complexity of real-life problems. If we are distracted or preoccupied with our own agenda, we don't really listen or hear what someone is telling us, especially if we don't like what is being said. If we are trying to make an impression, we parade the data that is favorable and suppress the facts that tell a different story. While paying attention to the facts seems so self-evident, it is also the most susceptible to our deepest emotions and private agendas. "Pay attention"—or, as business puts it, "speak with data"—is the most fundamental moral operation in our personal life as well as in the business world. Our neglect of this operation will poison the whole well.

> Consider some instances when you made bad decisions. How often did they involve the fact that you did not have adequate data? Then ask *why* your data was lacking. How often did it reflect your own preoccupations?

Explore Intelligently

At some point our questions for data and facts turn to making sense out of the data. What does it all mean? We try to find how all the pieces fit together intelligently. We struggle to discover what is really going on. Notice that it is still the question that is driving us, but it is a different kind of question. The Who? What? Where? When? become the Why? How? What does it mean? *Explore intelligently*. Not to move to this next set of operations is to stay at the level of data. The response to every action is a more violent reaction or, as it is more commonly termed, a knee-jerk reaction. Business and business leaders are particularly susceptible to this type of response because business is all about doing and making. Bad performance is met by outbursts of anger, and worse performance is met by even greater outbursts. Favorable results lead to spontaneous praise and celebration. But in both cases more heat than light is generated. To have the facts is only the first step in coming to a sound decision. Unless you are willing to allow the questions for meaning to have their full play, you will be short-circuiting an internal process that seeks to move us forward.

Blaming and praising are certainly two valuable responses to a situation. But unless we really understand what is going on, they can easily be misplaced. The Japanese have a business model that requires a person to ask Why? at least five times. For example:

1. Why do we have so much inventory? Because we need it.
2. Why do we need it? Because the customer wants it.
3. Why does the customer want it? Because he can't run short.
4. Why would he run short? Because of our long lead times.
5. Why do we have such long lead times?

There are at least three or more why's in this sequence that could lead to some positive solutions—other than the blame that would result by stopping at the first why. There are issues of longer customer commitments, identifying components with the longest lead time, and so forth. The point here, however, is not to solve an inventory problem but to recognize that the *data* of high inventory levels is only the first step in moving to a responsible decision. Only by following the further questions for understanding can the situation be met adequately, whether that be a business problem or a personal moral choice. Asking why five times is just a technique to help us not pass over the critical role of "exploring intelligently." To ignore this operation is to leave one in the bewildering world of data without a clue as to what is really going on. Even the best of responses to this world, then, is to unleash a flurry of frenzied activity that will only leave everyone breathless, a day late and a dollar short.

> Consider how many business goals or flavor-of-the-month initiatives are misplaced precisely because data is simply presented without adequate understanding. Can you think of examples, especially ones that are accompanied with praise or blame?

Judge Soundly

Again, at some point, our questions for understanding that generate various scenarios as to what is going on turn to questions such as Is it so? Is that really what's happening? Is it true? At this point, long explanations stop and answers are simply yes, no, maybe (with varying degrees of probability), or I don't know. While this type of question will probably lead us back to the data for confirmation and to understanding for adequacy of explanation, the final judgment always remains personal. It is interesting to note that the word "prejudice" comes from "*pre*-judge." There is nothing wrong with judging. The deficiency lies in judging *before* one has paid attention to the data and explored intelligently. The fact is we never have to make a judgment. Data hit us in the face and, unless our mental capacity is severely limited, we can usually understand explanations that are given. But when it comes to judgment, we can never take ourselves out of the picture. We can always say, I don't know or I need more evidence. We don't *have* to say yes or no. Am I being "principled" or just "stubborn"? No one can really tell me for sure. I have to decide, and no one can do that for me. Others can present data and offer explanations, but only the individual can make the judgment for herself. Precisely because judgment is so personal, it is the critical step of genuine morality. Consider that there is no issue of morality for a child until he is able to make a judgment, what we used to call "the age of reason." The fact that judgment is both personal and free makes it an indicator of morality. A person may have no control over the kind of data she can obtain and may have greater or lesser ability to comprehend that data, but she does have the ability to make or not make the judgment.

"Everyone complains about his memory but no one complains about his judgment" rings true *precisely because judgment is so personal.* Am I being courageous or reckless? Am I being prudent or procrastinating? Am I being ambitious or self-serving, clever or deceitful, selling or lying, convincing or exaggerating? The yes or no answer to this type of question is absolutely critical. For that is what makes the difference between fact or fiction, myth or reality, vision or illusion. While we can go to friends or confidants to help us sort out what's really going on, no other person can assume responsibility for our judgments. *Judge soundly* is at the root of every personal decision. Since judgment is so very personal, it is also open to the greatest personal deception. Our wants and desires, our hopes and fears, our loves and our aversions play such a decisive role in the judgments we make. What adds to the potential for the further distortion of reality is the fact that those judgments depend on the data we examine and the explanations we accept. Since judgment is so personal, we shy away from the obviously bad judgment. In its place, we tend to manipulate the data and distort the explanations to suit our underlying purposes. The devil as the "father of lies" and "prince of darkness" is an apt image because all falsehood is really a distortion of reality.

> Reflect on some tough judgments you have had to make. Did you vacillate between wanting to make the judgment right away and wanting to wait for a greater comfort level? What was influencing you and how did you finally resolve it? Does the imperative of *judge soundly* ring true?

Decide and Act Responsibly

Questions don't end with judgment. Once we have decided about the truth of the situation, questions such as What are we going to do about it? arise spontaneously. Now, however, the answers are not words but action: about doing it. It's about changing the world. It's not about what *is*, as arrived at in judgment, but about what is *not yet*, the future that we are to create. On a personal level, it is the lifelong task of making ourselves the persons we become. On a societal level, it is about making the world the place we want live in. As we have seen in chapter 3, business is about the human activity of producing the goods and services that, together with politics, education, and religion, attempt to make the world a better place for all.

If, as we have seen, judgment is an extremely personal moment, then deciding and acting responsibly is even more so. For what is "not yet" will only come to be from our own values. It is what we consider important that will move us to action. The operation of questioning at this point takes us to where our personal values are operative, often deeply embedded in our whole psyche and uncovered only in peeling back the motives and reasons for acting. It is what we explored in chapter 4 under "Discovering What Matters." It is why the ever-deepening understanding and assimilation of our values are so critical to all our activity. It is also why that discovery is a lifelong task. It is primarily our actions and not navel-gazing that really tell us what we value and where our loves are. *Deciding and acting responsibly* brings the intentional dynamics of consciousness to its highest fulfillment. "Moving beyond the present moment" reaches its natural goal, and morality finds its fullest expression. The whole movement is a process of self-transcending. Beginning with a basic awareness of the world, we move through understanding to judging to acting out of values that matter to us. The intentional dynamism that urges us on reveals itself in the question. Integrity or authenticity, then, is the self-transcending responsiveness to the questions as they arise in our life.[10]

> We have all experienced cynics and naysayers. They can be very bright and their judgments can be right on target, but they stand on the sidelines at best. There is probably some of that in all of us. The real issue is moving to the fourth level of responsible action. Discuss how you might effect change, both in yourself and in others.

A Self-Correcting Cycle

There is at least one more critical aspect to these four patterns of operations. They form a constantly repeating cycle. We move naturally and spontaneously from paying attention, to exploring intelligently, to judging soundly, to acting responsibly. They are not something we first learn to do and then follow the rules. This tends to be counterintuitive, since we are first confronted in life

---

[10] For a fuller exploration of the issue, see Bernard J. F. Lonergan, S.J., *Method in Theology* (New York: Herder & Herder, 1972), chap. 2, "The Human Good."

with rules, whether of our parents, of our culture, or of our religion. We learn the rules for good manners, trendy styles, proper behavior, the rules of the road for driving, for competent scholarship, for business success, and personal happiness. On the other hand, the operations and the questions we are identifying come from within; they are not handed down from the outside. They become the "shoulds" of our life, not from some external pressure to conform but from our own internal dynamism. They are our own consciousness in action through our own questions. The questioning keeps repeating itself, moving us forward. While we can learn to do it better, to be more in tune with our questioning, to be more open to the questions that arise, to be more aware of the different types of questioning operations, and so to respond to the process more effectively, we can't change the process. That would be accomplished only by examining different data, asking more questions and coming to different understandings and judgments—a process that uses the very dynamics we are affirming. That process, by its nature, is self-correcting because the cycle keeps repeating itself. Data that are missed on a first pass or are changed as the result of prior action now become the basis for new or more nuanced understanding. Better understanding and explanation lead to sounder judgment. More accurate judgment leads to more significant action. Action, in turn, changes data and opens up the process once again. It is this self-correcting dynamism that allows us to go forward in the hopes of improving. None of us is totally integrated, in complete harmony with ourselves and others. We are all some blend of authenticity and inauthenticity. We all have our own unique "next step" to take, if we are open to it.

Not only is the process self-correcting, it is also self-assembling and totally interactive. To stop the process at the level of data is to be in a stance of constant knee-jerk reactions. To stop at the level of intelligent exploration is to constantly explore options, to be entranced by endless possibilities, to be seduced by one plan after the other, to be dazzled by the smorgasbord of bright ideas and latest fads—but never to commit to or champion any of them. To stop at the level of judging soundly is to be right on target with the analysis of the situation, to know exactly what needs to be done, but to stand aloof and criticize others for not solving the problem. It is the stance of the cynic or constant complainer. Only the person or organization that works through all four levels of operations will bring forth the fruits of solid achievement.

Not only do the four types of operations form a whole, but they are also completely interdependent and interactive. One's understanding will only be as good as the data it is trying to understand, and one's judgment will only be as accurate as the understanding it is trying to judge. Correspondingly, one's actions cannot be better than one's judgments. The idea is only as good as the data it explains, and the judgment is only as true as the understanding that makes the data intelligible. Theories can be brilliant but not really explain the data at hand. Just as dangerous is the person full of goodwill, eager to help, but without a clue as to what is really going on.

A final and striking example of both the effectiveness and validity of the dynamism of the four levels of questioning can be found in the original English practice of "trial by jury." Why has this practice, despite its limitations, not only endured but expanded over the centuries as the best attempt to render at least a rough approximation of justice? Consider how it is grounded in the following intentional dynamics of the human person:

witnesses	bring data	pay attention
attorneys	propose competing explanations	explore intelligently
jury	decide which explanation is true/false	judge soundly
judge	direct the process and pass sentence	act responsibly

Not only does the process recognize that each set of operations is different but, even more importantly, that the fairness of the process is protected by having each group of persons be responsible for only one operation. The greatest miscarriages of justice occur when the same person is jury, judge, and executioner. In our own moral life, of course, we don't have the same type of checks and balances provided by different people being responsible for the various levels of questioning. By the same token, it also assures that we are the one-and-only version of ourselves.

This exploration of the conscious dynamism of the human spirit has numerous applications. We have examined several: a touchstone for determining integrity, a grounding of personal morality, an understanding of the integral link between morality and integrity, and a call to transformation and self-transcendence.[11] What might be more surprising is to recognize that what we now consider to be sound business practices are such because they, too, are grounded in this internal dynamic of our consciousness. Consider the following.

---

[11] What we have not discussed is its relation to the perennial epistemological problem of subject and object, or subjectivity to objectivity. A large part of Lonergan's personal effort was to explicate how objectivity can be reached only by authentic subjectivity. Only in judgment do we reach the true or the real. A brief summary can be found in Lonergan, *Method*, chap. 3, "Meaning."

Brainstorming. Why does it work? It is effective to the degree that it gives free reign to the first two types of operations: paying attention and exploring intelligently. By not allowing judgment, or prejudgment, to enter into the dynamics, the path is open for a free flow of all potential data and possible understandings. The constrictions of true or false, doable or not, do not come into play at this point. Only after all possible data and understandings have been aired is there any attempt to bring them to some type of judgment and action.

Teamwork. Why has it become essential? Our world has become so complex that there are far more data and potential explanations than any one person could ever master. Obviously, the more adequate the data and the more thorough the understanding, the better the judgments and actions can be.

Continuous improvement. This business practice has become fundamental to business success in our times. It is also reflected in such movements as Kaizen, (Imai), Total Quality Management (Deming), Continuous Process Improvement (Hammer), and The Learning Organization.[12] Why have they become so basic and successful? Is it not because they derive much of their strength and effectiveness from the fact that they are concrete applications of the basic cycle of self-correcting operations that move us forward? Every improvement and every corrective action leads to further data which are then brought into the dynamic to create better understanding leading to changes in operations. This new cycle produces further data which start the process over again. People can easily tie into these operations because they resonate with their own internal dynamic.

Leadership. No matter how many people are involved in researching data, analyzing the numbers, doing market research, forming opinions, exploring options, there comes a time when someone has to take charge. Since judgment and decision are, by their nature, extremely personal, some *one* has to take responsibility. Others can agree or disagree, but finally everyone needs to buy into the decisions made. Teamwork and cooperation, as critical as they are, can never take the place of someone to make final judgments and decisions. Peter Drucker is clear on this point. As much as he is a strong advocate of flattening the layers of an organization and of creating greater transparency, he also states that talk of the end of hierarchy is "blatant nonsense." While there is no single right form of organization, it must have clear lines of responsibility and have a final authority.[13] There is an important corollary. Since judgment and decision making are the most personal human activities,

---

[12] Peter Senge, *The Fifth Discipline: The Art and Practice of the Learning Organization* (New York: Currency, 2006).

[13] Peter F. Drucker, *Management Challenges for the 21st Century* (New York: HarperCollins, 1999).

it would follow that the tendency in business to push decision making down to the lowest level possible would also empower the most people. We naturally own and take responsibility for our judgments and decisions in a way that we never could in just presenting facts, offering opinions, or following orders.

Truth telling. At a time of huge corporate scandals, this hardly seems like a dominant characteristic of business. Actually the opposite is true. It is precisely the neglect of truth that has led to business disasters. Truth is not the same as a spreadsheet full of numbers. Numbers are only data that require the additional human and moral operations of interpretation and judgment to arrive at the truth. If arriving at the truth is a profoundly human activity requiring integrity and self-transcendence in addition to data and intelligence, then telling the truth is an important quality for success in business. Adding more and more levels of regulations and oversight will definitely add cost to any operation but will not guarantee greater truthfulness. What is needed are people who are in touch with reality. Business is always about results. "*Spending time in some alternate universe that does not exist to make the one we are living in feel better*" is a recipe for disaster.[14] The point here is the recognition that "telling the truth" is an authentic human achievement, and "not telling the truth" is a moral rather than a technical failure. Recent business scandals give adequate testimony to that fact.

INTEGRITY/AUTHENTICITY AND LEADERSHIP

When we ask the question What makes a leader? we usually end up with a list of outstanding qualities. As good a list as any can be found in C. Napolitano and L. Henderson's *The Leadership Odyssey*.[15] There, the qualities are explored under the rubrics of "Values: Qualities of Being" and "Perspectives: Habits of Mind." Each one has a long list of attributes. Thus, under "Qualities of Being" we find the following:

vision	integrity
passion and courage	optimism and self-confidence
focus and discipline	flexibility
tenacity and resourcefulness	humanity
self-renewal	balance

---

[14] Cloud, *Integrity*, 109. Part 3, "Oriented Toward Truth," is a dose of reality that every successful business needs to heed. The book's subtitle, *The Courage to Meet the Demands of Reality*, is indicative of the general thrust of the book.

[15] Carole S. Napolitano and Lida J. Henderson, *The Leadership Odyssey: A Self-Development Guide to New Skills for New Times* (San Francisco: Jossey-Bass, 1998), 13-55.

Similarly, under "Perspectives: Habits of Mind," there is an equally impressive list:

embraces change	tests assumptions
shifts paradigms	thinks holistically
tolerates ambiguity and paradox	trusts intuition
takes risks	seeks synergies
models values	

While all of these qualities are worthwhile and can surely be an asset for any leader, they suffer from one fault—they don't *all* exist in *any* leader! You don't determine who is a leader by identifying each of these characteristics in any one individual. In addition, you can keep finding endless variations on the lists themselves. These qualities make a good wish list, but they are hardly constitutive of leadership. If someone only became a leader to the extent that he possessed all these qualities, the existence of any leader would be in doubt.

AN EXERCISE

Name some examples of persons you would call leaders, either alive or dead. Make your own list—from your personal experience or from historical figures such as Winston Churchill, Mahatma Ghandi, Abraham Lincoln, Mother Teresa, Michael Jordan, just to start you thinking. Make your list before you continue reading. Now try to identify the qualities each person exemplified that make you consider them a leader. What becomes clear, I believe, is that no *checklist* of specific virtues and mental abilities will be common to your list. This becomes even clearer if you can do the exercise in a group. It must be something else that defines a leader because we do, in fact, recognize leaders even if we are unable to define them.

Review your list, and see if some form of *integrity/authenticity* is not critical to your choice. If this is so central to leadership, then we need to see how we might promote this quality in ourselves and in others.

Self-Determination

The first critical step to authenticity is to recognize that we are drifting, that our words and our deeds, at least initially, are really the words and deeds of others. What others are doing is our guiding star. Either consciously or unconsciously, it determines our living. This may not even involve any dishonesty or hypocrisy in itself, though it rarely remains that way for long. Just as the infant at some point takes the spoon from her mother's hand and says, in effect, "Let *me* do it," so there comes a moment when we realize that we really make ourselves the person we become by the choices we make. It is the critical moment of personal morality. Another determination of that moment is when we recognize that we can make a difference. At that point we no longer just share in the world of other people's ideas and values but become a *source* of value in our own right. At that point we have passed from an ethics of conformity to an ethics of achievement. It is this type of morality that is so critical for business because business itself is about achievement, about making and doing.

Growth in Authenticity

If we are all some mixture of authenticity and alienation, of loving and not loving, of egoism and transcendence, then how do we know whether our responses are authentic or not? An answer to that question takes us back to the inner dynamism revealed in consciousness through the question. The most any person is capable of is to be as open and honest as possible to the questions that do arise within her—as they arise, in the context they appear. We are unable to do more, but to do less is to move away from authenticity and to become alienated from our own self. The questions of the child and of the old man are not the same. The question of the CEO and the production-line assembler may not be the same. But they can all be authentic or inauthentic. It is only as we respond honestly to the present question that the next one can arise. The easiest way of avoiding a more difficult question or choice is not to deal with the immediate question. If a business doesn't ask the question of whether its product is being advertised honestly, it will never have to deal with the question of whether its product is of any real benefit to anyone at all.

The obstacles to personal authenticity are myriad: ego, conflict avoidance, grudges, prejudices, laziness, fatigue, impatience, shortsightedness, emotional distortion, fear of any number of specters, anxiety, self-doubt, and so on. We can each name our own, and they will probably differ over a lifetime. The most we can hope to do is to respond as openly and responsibly as possible to the question before us at this moment. In that question we can find the way forward through our own inner drive to transcend our present self at this present moment.

Our alienation, then, is regrettable but hardly surprising. What is a far greater danger is ideology, the personal or cultural *justification* of our inauthenticity. It is adopting the lame excuses, the rationalizations, the unexamined assumptions of our family, our race, our nation, our world at this moment in history as the basis for what is right. It is the glib answers such as "business is business" to any question beyond immediate profit. Ideology of any kind, whether to the right or to the left, is the greatest threat to personal morality and to business success precisely because it prevents further questions from even arising or being taken seriously.

Perhaps we can better appreciate at this point the need for balance and self-renewal in personal as well as in business life. A person without balance of head and heart, of work and family, of activity and retreat, will not allow the real issues to arise. Questions that go beyond the individualist point of view will not be addressed. The nagging doubt, the uneasy conscience, the uncomfortable "shoulds" are always put off for another day. Alienation from ourselves grows quietly deeper until we no longer know what is truly our own word and deed. Our own rationalizations grow stronger and the possibilities of real change, whether personal or business-wise, grow dimmer. And just as there is a spiral of achievement that continues to build on prior success, so there is a spiral of decline that leads to further and further contraction of choices until it results in atrophy.

Summarily, when people intelligently and responsibly ask and answer questions, and act on those answers, problems get identified and solved; new ideas are not squelched; *progress* is promoted. On the other hand, when people don't pay attention and explore intelligently, problems tend to get overlooked until it is too late to handle them easily. Situations and people are misunderstood; people act on the basis of supposed facts and theories that are not true. Decisions are based on disvalues, and compromises head for the easiest but least effective course of action. *Decline* sets in until the only thing that still makes sense is making money. The spiral of decline has reached the bottom. Business is no longer about producing valued goods and services. There are two options. Close the business, or manipulate the books in such a way as to show that money is still being made!

Nurturing Interiority

The notions of renewal and retreat have always been integral to every religious tradition. The interesting development is that they are now becoming important to business as well. It is somewhat paradoxical for business, which is so focused on doing and making, to recognize the value of "not doing." It does make complete sense, however, when we come to appreciate the importance of personal values in the business enterprise. We are all in the process of *becoming*—led by the dynamism of our questioning and our loving. Unless we pay attention to that dynamism, our only response will be more frenzied activity, putting out one brush fire after another, overextending ourselves till stress or burnout wins the day. Self-renewal—and business renewal—means stepping aside, a quiet walk, a weekend away to allow the dim voices within to get a hearing, to allow the voice of others to enlarge our single vantage point. Whether the retreat be as a business group or as an individual, a number of basic conditions are recommended as critical to success.[16]

Set aside a minimum of three days. The whirlwind of constant activity needs to slow down. Anything in motion tends to stay in motion. And it is the constancy of demands, responses, and stress that keeps anything new or different from coming to the surface. We want quick fixes, including the quick fix of a retreat.

Locate in an unfamiliar setting. There is a tyranny about the familiar: the same office, the same routines, the same faces, the same products, the same problems. They all tend to dull the senses and give one a false sense of comfort and security. Obviously, the same holds true of the extensions of our work, such as cell phones and laptops.

Embrace the uncomfortable. Allow the uneasy questions to arise and be heard. Listen to the feelings that make us uncomfortable. We often ignore feelings in our daily preoccupation with thinking and making decisions. The fact is we are feeling creatures. Our feelings will reveal our deeper agendas. Watch for signs of discomfort: frustration, worry, guilt, sadness. They tend to come to the surface as we relax. They can also lead us to the places where we find peace.

Allow unconscious motives to surface. This may well require the help of others, perhaps a coach, a friend, a confidant, sometimes even a person hostile to us. Here is a list that can get us started in discovering some possible unconscious motivation:

- I want to be liked.
- I am smarter than those around me.
- It's better to be reasonable than unreasonable.
- I don't make mistakes.
- Tasks are more important than relationships.
- I want to stay safe and comfortable.

---

[16] Witmer & Associates, 2003, www.witmerassociates.com, etips no. 9, "Renewing Yourself and Your Career." They offer many helpful services for training, development, and personal coaching.

- Ego is bad.
- I must protect my position.
- I must control this situation

More consideration will be given to this subject in chapter 8 on moral development. The important thing is to find ways continuously to nurture our spirit because leadership and authenticity are not some fixed stage of development or established position of authority but an ongoing process by which we achieve our main task in life—to give birth to the one and only version of ourselves. Perhaps Jack Welch's words are beginning to sound familiar: "A leader in times of crisis can't have an iota of fakeness in him. He has to know himself—and like himself—so that he can be straight with the world, energize his followers, and lead with the authority born of authenticity."[17]

QUESTIONS FOR REFLECTION

1. If you have not carried out the exercises boxed in the text, do so now.
2. Do you think Jesus was a leader? Why or why not?
3. Consider how Jesus used the *question* in so much of his teaching: answering questions with questions; using questions to draw out the meaning of a parable. Come up with examples.
4. Expand on the relationship of law to morality. In what ways are they similar and in what ways are they different?
5. "To him who has, more will be given, to the other all will be taken away." Is the meaning of this seemingly "unfair" biblical verse enhanced with our description of *progress and decline?* Is the verse a good business model?
6. Reflect on the role of prayer and morality, especially if morality is based on the self-transcending dynamism of the human spirit and prayer is the stance of absolute openness to God.
7. How does a religious experience of being loved by God promote true integrity/authenticity?

SUGGESTIONS FOR FURTHER READING AND STUDY

Bakke, Raymond, William Hendricks, and Brad Smith. *Joy at Work: Bible Study Companion.* Seattle, Wash.: P V G, 2005. How the personal values of one person laid the foundation for a different way of running a large corporation.

---

[17] Jack Welch, "Five Questions to Ask," *Wall Street Journal,* October 28, 2004.

Cloud, Henry. *Integrity: The Courage to Meet the Demands of Reality.* New York: HarperCollins, 2006. The critical role of truth in a business operation.

Lonergan, Bernard J. F., S.J. *Method in Theology.* New York: Herder & Herder, 1972, part one, 3-124. A general introduction to the seminal thought of one of the greatest philosophical thinkers of our times.

———. *"Existenz* and *Aggiornamento."* In *Collection: Papers by Bernard Lonergan, S.J.,* ed. F. E. Crowe, 240-51. New York: Herder & Herder, 1967. This and the following article are good introductions to Lonergan's thought on the self-transcending dynamism of the human spirit.

———. "Dimensions of Meaning." In *Collection: Papers by Bernard Lonergan, S.J.,* ed. F. E. Crowe, 252-67. New York: Herder & Herder, 1967.

Secretan, Lance H. K. *Inspirational Leadership: Destiny, Calling and Cause.* (Canada: Macmillan, 1999). The fact that he writes a regular column in the business journal *Industry Week* is itself a telling recognition of the role played by the human spirit in business. Web site: secretan@industry week.com.

6

Ethics as Culture

A company's values—
what it stands for,
what its people believe in—
are crucial to its competitive success.
Indeed, values drive the business.
Robert Haas, CEO of Levi-Strauss

In the previous chapter we looked at morality and integrity from the perspective of the individual person. After all, there is nothing more personal than the exercise of one's freedom. We make ourselves the persons we become through the moral choices we make over a lifetime. Our very identity is at stake. "The devil made me do it" is humorous precisely because of its blatant incongruity. If there were no personal freedom, there would be no issue of morality. Dogs and cats can be well behaved or ill behaved, but only human beings are capable of being moral or immoral. In the depth of consciousness, what we call conscience, each of us stands alone before God.

However, if we sometimes talk about the bad apple spoiling the whole barrel, is it not also true that a bad barrel spoils the apple? In other words, while morality is indeed the most personal dimension of who we are and what we do, it is a rare individual who can stand alone in the face of immense pressure to conform. "Everyone does it" usually settles the argument. Loyalty to the group, as sociologists are fond of repeating, is one of the most powerful norms of behavior. No one wants to be ostracized; we need to belong. In the United States we have an added problem: the myth of the rugged individual, the frontier conquered by the courageous and isolated pioneer, the sheriff who rides into town and single-handedly takes care of evil and corruption. "Anyone can be a millionaire" and "you just need to pull yourself up by your bootstraps" reflect a can-do attitude that is surely admirable but only tells a part of the story. Most people are not as totally internally directed as the American myth might suggest. In fact, the reality is probably more what Princeton anthropologist Clifford Geertz envisioned when he says that a human being all alone in nature would not be a noble, autonomous being, but a pathetic, quivering creature with no identity and few defenses or means of support.[1] Our identity is created in the tension and balance between the individual and the community. While authentic morality moves us to responsibility for our words and deeds, those words and deeds are deeply influenced by the words and symbols, the art and play, the politics and history of our culture. Our relationships with others, both past and present, play a critical role in the formation of our moral identity. It is those relationships that form us into communities. For most of us, that includes the communities of family, church, neighborhoods, friends, and work.

Business, then, whether privately or publicly owned, is not just a random collection of individuals, but an extraordinary community different from all others. It is a social institution but independent of the state. Unlike the family, it is a freely chosen community. It is not a church, not a state, not a family, not a welfare agency. It is an economic association with distinct goals and responsibilities that can command more time and effort than a family and more loyalty than a state, yet remain relatively independent of both. This can, no doubt, have ambiguous implications, but it does allow for another level of civil society that is not simply a captive of the state or the family. It is primarily a *human* community formed by the human activity of providing for one's existence through work and commerce. It is significant to note that cultures without a strongly developed business economy tend to be dominated by family, tribe, state, or religion. Business, by creating a different type of community, enlarges the notion of civil society by mediating between the family and the state. It enriches the range of human associations by adding another distinct type of community to the compulsory and free associations that compose the total human community which is, in our times, truly global.[2] In fact, it is hard to imagine that democracy could be a viable form of government without the kind of independence that business brings to a people.

Since business is indeed a community, then it is not enough to think that the demands of business ethics can be satisfied on an individual level. To talk only about "bad apples" or simply to insist that everyone sign a code of ethics can imply that ethics is strictly a personal matter between the individual and his conscience. It effectively takes the company off the hook. It also suggests that an individual either is or isn't moral, and there isn't much anyone can do about it. In reality, there will be some who will deliberately choose bad things. There will also be those who try hard to do what is right. The majority, however, will tolerate whatever seems to be the standard. It is that standard which

---

[1] Robert C. Solomon, *A Better Way to Think about Business: How Personal Integrity Leads to Corporate Success* (New York: Oxford University Press, 1999), 45.

[2] See Michael Novak, *Business as a Calling: Work and the Examined Life* (New York: Free Press, 1996), 125-28, in which the author emphasizes the role of business in building communities.

is the achievement, not primarily of the individual, but of the entire group. Just as the values of a company are embodied in every aspect of its operations and become its culture, so, too, its moral standards are embodied in the culture. Ethics, then, while always extremely personal, is also an organizational issue that has everything to do with the development of an ethical culture.[3] Some might dismiss culture as being "fluff" or the "soft stuff" of business— the pizza parties and celebrations organized by the human resource department. In fact, culture is the set of meanings and values that permeates every aspect of a business or a society. It's about disciplined people who engage in disciplined thought and action. Its assumptions drive the whole business effort, as we have seen in chapter 3, on core values. Nothing less holds true for a company's moral culture. Most formation in business ethics (as most other aspects of business skills) will take place in the business organizations where people actually live out their day-to-day decisions. How those decisions will be made will be the result, by and large, of the company's ethical culture. That culture can be approximated by focusing on key formal and informal elements that can and must be identified and managed if a company is going to take seriously its responsibility to foster an ethical culture Is it worth the effort? Consider the following:

- A *culture of integrity* prevents Enronesque disasters from occurring and builds loyalty among customers and employees.
- A *compelling brand* evolves from consistent application of ethical guidelines.
- A *competitive advantage* ensues when people feel free to speak the truth, to ask tough questions, to disagree, and to argue.
- A *productive workforce* flourishes when employees spend their time and energy on the business they need to conduct, not on destructive politics and dysfunctional relationships.
- *Consistent leadership* that makes ethical behavior an integral part of everyone's job builds unstoppable momentum for the company.
- *Positive morale* results when employees are treated and treat one another with honesty and respect.[4]

Our analysis of the moral culture of a business must take us to every aspect of the business. James Collins and Jerry Porras remind us that a company's val-

---

[3] Lynn Sharp Paine, "Managing for Organizational Integrity," in *Harvard Business Review on Corporate Ethics* (Boston: Harvard Business School, 2003) 85-112, in which she argues that companies need more than compliance-based ethics programs designed by lawyers. That "more" is an ethical culture.

[4] Henry Cloud, *Integrity: The Courage to Meet the Demands of Reality* (New York: HarperCollins, 2006), 240.

ues must be translated into "the very fabric of the organization—into goals, strategies, tactics, policies, processes, cultural practices, management behaviors, building layouts, pay systems, accounting systems, job design—into *everything* that the company does."[5] This is hardly fluff or frosting on the cake. Real cultural change will probably involve terminating employees who cannot or will not buy into that culture.

FORMAL ELEMENTS OF AN ETHICAL CULTURE

In analyzing the components of a strong moral culture, we will follow the list of contributing factors as outlined by Linda Treviño and Katherine Nelson in *Managing Business Ethics.*[6] The major division is between *formal* and *informal* elements. The formal elements are identified as leadership, organizational structure, policies, reward systems, selection and training, and decision-making process.

Leadership

The single most important element in determining the ethical culture of a company is its leadership. And that tone is set at the very top. Unless the president or CEO makes clear ethical decisions, a lack of integrity will run through the whole organization. Department heads and their reports will follow the cue set by the chief executive, and the rest is an easy downward flow to everyone else. As we have seen, leadership and morality are integrally linked. What the leader stands for is what will be played out in the day-to-day drama of hundreds of business decisions. The role of the leader in setting the business culture is most clearly seen in the role of the founder of a business. Most businesses derive their distinct culture from the words and deeds of their founder. "What would Walt do?" was the guiding question leading the development of the Disney empire. "We use everything but the squeal" was the result of Armour's obsession with not wasting anything in his meat-processing business.

That the leader sets the tone is a commonplace. How the leader accomplishes this is a more difficult matter. Very few, if any, chief executives will say that they expect people to act immorally. More indicative is whether the CEO ever talks about ethics. It is not enough for a CEO to merely *presume* ethical

---

    [5] James C. Collins and Jerry I. Porras, *Built to Last: Successful Habits of Visionary Companies* (New York: HarperBusiness, 1994), 201.
    [6] Linda Klebe Treviño and Katherine A. Nelson, *Managing Business Ethics: Straight Talk about How to Do It Right*, 2nd ed. (New York: John Wiley & Sons, 1999), 204-28.

behavior. Silence is consent. An unethical vice president or manager has as much support for not acting ethically as for acting ethically. A first test then is whether the CEO speaks out clearly for company values that include clear ethical conduct for all.

At a second level, however, there is the tougher test of not only what the CEO says but what she does. A culture of candor and transparency starts at the top. Is the CEO not only open to, but also insistent on, hearing bad news? Does he immediately react with blame, or does he shoot the messenger? Does he admit his own mistakes? Does she always sugarcoat bad news with half truths in communicating with employees? All of these behaviors will communicate deep-seated messages about the ethical culture of the company, and even more importantly, promote the same in everyone else. If the managers who lead the company stop telling the truth to their employees, deception will ripple throughout the company. Employees will then lie back to their managers and to one another. How will executives find out what is and what is not working at their companies if they do not promote a culture of telling the truth. The problem only grows more complicated by the fact that the higher an executive climbs, the easier it is to distance himself from problems. Top officials tend to surround themselves with yes people who filter out bad news. However, no one is really fooling anyone. The consulting firm Towers Perrin recently conducted a survey of one thousand Americans working in a broad cross-section of industries. The message to management was simple: "Tell it like it is." Only slightly over half of the survey respondents believe that their company generally tells the truth. Equally troubling is that they believe their employer is less truthful with them than with customers or shareholders. Most feel that their organization is trying too hard to spin the story.[7]

A more subtle message is sent by a CEO's personal compensation. The role of a CEO in contemporary business has never been more crucial. In more traditional times, the CEO's role might be more like a supermanager steering the corporate ship in steady waters. However, when change is the only constant and decisions are made in a global context, the role of the CEO becomes extremely critical and far-reaching. His decisions can easily make and break companies. High salaries are not only justified but required. Do not rock stars, actresses, sports stars make as much and more? But what about salaries that are completely out of line with other officers or that are based on meeting only short-term objectives that can be more easily manipulated (e.g., short-term stock options)? What about less-than-full disclosure of the complete compensation awarded to top management, especially when more of it is hidden

---

[7] *Towers Perrin Monitor* (January 2004). Monthly HR newsletter published by Towers Perrin (www.towersperrin.com).

(e.g., in bonuses, options, termination and retirement benefits) than is disclosed? Perhaps the most devastating consequence of these practices has less to do with the amount of money involved and more to do with their impact on the ethical culture. Does it not send the message that it's OK to grab all you can get? And keep it quiet! Why should other managers—in fact, why should anyone—exercise more restraint than what they witness at the top? Reform, I believe, needs to start with transparency and with compensation based on performance for long-term growth.

The visibility of top management's commitment to ethics and values cannot be overestimated. Charles O. Prince was appointed CEO of Citigroup, the world's largest financial services firm, in 2003. He decided that talking more about culture and values is exactly right. "We have to have the right moral compass that steers us down the middle of the road." Consequently, he intended to devote more of his time in 2004 talking to both employees and customers about values. His concern, though, is to internalize a strong code of ethics. As he says, "You can't think of this in terms of control . . . You can't expect to have policemen lined up along the side of a road saying, 'you can't drive here.'"[8]

There is another aspect to the leadership role that has surfaced since the corporate scandals of the past ten years. That issue is the role of the board of directors with respect to corporations. How independent is the board? Supposedly the board represents the interests of the shareholders, which, as we have seen, ties in to the interests of all the stakeholders in the long run. But how independent are the directors if (1) the directors are picked by the CEO; (2) the CEO is also chairman of the board; and (3) the CEO sets the board agenda? None of these conditions leads inevitably to unethical behavior, but they surely weaken the checks and balances that make top management accountable to something beyond itself. One of the needed reforms would lead to boards that maintain a stronger independence. Independence does not imply hostility or antagonism to management; it does, however, mean that management will be held accountable. There is more work to be done along these lines.

Organizational Structure

Our first inclination is to think of ethics in personal terms, and rightly so, but ethical behavior is strongly, if often unconsciously, influenced by the structures

---

[8] Mitchell Pacelle, "Citigroup CEO Makes 'Values' A Key Focus," *Wall Street Journal*, October 1, 2004, C1.

of an organization. This is not to say that structures can be moral or immoral. Rather, structure sets patterns of behavior that become invisible unless they are examined explicitly. Indeed, the more anything remains just an assumption, the more it has free reign (e.g., the assumptions of the recent past about the roles of women and men in business). The structures in modern organizations have not changed much since the Industrial Revolution three hundred years ago, at a time when the military model of command and control dominated organizational thinking. It is a bureaucratic model that provides a hierarchy of clearly defined authority, a division of labor into specialized roles and skills, a standardization of activities into defined procedures, and a stress on competency and efficiency. While bureaucracies have advantages, such as providing stability, clear performance, and role expectations, as well as defined paths of career advancement, they also have built-in dangers that need to be examined.

Bureaucracy is grounded in the idea of legitimate authority. Just look at a company's organizational chart. Everyone, including the president, reports to someone. That authority can be extremely comprehensive, especially when it includes authority over life issues such as hiring and firing. A job is not just a hobby; it is a livelihood that provides essential support for oneself and perhaps a family. The pressure simply to obey and conform is immense. Not only are the stakes of making a living high, but also there is a natural tendency to obey authority figures, no matter what they order, simply because it is an order. History (e.g., Nazi concentration camps) and sociology (Milgram experiment) are filled with corroborative examples and experiments. People allow themselves to be freed of responsibility as long as the action in question is being ordered by a legitimate authority. Another factor diminishing a sense of responsibility in a bureaucracy, particularly if it is large, is that the person doesn't necessarily see the results of her actions. The manager who fires an employee turns the person over to the human resources department to mop up the mess and to try to assist the person to move on with his life. The worker who produces a shoddy product doesn't have to go with the salesperson who must deal with an angry and frustrated customer. Bureaucracy inserts psychological distances that insulate people from the consequences of their actions.

The tendency to rely on authority figures and to distance oneself from consequences tends to diminish personal responsibility and, consequently, morality. Everyone finds someone to blame, either above or below. Much effort and posturing (memos, e-mails, double-talk, "not my job," "just doing my job") are put into diffusing responsibility. Tracking responsibility is difficult, time consuming, and rarely done well. These are not inevitable consequences of a bureaucracy, but they are structural fault lines. Responsibility, and consequently ethics, can become so diffused that, at the end of the day, no one is really responsible for anything.

However, countermovements are also emerging. Managers telling workers what to do, when to do it, and how to do it is giving way to a greater sense of participation in decision making and to greater accountability of each person for what one does. In business terms, push the decision making down as far as possible. A higher level should not make decisions that can be made at a lower level. Everyone is responsible for results. This model can unleash results that are hard to even imagine in a strictly bureaucratic model. A poster-child example of this newer model is Nucor, all the more convincing because it comes from an old-line manufacturing sector, steelmaking.[9]

No matter what organizational model is employed, and there are many varieties, an ethical business culture will also have some built-in safeguards. Can employees, for instance, go over their manager's head without retribution? Are real decision making and, consequently, responsibility pushed down to the lowest possible level? Do managers listen only to favorite employees? Are some departments off-limits and untouchable by others? Are the individuals within a group held accountable for the group's decisions? Are dissenting opinions aired? Are layers of bureaucracy being decreased rather than increased? Are people encouraged to see the whole picture, to buy into company values, or only to focus on their narrow sphere of activity? Is information about company performance shared with all? These are important questions in determining the ethics of the culture.

Roles

There is another critical function played by structure, and that is the creation of roles. Roles follow from functions in an organization and are guided by expectations. Consequently, they are strong forces for guiding behavior, and workers are powerfully influenced by the role they play. This has both positive and negative implications for an ethical culture. Accountants, for instance, tend by nature, training, and role to hold tight to data, to measure accurately and scrupulously, but not to risk and dare. Salespersons, on the other hand, sell promise, possibility, dreams—sometimes far removed from hard data. As the quip goes, "I'm not lying, I'm selling!" Or, as a seasoned manufacturing supervisor put it, every salesperson thinks he's a magician—just saying so makes it happen.

As long as the different roles are kept in balance and talking to one another, there is a natural set of checks and balances. Within the structure of roles, ethical problems can occur in at least two ways. There is a natural tension, inher-

---

[9] "The Art of Motivation," *Business Week Online* (www.businessweek.com), May 1, 2006.

ent in the roles themselves, between, for example, sales and manufacturing, manufacturing and purchasing, engineering and sales, accounting and almost any other role. If any one role becomes so strong as to simply override the others, then power and not truth becomes decisive. Jockeying for position, political influence, personal favoritism become the hot issues. Respect for the less-powerful role is diminished, and the person in a conflicting role is degraded. Questions are no longer about facts but about turf and power. How a company handles this kind of conflict will give some indication of the ethics of the culture.

The other danger inherent in roles occurs when the demands of the role itself are in conflict. The role of the human-resource manager, for instance, is to promote the best interests of the company and of the individual employee. The role of the customer-service representative is to satisfy the customer and to protect the reputation of the company. The conflicting demands of a given role can pressure employees to be dishonest or shortchange one aspect of the role. While some of this tension is inevitable, an ethical culture will recognize these inherent conflicts and try to minimize the temptation simply to cop out in favor of one or the other side of the tension.

Policies—Formal Codes of Ethics

The cynical response to the issue of formal codes is to note that you could purchase a brass plaque bearing the Enron Code of Ethics on eBay for a dollar.[10] In effect, no amount of ethical codes will create an ethical culture or develop ethical people. Nonetheless, ethical codes continue to multiply. Most businesses today have initiated some type of ethical policy. The issue is no longer voluntary for U.S. corporations. The Sarbannes-Oxley Act of 2002 mandates not only corporate policies and signed ethical compliance statements from employees but also requires elaborate levels of control for all financial transactions.

Will corporate conduct of business be more ethical as a result? The probable answer is "it depends." In general, there seems to be some evidence that employees working in organizations with formal codes of ethics engage in less unethical behavior.[11] But the reason probably lies more in the fact that most companies with formal codes also pay more attention to some of the other elements that help create a total ethical culture. The cheating or dishonesty of

---

[10] Jeffrey Hollender and Stephen Fenichell, *What Matters Most: How a Small Group of Pioneers Is Teaching Social Responsibility to Big Business and Why Big Business Is Listening* (New York: Basic Books, 2004), 31.

[11] Treviño and Nelson, *Managing Business Ethics*, 216-18.

fellow employees will far outweigh any code in determining one's own ethical behavior.

The form of the code can also be significant. The more general the code, the less effective it will be in determining behavior. Most codes come out looking the same. There is a prominent dedication to the customer as top priority. This is followed by a statement of respect for the individual as the company's greatest asset, an emphasis on teamwork, an insistence on integrity, some reference to innovation and excellence and, more recently, a concern for the environment. Even something as specific as "bribery is forbidden" will have little impact without some attempt to define specifically what constitutes gift giving and receiving, what are legitimate payments for getting goods through customs, and when is it ethical to hire intermediaries to "get things done."

A good code of ethics will have clear policies in four key areas: (1) gifts and gratuities; (2) political contributions; (3) entertainment/business development; and (4) bribes and kickbacks.

There are many aids in helping companies develop codes. One of the best can be found in *Absolute Honesty*. It not only outlines a process for developing a code but directs you to a Web site—www.maguiregroup.com/ethics.htm— for a good example of what it might look like.[12]

The strength of a code of ethics is that it can objectify the expectations of an ethical culture. In times of critical moral-decision making it can provide a stable framework of company values. It can state what is at least professed to be held in common by all and what the company would like to be at its best. Most people look outside themselves for guidance in making moral decisions. While the role of fellow employees, leaders, and managers, as well as past practice, is probably more decisive, the fact of a clear code of ethics, particularly if it is specific, can be an external guide to moral behavior. It can be a starting point for discussion of ethical issues. It also has the advantage of being enforceable by external punishment—not a noble motive, but at least it sets some definable outside limits.

On the other hand, the limits of a formal code are the limits of any ethics of compliance, as explained in chapter 5. A formal code overemphasizes the threat of detection and punishment, tends toward minimal external compliance, always needs further interpretation for the specific case at hand, reduces expectations to a minimum, and cannot address some of the root causes of misconduct. A code also tends to overlook the difference between the legal

---

[12] Larry Johnson and Bob Phillips, *Absolute Honesty: Building a Corporate Culture That Values Straight Talk and Rewards Integrity* (New York: AMACOM, American Management Association, 2003), 235-39.

and the ethical. To the skeptic, it can look more like window dressing or else nothing more than liability insurance for senior management. If nothing else, however, one can at least point to an ethical code as a first step toward an ethical culture.

Reward Systems

Business is about doing and making. The free-market economy is grounded in results. Luck and timing can always play a role, but basically business is built on the expectation of a return on investment, whatever form the investment might take. Not only do we expect a fair return on created goods and services but also on the time, skill, and effort of the individuals who make it happen. There is still a fundamental belief that knowledge, skill, and hard work will be rewarded—at least in the long run. That assumption provides the incentive for many to reach for excellence in what they do. Unfortunately, this tie has been weakened in our own times as a result of so much business restructuring that has led to massive layoffs, downsizings, and reorganizations that weaken the link between performance and reward.

This link, though, is most basically weakened by a lack of fairness in a company's reward system. The issue is succinctly summed up by Robert Jackall:

> What if men and women in the corporation no longer see success as necessarily connected to hard work? What becomes of the social morality of the corporation—the everyday rules-in-use that people play by— when there is thought to be no fixed or, one might say, objective standard of excellence to explain how and why winners are separated from also-rans, how and why some people succeed and others fail. What rules do people fashion to interact with one another when they feel that, instead of ability, talent, and dedicated service to an organization, politics, adroit talk, luck, connections and self-promotion are the real sorter of people into sheep and goats?[13]

There is a basic business axiom summed up in the words "what gets measured and rewarded gets done." On that basis, an analysis of the reward structure of a business says more about the values of the company than any formal code of ethics. Here are some telling aspects that need to be examined to discover the operative values of a business. Some concrete questions can help us unearth the real messages being sent about what is most highly valued. It

---

[13] Solomon, *A Better Way to Think about Business*, 59.

really follows another basic business axiom, "If you want to know what's going on, follow the money."

Short- vs. Long-Term Results
Are all rewards based on short-term results? The short term allows for much easier manipulation. Are short-term results being generated at the expense of long-term growth and profitability?

Compensation Structures
Are compensation and wage increases based on merit? Once there is a general sense that wage increases are a function of politics, then the door is wide open to deception, posturing, and allegiances.

Evaluations
Are evaluations and goal setting used to motivate performance? Are there checks and balances in place to protect against arbitrary or biased reviews? Every evaluation should be reviewed by at least the next higher level of accountability. Occasional 360-degree evaluation feedback based on input from peers and subordinates in addition to immediate supervisors can provide balance. Are supervisors themselves evaluated? A disturbing issue that has entered into some performance reviews is the requirement of ranking hierarchically all direct reports and then firing the bottom 20 percent. The mere fact of ranking has some merit in that there is a tendency simply to even out every evaluation without making realistic or tough judgments. There are two problems, however. While some will always be better than others, it does not automatically mean that the others are inadequate. An even more sinister problem arises when the evaluation is based exclusively on financial measurements. At that point numbers can no longer be trusted as everyone jockeys to present the "right" numbers. One of the underlying faults with Enron was an evaluation system that was blatantly based on meeting numbers without any other consideration. Any failure to meet quota resulted in quick dismissal.

Discipline
While people generally learn about what is important to a company by what gets rewarded, they learn even faster by what gets punished or what doesn't get punished. Disciplinary action will tell you what a company is serious about. No one can be serious about everything. We exhort, encourage, persuade in an effort to move us to certain types of behavior. But the real test is what gets punished. If submitting padded expense reports is winked at when done by a "successful" salesperson but is punished in one who is having trou-

ble meeting quotas, then the lesson is clear. The powerful, whether as a result of performance or position, are not held to the same standards as others.

For discipline to be an effective learning tool, there are some key considerations that must be met. First, what is being punished must be clearly wrong. If the evidence is not conclusive, it is better to be attentive and wait for clearer evidence. The positive effect of punishment comes largely from what is perceived as fair by others. While there are times when facts can't be aired in public, the "grapevine" will assess whether punishment is administered fairly in most cases. Second, if the person just happened to be caught at what is common practice or excused in others, then the only real lesson that punishment teaches is that it is arbitrary or capricious. The moral then becomes "don't get caught." Third, punishment must be administered evenhandedly. Does it apply at all levels of the organization and in all departments? While punishment is rarely easy to administer, it is a critical aspect of a reward system. If you never discipline, you are sending the signal that you are not serious about anything.

Promotions

While compensation effectively rewards what a company considers important, it often remains private and confidential. Promotions and awards, on the other hand, are publicly celebrated forms of reward. Who gets promoted and who doesn't solidifies a company's culture. Even more significant is the continuity between stated values and the promotion process. Consider the effect of promoting or granting bonuses to an engineering manager whose success is known to depend on some unethical practice or on a special connection to the CEO. Nothing will promote cynicism or hypocrisy quicker. Actions will always speak louder than words. Promotions are extremely high-visibility actions and require careful consideration about the message being proclaimed from the rooftops.

Incentives

A number of years ago, Sears, always known and valued for its delivery of basic value to middle America, was rocked by a huge scandal. Car owners were being told by the Sears Automotive Division that they needed to replace their batteries even though there was nothing wrong with their existing ones. Replacement battery sales increased dramatically. The board of directors acted decisively, demanding a revised full-blown corporate ethics policy. The root cause, it was discovered, was that a new incentive program was instituted that rewarded employees based on increased battery sales. Sears swiftly changed its program, but the issue of incentives is one that needs constant scrutiny. When all incentives and bonus programs are based completely on narrowly defined financial goals, then one and only one message becomes clear: there is only one thing that matters—bottom-line results.

Whistleblowers

While this is not a common situation, it is becoming more important as bureaucracy is being thinned out, responsibility is being pushed down, and checks and balances are being streamlined. It is the issue of reporting wrong-doing. It is difficult at best. Even the words are distasteful and odious: squealing, tattling, ratting, snitching, turning traitor. Most whistleblowers are not expecting to be rewarded. They do, however, expect to be safe. Does the culture of the organization provide for some type of hotline or recognized person where wrongdoing can be reported without fear of recrimination?

Office Untouchables

Are there some people in the company who always seem to survive, no matter what? In a survey of 963 survey respondents, nearly 93 percent agreed that such is indeed the case.[14] These untouchables come in two varieties. There are the superstars at the top who behave atrociously. They are the prima donnas and hotheads who make the numbers and consequently are given free rein. The message is clear: "Bring home the bacon and you can do what you want." They confront others with the implied or expressed question, "Do you want me to close deals (introduce change, complete projects) or play nice?" On the other end is the "nice, sweet" retiring person who does almost nothing. It could be someone resting on prior laurels, or nearing retirement, or just lucky enough to always pass under the radar screen. Or it might be someone who has been poorly managed over a period of time and for whom everyone now feels guilt or threatened by potential lawsuits. Both types of untouchables undermine the morale of others and give a lie to the basic assumption that promoting company values gets rewarded.

Selection and Training

When I took on a position as human resources director with a new company, I realized that there was a problem with drugs in the plant. Accordingly, I initiated a new policy requiring drug screening for new hires. To my dismay, I discovered that most of the hires, seemingly qualified, were failing the drug

---

[14] Jared Sandberg, "Colleagues You Wish You Didn't Have Seem the Most Secure," *Wall Street Journal*, October 10, 2006.

test. I began to wonder if there were really drug-free candidates in the area. Then, after a few months, there were no further problems with new hires passing the drug screen. What I began to realize is that a preselection change had taken place. The word on the street was that the company hired without any testing. When it changed to the realization that the company tests everyone before being hired, the applicant pool also changed. The hiring process is indeed an important element in developing and maintaining an ethical culture. What criteria a company uses to hire its new life blood has long-term consequences. Has the candidate lied on the application? Does the company check and dismiss a candidate who falsifies information? Does the applicant talk lightly of getting to results without considering the cost? On the other hand, does the company present the position realistically? Are difficulties about the job glossed over? Are unfounded and nebulous hopes of advancement or compensation dangled alluringly? Hiring decisions will impact the company for many years. If they are based on false premises, then further ethical consequences can be expected.

Decision-Making Process

Realistically, what does the decision-making process have to do with morality? Surely, process as process is value free. But, as discussed under organizational structure, many values are embodied in the structure itself. If, for instance, every decision is driven solely by quantitative cost/benefit considerations, then the only operative value becomes immediate profit. Obviously, every business decision must include a cost/benefit analysis. But, if a CEO or manager wants only to "see the numbers," if all decisions are made in the accounting department, if broad-based involvement of all relevant departments is not encouraged, if personnel decisions are based only on cost, then talk about company values is reduced effectively to immediate financial considerations. Ethical and other values do not even have a chance of being heard.

One telling way of determining whether a company has lost its sense of values is to determine its practices of fair exchange with its customers. Here are four questions to consider:

1. What promises does the company make to its customers and can it deliver on them?
2. Do the company's operations from marketing to sales to delivery respect the dignity of the customer?
3. When the company fails a customer, how fast does it move to make amends? Does it acknowledge problems quickly?

4. Does the company make meaningful changes in response to customer needs and feedback?[15]

INFORMAL ELEMENTS

We have been examining the six elements that determine the formal culture of a company. They relate to systems that can and must be managed if a company is to have an ethical culture. They can be identified clearly and evaluated. They can also be developed and improved or ignored and allowed to deteriorate. However, there are also more intangible elements that constitute a culture. These elements are more difficult to measure, but they can be just as decisive in determining that culture. They comprise the more elusive yet very tangible aspects of a company's culture and are captured in phrases such as "the way we do things around here." Again, following the outline of Treviño and Nelson, they can be categorized as heroes and role models, rituals, myths and stories, language of ethics, diversity, reality checks, and the grapevine.[16]

Heroes and Role Models

These figures are the ones who not only profess a set of values but embody them. They are the symbolic carriers of the values and meanings that a business is all about. Often they are the original entrepreneurs who had a vision and a passion about some product or service that would be valued in society. Sam Walton of Wal-Mart, Tom Watson of IBM, Jack Welch of GE, to name but a few, were not only leaders or founders of their businesses but symbolized what made the business great. This does not make them moral exemplars, but it does give us a clue about the moral culture of their company.

These heroes are easy to identify. More difficult perhaps, but even more important, is to determine who is actually looked up to or respected in the company's current operation. Heroes can be enshrined with appropriate pictures and plaques, but the people who are admired today by the employees within the company are the real drivers of the current culture and values. There is no simple way to determine who they are, because they are not automatically identified with formal positions, not even with the position of CEO. Usually they can only be identified by people within the organization through such questions as, "Who do people really look up to or respect?" or "Who are the go-to people?"

---

[15] David Batstone, *Saving the Corporate Soul & (Who Knows?) Maybe Your Own* (San Francisco: Jossey-Bass, 2003), 104-5.

[16] Treviño and Nelson, *Managing Business Ethics*, 223-27.

> Review the people in your own organization. Pick out the ones who are most admired and respected. More importantly, ask yourself *why* they are looked up to. The answer will give you a good clue to the real values and moral climate of a company.

Rituals

What a company celebrates will give another clue to what a company values. To proclaim that "employees are our greatest asset," yet not recognize things like years of service or retirements or other important personal milestones is to undermine the original statement. A CEO once said, wisely, that retirement celebrations are really less for the one leaving than for the rest who remain. It says something to everyone about the value of the individual person. The practice of employees voluntarily taking up collections or signing cards for a fellow employee who is on extended sick leave, or who suffered a death in the family, is another indication of company values. An important aspect of celebration is to observe who gets recognition and why. Is it consistent with formally stated values and policies? Is recognition given only for bottom-line performance? Are other values recognized and awarded?

Rituals can also indicate whether a company has any interest in the larger community in which it operates. Does the company participate in things like community blood drives or United Way campaigns? Do Christmas rituals and celebrations also consider the needs of the less fortunate? Does the company contribute outright to charities? Does it participate in some form of matching employee contributions to voluntary organizations? Not every business is in a financial position to make large contributions, nor is there some magical number that validates its good intentions. The point here is to recognize that a company's rituals and celebrations do reflect its culture and values.

Myths and Stories

Where there are heroes and role models there will be myths and stories that concretize and symbolize the values in question. Johnson & Johnson's prompt response to the Tylenol tampering incident has become legendary. While the tampering was very localized and involved relatively few bottles, J&J's action was immediate and decisive. All Tylenol products were removed from the supply chain, from manufacturing to distribution to retail shelves, at considerable cost to the business, but the reputation both within and outside the company was solidified: J&J puts the safety of customers above every other consideration.

Stories that go back to an early time, and even become mythical elaborations, play a role in determining company culture. A company I worked for would repeat the story of how it made a special fuse for munitions during the Korean War. Since it did not cost as much as had been estimated originally, the company returned a check for the difference to the U.S. government. Surely there could have been all sorts of rationalizations for not doing so, including the fact that it could possibly get the government procurement office in trouble. It is not surprising, then, that the same company some fifty years later immediately undertook the costly job of replacing a potentially faulty capacitor in every unit around the world that contained that particular capacitor. The issue in stories of this kind is that there are situations where company values are the controlling factor. Decisions are made not on the basis of inherent ambiguity, short-term loss, potential justifications and rationalizations, but on an overriding consideration of company values. These are the myths and stories that establish, reinforce, and communicate the operative values in the life of a business much more effectively than any formal code of ethics. They should not be lost to future generations.

Language of Ethics

At first blush, you might ask what does language have to do with ethics? On further reflection, however, language can indeed frame how an issue is perceived. Linguistic analysis and the sociology of language would say that a person's entire worldview is determined by language. Without entering that philosophical debate, it is reasonable to say that words are not neutral. They play a large role in delineating values. Is it abortion or free choice? Is it a layoff or right-sizing? Is it collateral damage or unintended killings? Is it a demotion or a lateral move? Is it early retirement or forced termination? The words we use say something about the values implied. Even to say "business ethics" is jokingly referred to as an oxymoron.

A business, then, that shies away from even using the language of morals or ethics probably will act less ethically than the one that raises explicit ethical concerns in its deliberations and decisions. It matters if it is OK for people to talk about the ethics of a situation. If people feel uncomfortable even in raising the moral question, then the impact of ethics as a cultural value diminishes. On the other hand, there is often a hesitancy to use explicitly ethical language when discussing business decisions. This is partly due to a larger cultural issue of being judgmental about someone's moral decisions. In general, we would rather not have to deal with other people's moral choices. It's just too personal and people react defensively too quickly. We would rather talk about shared values and integrity. That can be fine in most cases as long as we also recognize that some decisions might indeed be unethical and that such questions need to be addressed head-on. Fundamentally, ethical questions need to be recognized as legitimate concerns in a business decision. If such concerns are considered as extraneous to the decision or are reduced to idealistic or legalistic considerations, then the main message of this book is called into question.

To use words like "right sizing," "lateral move" or "early retirement" can have a place in public announcements of a company as long as they do not camouflage the moral considerations involved in these actions. The corresponding words of "layoff," "demotion," and "termination" have a way of bringing moral considerations to the fore. For instance, to lay off a person through no fault of his own, while necessary and justifiable at times, must still be recognized as a serious event that should not be undertaken lightly. Further, the nature of business as a bureaucratic organization only further minimizes taking full responsibility for the consequences of decisions made.

Bureaucracy, especially in larger companies, presents a further danger with regard to language. It is too easy to pass off ethical considerations to the ethics person/department just like sales departments pass customer orders on to manufacturing. Managers, even when acting for sound moral reasons, often are reluctant to explain their actions in moral terms. Reasons can be many: not wanting to become too personal, not wanting to appear idealistic, not wanting to appear "soft" rather than "hard-nosed, efficient, business driven." Still, it is the manager making the decision who is also most credible in explaining the moral reasoning implied in that decision. If a manager is comfortable talking about the ethical considerations, then others are being invited freely to discuss ethical dimensions as well. As a result, the confirmation and development of the ethical culture of the company is promoted. Ethics, like sex, is something that each person must deal with. Relegating it to a specialist is like parents leaving all sex education of their children to a school teacher.

Diversity

Another indication of how well the formal elements of a culture are working is to see how a business values diversity. Diversity is such a complex social, moral, and organizational issue in our times that it can be a good cultural and ethical barometer. Good companies have moved from *discriminating against* to *tolerating* differences. Still better companies have moved on to *valuing and embracing* differences. They have begun to realize there is a richness and strength in diversity. The diversity that stems from gender, race, and age can be a source of opportunity and enrichment for all. To put the issue negatively, how can a company say that it rewards based on merit, that it is open to new ideas and possibilities, that it values independence of judgment and thinking and at the same time be totally dominated by young white males—or Hispanic females, for that matter?

The value of diversity is ultimately rooted in the deeper recognition and appreciation of the unique gifts, talents, and skills that each individual and each identity group bring to their work. Diversity has become so entangled in the legal and political issues of discrimination that the richer and more comprehensive meaning of the term easily gets lost. How does the company culture encourage the development of each person's talent? How does it provide opportunity for each person's gifts to be recognized and utilized as fully as possible? Conventional wisdom about management says that no one deserves special treatment; no one should be treated differently. Perhaps there is more wisdom in saying that *everyone* should get special treatment.

There is no doubt that the recognition of diversity in all its aspects creates its own problems for management. Recognizing differences also means that there are fewer common frames of reference. Learning how to maintain the critical tension between the need to honor individual differences and the need to create a cohesive unity will be a challenge. A deeper issue lies in management's ability to give honest feedback or corrective action. It is a fact that there are two groups, racial minorities and women, who are least likely to get honest critical feedback on evaluations. Managers are often unwilling to take on that task precisely because it can be a challenge to their own adequacy in dealing with diversity. Yet, critical feedback, as we shall see in chapter 8, is extremely important in promoting the development of any person.[17]

Reality Checks

Reality checks are a more recent phenomenon in the business world. Business has become so complex; decisions need to be made so rapidly; issues, and even paradigms, are constantly changing; the consequences of actions are so far reaching—all these factors make decision making ever more difficult. Managers and employees are finding themselves seeking out a person of integrity and wisdom from within the company for a "reality or sanity check." This is

---

[17] Carole S. Napolitano and Lida J. Henderson, *The Leadership Odyssey: A Self-Development Guide to New Skills for New Times* (San Francisco: Jossey-Bass, 1998), 72-75.

an opportunity to air the issues, raise the questions, and look for feedback without any official consequences. It is not a formal position but an informal acknowledgment that some people are more trusted and respected to provide that kind of feedback. They are people who speak their minds freely without having to be politically correct because they don't have their eyes on the corner office. These people may have little or no formal position of authority. In some companies they may gain the title of an ombudsman. They become the keepers of the company's ethical standards and values, its heart and conscience.[18] Who they are and what they stand for will tell you much about the culture. By the same token, anyone responsible for making tough decisions should have someone who can fill this role for her. In traditional cultures, this function was probably carried out by the elders or a recognized wise man or woman.

The Grapevine

Every organization has a grapevine, that is, the informal flow of news, opinions, rumors, attitudes, coming events. It is usually never all right or all wrong. Contrary to the formal elements of a culture, it is not something that management can control—which is exactly why it thrives. A company that communicates well with its employees and that strives for openness and transparency will have a less active grapevine but will never eliminate it. The issue here, however, is not the existence of a grapevine but how divergent is it from the formal elements of a culture? Is the formal communication (written and spoken announcements) consistent with the informal (grapevine) communication? If there is a deep inconsistency between the two, then not only must one question how valid the formal culture really is, but also whether that very inconsistency doesn't add hypocrisy to the list of unethical elements in a company's culture.

CONCLUSION

What began as a simple analogy of the apple and the barrel has taken us through six formal and seven informal elements of a company's ethical culture. I hope that this process has shown us how complex and how absolutely important culture is to the ethical operation of a company and of each person in it. Ultimately, it is not a dilemma of either the apple or the barrel, either the

---

[18] This is a role not often referred to in business literature. An article by Carol Hymowitz provides a quick insight into its workings. "Often the Go-to Person for Company Insiders Isn't Known Outside," *The Wall Street Journal*, November 23, 2004.

individual or the company. Each has a definite influence on the other, so that neither can take the place of the other. However, a strong ethical culture can more easily thrive with an unethical individual than an ethical individual can thrive in an unethical culture. Ethical culture is really a make-or-break issue. No company culture is morally neutral or value free.

The real challenge here is to assess the ethical culture of a company. Obviously it is not some quick checklist or formula, nor is it possible to give each of the thirteen elements a simple yes or no and add up the score. No one company has all the elements completely in place. In addition, some of the elements work better for one company than another. One very strong element, for example, leadership, can compensate for a number of other less developed elements. Smaller companies might work more effectively through the informal dimensions while larger corporations need more formal reinforcements. All the elements, however, are indications and points of reference for determining just how effective the ethical culture of any company really is and what might be done to improve it. That culture, like the company itself, is a living reality composed of people in various stages of moral development who, for a wide variety of reasons, are united to produce the goods and services that make the business what it is.

QUESTIONS FOR REFLECTION

1. Take your own company through the thirteen elements of formal and informal ethical cultures. Write an evaluation of your company's ethical culture.
2. Use the selected questions presented in *Managing Business Ethics*[19] for auditing your company's ethical culture. Which elements are strongest? Which improvements will make the greatest difference. Stay specific.
3. Take the four questions for evaluating the fairness of a company toward its customers in the section "Decision-Making Process" earlier in this chapter and substitute the word "employee" for "customer." Do both exercises. What does it tell you?

SUGGESTIONS FOR FURTHER READING AND STUDY

Batstone, David. *Saving the Corporate Soul & (Who Knows?) Maybe Your Own*. San Francisco: Jossey-Bass, 2003. Batstone has been a strong voice in corporate ethics, nationally and internationally, for many years.

---

[19] Treviño and Nelson, *Managing Business Ethics*, p. 232.

Center for Ethical Business Cultures (CEBC) at the University of St. Thomas in St. Paul, Minnesota, has an Integrity Measurement Program that attempts to measure a company's ethical performance by benchmarking it against a national database.

Ethics Resource Center of the Society for Human Resource Management (www.ethics.org) conducts the annual National Business Ethics Survey (NBES), which studies ethical trends in for-profit, not-for-profit, and governmental sectors in the United States.

Harvard Business Review on Corporate Ethics. Boston: Harvard Business School, 2003. A collection of articles that are specific and to the point, as can be seen from some of the article titles: "Ethics without the Sermon," "Why 'Good' Managers Make Bad Ethical Choices," "Managing for Organizational Integrity."

Treviño, Linda Klebe, and Katherine A. Nelson. *Managing Business Ethics: Straight Talk about How to Do It Right.* Second edition. New York: John Wiley, 1999. A "how-to" book on managing the ethical culture of a business.

7

Moral-Decision Making

You shall not murder.
You shall not steal.
You shall not bear false witness against your neighbor.
Exodus 20:13, 15, 16

The Decalogue, the great ten words that ground the Judeo-Christian moral tradition, leaves no room for doubt. Thou shall not murder, steal, or lie. There is no middle ground. The imperatives are absolute, all the clearer since they are couched in negative terms—what *not* to do. No doubt the first line of morality is the basic issue of right vs. wrong. And at a fundamental level, that is indeed the choice. Sound values do raise tough choices, and tough choices are never easy. We know we are dealing with a tough choice when the temptations to avoid it become ever more enticing. We can all recognize the familiar ring to phrases such as "Everybody does it," "It won't hurt anyone," "Nobody will know," "Just this once," "It's just business," etc. While we might waver in our own resolve, we at least know what we are dealing with: a tough choice between right and wrong—"don't murder/inflict harm, steal/cheat, or lie."

In prior chapters we have dealt with many general ethical considerations, such as the role of values in business, the meaning of morality in personal living, and the relationship of personal morality to an ethical culture. Perhaps you are finding yourself saying, "Well all that's fine, but I still need to know what to do. What's right and what's wrong, and how do I know the difference?" In this chapter we will address that issue. Nonetheless, if you looking for quick and easy answers, you will probably be disappointed. If morality is the deepest exercise of our personal freedom, then it takes on all the complexity of human living. Fundamentally, however, the issue *is* simple. The basic moral imperative, as articulated in every religious and cultural tradition, is clear: Do good and avoid evil. Right vs. wrong—that's the choice. Indeed, the tests for right vs. wrong are fairly straightforward. Here are a few:

- *Is it legal?* While the legal and the moral are not equivalents, as we have already seen, business is not a private affair. Commerce is a public function that involves the entire human community. In that sense the community has every right to regulate its exercise. Laws and ordinances and regulations of government become the common expression of that public oversight. No one really questions that business is obligated to the law of the land. The legal is the first threshold of business ethics. The fact that it can create huge dilemmas in a global economy will be taken up in chapter 9.
- *What if it showed up in the newspapers?* What everyone sees and thinks does not create right and wrong. However, our ability to explain or justify our actions before others can be a good test of the integrity of our action. If we would become ashamed to have our action become public, then we need to go back and ask why. Our easy rationalizations wear thin quickly in the light of scrutiny. It is not the fact of an action appearing in the newspapers or on TV but how we would react to that publicity that gives us a clue to the morality of the act. It is also called the "Mom test." How would you feel explaining it to your mother?
- *What does my gut say?* An uneasy conscience or an emotional churning does not automatically mean that our actions are wrong. Tough honest decisions can also take us through a period of similar uneasiness, but that uneasiness demands that we revisit the reasons for our actions and scrutinize our motives as honestly as we can.
- *Who gets hurt?* An action that is clearly wrong will hurt someone. Again, honest actions can also hurt others, but the question is *who* gets hurt. Does the action rob or cheat someone else? Are innocent people being taken advantage of? Is the issue of competitive advantage being decided on dishonest or unfair premises? By considering who gets hurt and *why*, it is usually possible to discover basic issues of right and wrong.

While the recognition that a choice is a right vs. wrong issue does not necessarily make the decision any easier, it does place the issue squarely in the framework of basic moral choice. The outcome has more to do with one's moral integrity than with the ability to decide what the right course of action might be. There is, of course, another issue that is of greater concern to many. It is the issue of moral relativism, that the meaning of murdering, stealing, and lying are different for different people depending on their point of view. That is a broader issue than can be treated here.[1]

---

[1] Rushworth M. Kidder, *How Good People Make Tough Choices: Resolving the Dilemmas of Ethical Living* (New York: Fireside, 1995), 38-56.

THE MORAL DILEMMA

While issues of right vs. wrong tend to be clear, they can require deep moral courage. To choose what is clearly right in the face of potential job loss, alienation from others, or financial loss can call for true heroism. The redeeming feature, of course, is that at least one lives with the conviction that he stands on the side of what is right and just and honorable. A different type of moral courage is called for when the issue is not right vs. wrong but rather right vs. right. What is the adequate moral response when one is forced to choose between two positions, each of which is rooted in one's basic core values? Nor is such a choice far-fetched. Since the good, as we have continually repeated, is in things, we cannot simply make *mental* distinctions that separate the good from the bad. The world about us is complex and ambiguous. Many decisions involve choices in which there is genuine value on both sides. The issue, then, is no longer dealing with the temptations that come from choosing what is right precisely because it is right, but from the dilemma of choosing among conflicting values. This type of choice is not unique to business. It is common to all aspects of life. Some examples:

- choosing the most fuel-efficient and pollution-free car vs. the sporty or prestigious one
- choosing between two political candidates, each of whom stands for some of what we believe in
- choosing between the values of urban vs. suburban living
- choosing between artistic freedom and acceptable social norms
- choosing between time devoted to career and time devoted to spouse and children
- choosing between money for a needed vacation and money for the children's education
- recognizing the civil rights of gay unions and the distinctive nature of marriage
- recognizing the rights of privacy and rights of public safety.

All of us are constantly making choices that by their nature exclude other values. There are times when these kinds of choices have far-ranging implications for our lives, for example, exchanging a high-paying job for a lower-paying one that I enjoy much more. Reflection and discernment are in order for that type of decision. We make most of our choices without too much thought. We choose based on the particular values that make us who we are. But when these choices affect the social order or the future of a business enterprise and impact the lives of others, then the moral implications are much more prominent. How do we make these kind of choices which also call for a type of moral courage that is different from what is demanded in the right vs. wrong choices.

Four Paradigms of Moral Dilemmas

Rushworth Kidder, in his outstanding work *How Good People Make Tough Choices*, helps work toward the resolution of ethical dilemmas by identifying four basic types.[2] By becoming aware of these fundamental patterns that set up the ethical dilemma, we also become more aware of the conflicting values that create the tension in the first place. We are also reminded why ethical dilemmas are so common. The world is not divided into abstract entities that can be logically divided into mental categories expressed in words. Still, words and distinctions are very helpful for identifying elements in a complex and concrete situation. Here are sets of words that Kidder says can help us identify situations that we can easily recognize as dilemmas in which the issue is not right vs. wrong but right (one value) vs. right (another value). These are the kinds of situations that make it hard for good people to make tough choices.

Short Term vs. Long Term

This pattern "reflects the difficulties arising when immediate needs or desires run counter to future goals or prospects."[3] It is a dynamic that runs through every business operation. Here are just a few examples:

- Do I use inventory scheduled for future promised delivery to make a present opportunistic sale with the hope that the inventory can be replaced in time?
- Do I lay off employees now to avoid probable greater losses next year?
- Do I leave a secure job now to start a new career in an uncertain field?
- Do I save jobs now by temporarily underfunding pension obligations?
- Do I prevent loss of morale now by not communicating probable difficulties down the road?
- Do I shore up current quarterly earnings by prematurely shipping next quarter's orders?
- Do I sacrifice time with family now to advance the future of my career?
- Do I accept a lower quality standard at the beginning of a start-up in order to ensure viability until it grows more mature?

---

[2] Kidder, *How Good People Make Tough Choices*, 114-44.
[3] Kidder, *How Good People Make Tough Choices*, 113.

• Do I decide for jobs now at the expense of possible long-term environmental damage?

Some balancing of these types of short-term/long-term dynamics is part of every business. Business executives are constantly challenged to make decisions that must account for both the short and the long term. There is no magic formula to resolve these issues. However, it can be helpful to be aware that the issue comes from a dilemma of competing values. There is no automatic right answer, as in a right vs. wrong situation. Any one of the above examples could be decided so totally one sided that it could be transformed into a right vs. wrong issue.

Perhaps one of the distinctive features of this particular paradigm is that more knowledge can help significantly in resolving the dilemma. The more one understands of the short-term and long-term consequences and how they interrelate, the easier it becomes to resolve this type of dilemma. Knowledge becomes a key factor in choosing. In the examples above, for instance, how much easier it would be to make the decision if you knew exactly what the environmental impact would be in the long run or what type of orders the company can realistically expect next year.

This tension, though, is more than a question of additional knowledge. It is one of the most fundamental dynamics of human existence represented in such issues as present pleasure vs. long-term gains, today vs. tomorrow, this world vs. the next. Every religion recognizes the tension between the short and the long term through the practice and theology of some form of self-denial. Healthy self-denial is never an end in itself; rather, it is a way to something more, whether that *more* is reward in some future existence or a deeper connection with the interdependence of the total universe.

Another way of understanding this paradigm is to think of it in terms of risk vs. benefit. Everything we do has some risk to be measured against its perceived benefit. How much insurance do we buy? And for what risks— health, house, liability? How often do I get a medical check-up? I do a risk vs. benefit analysis every time I travel anywhere—by plane, train, automobile. There is a short-term risk of safety vs. the long-term benefit of getting to where I would like to go. A risk-free childhood would condemn a child to permanent infancy. We balance out short term vs. long term almost instinctively. The more we know about the potential risks and benefits, the more confidence we have in our decisions. At its core, however, we are dealing with a dilemma that only a free personal choice can resolve.

The dilemma of short term vs. long term has two large implications for all business that goes beyond the day-to-day decision making of producing goods and services.

The first implication relates to economics. There is a constant pressure for short-term results. After all, unless there is a profitable "now," what difference do all the great promises and projections really make? Are they merely wishful thinking, or are they based on solid achievement? Holding companies accountable for present performance is the first, and necessary, step to a prosperous future. But what happens when the tension of the short term and long term collapse completely into the short term. Then it seems that the focus on producing valued goods and services contracts into instant profitability, quick fixes, short-term accounting, and ill-advised mergers and acquisitions. Instant gratification takes over, and the kind of corporate self-denial that keeps investing in research and development, that fosters long-term relationships, and that is concerned about developing its own people gets overridden. To complicate this natural tension of long term vs. short term is the phenomenon that we have explored previously under the title of ultracapitalism. Instead of maintaining the healthy tension involved in every dilemma, it tips the scales completely to the short term.

The second implication relates to environmentalism. This is a classical case of short term vs. long term. It also raises some of the most challenging issues for business in our day. There is no quick fix or easy formula. The natural tension inherent in the short- vs. long-term dynamics tends to polarize people at opposite ends of the spectrum. Is it always right to focus on the long term? Certainly not. The vast increase in population—some say about four million every four days—needs to be fed, housed, and helped to be productive. Is it always right to focus on the short term? Certainly not. In that case there may be no future for anyone. At this point it is important to recognize environmentalism as the type of issue that needs to be understood as a dilemma that has no single or simple morally correct response.

Individual vs. Community

This pattern reflects the tension involved in the dynamics of "*us versus them, self versus others, the smaller versus the larger* group."[4] Nothing is more critical in the development of a society or an organization, business or otherwise, than the dilemma here identified as individual vs. community. This tension is particularly acute in the United States because of its unique history. It can legitimately be argued that the United States is the first nation to be brought together on an entirely new basis. Until the formation of the United States, a people came together in some type of unity based on a common factor. The most common denominator was the unity created by the family, which had its natural extension in the tribe. The city-state, the empire, the nation were all

---

[4] Kidder, *How Good People Make Tough Choices*, 113.

further forms of unity created under a common unity of tribe combined with geography and ruler. The unity was the preexistent given from which the individual as individual gradually emerged. The history of the United States, on the other hand, began not with some common unity but with individuals who left their common unity of nation and extended family to begin something new. It was a reaction against the common political, social, and religious unity that they found oppressive. Our constitution speaks of the "inalienable rights" of the individual; Ralph Waldo Emerson holds forth on "self-reliance"; Benjamin Franklin shows us how individual pluck and effort can achieve all things; personal freedom echoes like a mantra.

Yet a nation is what this group of people strove to become, granted, a *new* nation, a *more perfect* union, but still a unity of some kind. As we know, the experiment is far from over. How do we form a human community that can embrace the inherent tension between the individual and the community? This same tension, inherent in any group, from the emotionally charged bonds of the elemental family to the politically structured associations of a nation, is also operative in every business. John W. Gardner, a thoughtful advocate of the role of community has written, "Skill in the building and rebuilding of community . . . is one of the highest and most essential skills a leader can command."[5] All of our prior emphasis on teamwork, shared values, and the absolute necessity of a moral culture to nourish moral-decision making reinforce the realization that community is the other essential pole to the individual. The insight we have developed in chapter 3 is that great companies first create a community of performers who then create the products and services. That community has two moral voices: the moral voice of the community as a whole and the moral voice of the individual. They represent well the inherent tension between the community and the individual. That tension is reflected in business dilemmas such as the following:

- How does one deal with a sixty-two-year-old employee who has worked faithfully for twenty years but is unable to learn the new computer technology necessary to remain efficient? For the sake of the illustration, assume that there is no other position for him to be moved to and the company is losing money.
- A new employee is required to sign a confidentiality agreement declaring that, should she leave or be terminated for any reason, she will not join a competitor. What about her rights to make a living vs. the company's right to protect its business for the sake of all the other employees? And for how long? One year, two years?

---

[5] Kidder, *How Good People Make Tough Choices*, 130.

- A model male employee was asked to act as a temporary lead person on a production line. In a fit of frustration at one female's reluctance to do her job adequately he hit her in the face. While it was not intentional and was not a serious blow, there was no doubt that he hit her. She will not be satisfied with any less discipline than his immediate termination. Otherwise she will file a discrimination case against the company. Should the company risk an almost certain loss of this case in court, with its attendant damages, or fire a good employee?
- How many new safety procedures and how much costly safety equipment should a company invest in for the sake of some risk to the safety of an individual employee? What if the profitability of the company is jeopardized by the new procedures and expensive equipment, thus endangering the jobs of others? What if the risk is real but highly unlikely? How expensive is expensive relative to the risk? If risk is not zero, then what is a justifiable risk? And at what cost to the whole business?

It is important to keep in mind that the tension here is not between the individual, understood in terms of selfishness, greed, or egotism, and the community, understood as a choice for altruism or unselfishness. The rights of an individual and the common good of the community can be in legitimate conflict—a conflict that has no necessarily right or wrong answer.

Truth vs. Loyalty

This dynamic can be seen as "honesty or integrity versus commitment, responsibility or promise-keeping."[6] Truth, reached in judgment, takes us to what is objective. In that sense it represents something over against us. "It is what it is," as business likes to remind us. Truth is truth whether it makes us jump for joy or cry out in despair. Finally, every issue is only resolved on the basis of truth. Only the truth will make you free. Truth is the foundation of trust, and trust is the foundation of relations among human beings. Think of how much trust, based on truth, lies at the heart of business. Handshakes, phone calls, e-mails, credit-card numbers, ads, addresses—all move business forward at speeds that would be impossible if trust in the truth or objectivity of the process was always in question.

On the other hand, loyalty is intensely subjective. It focuses not on statements of fact but on personal commitment. It speaks not of what is separate from the person, as in objective truth, but of what is most intimate to the person, as in one's loves and allegiances. Could two such obvious values as truth

---

[6] Kidder, *How Good People Make Tough Choices*, 113.

and loyalty really be at odds with each other? Are we not taught, almost at the same time as we learn to talk, to always tell the truth? At the same time, are we not also taught that loyalty is a precious thing, and that we should be loyal to our families and friends? Is the dilemma not caught in the two proverbs "Honesty is the best policy," and "A friend in need is a friend indeed"? The dilemma of truth and loyalty can play out in the high drama between Thomas More and Henry VIII as portrayed in Robert Bolt's *A Man for All Seasons* as well as in something as ordinary as a letter of recommendation requested by a friend who has been involved in some ambiguous, if not actually immoral, activity. It can be a common occurrence in business. For example:

- I know a co-worker in our department is spending a lot of time on personal matters on the Internet. Our boss is complaining to us about not getting the work done. I talk to my fellow employee without results. Do I tell the boss what is going on?
- An employee comes to me as human resource director for information he needs to get a mortgage on a possible first-time purchase of a house. I know he is slated for layoff in a few weeks. I have been ordered to keep news of the layoff highly confidential. What do I tell him?
- I relate to the boss some information that is potentially harmful to the company. The information was told to me in strict confidence. The boss insists on knowing who told me. What do I do?
- At what point does truth or loyalty prevail when I am confronted with ambiguous behavior by the boss who promoted me to my present position?

Justice vs. Mercy

The issue behind this pattern is that "fairness, equity, and even-handed application of the law often conflicts with compassion, empathy and love."[7] There is a wholeness about life that cannot be captured in either justice or mercy taken by itself. At what point, for instance, do you give an alcoholic employee one more chance to get his life together, or do you terminate him for consistent violation of an attendance policy? Does it make a difference if he is a real contributor to the company effort? Or what if she is a long-time employee who has given many years of good service? At what point does compassion turn to enabling? And, if he successfully completes a rehab program but then falls again, is he given another chance to repeat the program? If so, is he given a leave of absence or terminated? If terminated, is it permanent or will consideration be given to rehiring him? And if so, when? What is the message

7 Kidder, *How Good People Make Tough Choices*, 113.

being given to others? Questions will continue endlessly. The issue will not be resolved by considering only external factors. At some point the resolution will be based on a personal decision determining how one balances justice and mercy. If the issue is pushed to either extreme, there will be a corresponding reaction. "Tough love" is a reaction to blind mercy. On the other hand, a simplistic application of the letter of the law, which attempts to focus on the justice pole of the dilemma, does not, in fact, do justice to the situation. The reality of this type of situation cannot be adequately understood by either pole of the dilemma, yet choices must be made. It is right to do justice. It is right to be merciful. Yet how can I do both? Words of blame can follow either choice: "bleeding-heart liberal" or "ruthless bottom-line tyrant."

While one might ask what does justice vs. mercy have to do with the bottom-line orientation of business, a little reflection will reveal just how extensively this dilemma operates in everyday business decisions.

- How are company rules applied? Rigorously? Without exception? Not taken seriously? Controlled by likes and dislikes? Arbitrarily?
- Does the company emphasize managers or leaders?
- Is the business climate demanding yet considerate?
- Are things like age, disability, years of service, personal tragedies, taken into consideration?
- Are terminations and promotions fair?
- Is being considerate to one person really unjust to others or even to the company's drive for excellence?
- Will a hard-nosed decision now send a salutary message to everyone else?
- Will a show of compassion send a message of favoritism or lack of resolve to others?

The claims of justice are very demanding. Rights and principles must be upheld, despite the pressures of the moment. Sympathy and compassion are not substitutes for equity and fairness. Justice is symbolized as a blindfolded woman holding the scales of justice. English judges wear wigs. In other words, personalities and private emotions are not to interfere with the impartiality of justice. This stern, even austere, face of justice is recognized as the first level of true love. There is no love, or peace for that matter, without justice. Only justice can resolve the conflicting claims of several loves. It must be absolute.

On the other hand, mercy is never blind. It looks intently at the individual, at the particular, at the differences that do indeed make a difference. It calls us to be compassionate, to rise above the dictates of law and social order and to embrace the individual, no matter what the sin or lack of merit. Love calls us to treat the individual as the absolute. Nothing in the entire universe is of more value.

The same issue has also been framed in other terms, namely, as masculine or feminine ethics. Without attempting to resolve the sociological debate of nature vs. nurture, there does seem to be some difference in the way that the justice vs. mercy dilemma tends to get resolved. In general, women tend to find greater moral worth in "caring," "relationships," and "wholeness," while men gravitate toward "fairness," "rights," and "abstraction." While this is surely a generalization, it does seem to tie into the mercy vs. justice dynamic. A one-sided application of either principle leads to distortion. Caring and building relationships can lead more easily to an emotionally charged world of oversensitivity, jealousy, and betrayal, while rights and abstractions open the way to impersonal, legalistic, and calculating behavior.

In the end, both justice and mercy make profound and unyielding claims on our very person. There is no automatic right way. Decisions favoring either pole of the dilemma can be heart breaking. But decide we must. In fact, only in the *making of the decision* is the issue resolved. Such is the nature of ethical dilemmas.

Summary Conclusion

What, then, can we take from Kidder's perceptive analysis of so much decision making that leaves us without clear-cut solutions? His identification of four paradigms that model different types of fundamental dilemmas in moral-decision making can help us in very distinct ways.

1. Recognizing the difference between right vs. wrong (don't lie, cheat, and steal) and right vs. right (real value on both sides) allows us to identify just where the difficulty of the moral decision lies. The tough choice in the face of right vs. wrong lies in the moral integrity of doing what is right. The tough choice in the face of right vs. right is in the moral sensitivity required to explore not only the facts of the matter but the matter of our own heart.
2. The use of the four models can help identify what the conflicting values are. This, in turn, can help illuminate what the real ethical choice entails. It also helps us to understand why there is a tension in the first place.
3. The use of paradigms or models, however, will never automatically resolve the dilemma. Indeed, no amount of additional information will resolve an ethical dilemma precisely because there are deeply held values on both sides of the issue. Resolution will occur only when an inter-

nal decision is reached about the values that are more important to us in this situation. Our choices at that point are intimate reflections of the kind of person we are, the experiences that have formed our moral character, and our moral development "As we are, so the world seems" is probably never truer than in our moral choices in the face of ethical dilemmas.

4. No amount of analysis or conceptualization will ever be adequate to the full reality of life itself. This does not mean that morality is simply relative but only that our own response to the world and to others is never completely adequate. Growth in wisdom and love are not only possible but reflect a lifelong calling. In the meantime, a genuine humility, a willingness to seek forgiveness, and an acceptance of one another as we are can be good companions on the way.

5. Since dilemmas always involve a tension of personally held values, culture plays a critical role in how dilemmas are resolved. Some cultures emphasize the group over the individual, loyalty over truth, short term over long term. Rather than simply judge another culture's way of resolving business tension as a right vs. wrong choice, it might be more enlightening and helpful to see how the culture tends to resolve those tensions in general. On the other hand, business can be deeply impacted if loyalty to family, for instance, becomes the decisive factor in every business judgment.

THREE MORAL PHILOSOPHIES

While recognizing that the conflict of values involved in moral dilemmas does give us insight into a situation, it still doesn't resolve the issue. If ethics is really such a personal choice, then why bother with analysis. After all, no amount of objectivity will give us clear answers to our ethical dilemmas. Flip a coin or go with the gut! Although the recognition of a moral dilemma is a necessary first step to a moral decision, it is not the last. Three different moral philosophies or overarching moral systems have been used traditionally to resolve moral issues.[8] A summary of each can not only bring us a step closer to better moral-decision making but can also give us insight into our own habitual way of making moral decisions. To call them philosophies is to encourage the appearance of a familiar glazing of the eyes. While they can

---

[8] Linda Klebe Treviño and Katherine A. Nelson, *Managing Business Ethics: Straight Talk about How to Do It Right*, 2nd ed. (New York, John Wiley & Sons, 1999), 80-84; and Kidder, *How Good People Make Tough Choices*, 23-29, 154-76.

certainly be explored in their full philosophical depth, they are also common assumptions that we use implicitly in all of our moral-decision making. If we don't reflect on the principles that are driving our decisions, then we are choosing and deciding without even being aware that there might be other principles to guide our actions. While these principles have a history of philosophical speculation and are taught in academic courses, they are grounded in the patterns of everyday experience and thought patterns.

1. Consequences

What's best for the most people? What are the consequences? What are the effects of other options? What's the net result? These types of questions follow naturally from an orientation based on utilitarianism. It's an orientation that fits naturally with the whole dynamic of business in its focus on bottom-line results. It's the moral equivalent of a cost/benefit analysis. It has the advantage of being easily understood by businesspeople. To maximize benefit and minimize harm is a great business as well moral axiom. It also has that other great business virtue of being calculating, effective, and forever realistic. Mere good intentions, Pollyannaish naivete, grandiose delusion must be exorcised for the sake of definable results and measurable benefits. Such an approach is also the basis of much public policy and social legislation. Policies are crafted based on how many people are helped: what will be the greatest good for the greatest number.

Without identifying the assumptions in this type of moral thinking, it is easy to be blinded as to how limited its application can be. The first and most important caveat is the recognition that we can never know what all or even the most significant consequences will be. When do we ever have all the facts, and when have we ever had such a clear vision of the future that we can be confident in determining what is the *best* benefit for the *most* people? Do we know the full consequences, both for the individual and for the business, of terminating even one person? Would we have thought differently about electricity if its first application had been for the electric chair? Unfortunately, the first use of atomic power was for the atomic bomb. Who could have known the consequences of the discovery of the transistor? People are notoriously poor speculators on foreseeing the consequences of personal actions, let alone public policies, on the future of the human race. The long-term consequences of slavery were never even imagined when slavery was introduced to the United States. Business can succeed with the utilitarian model only because its objective is very limited and clearly defined.

There is another important assumption in utilitarian thinking that must be addressed. What about the minority for whom this action is not the best? Can fatal experimentation with some human beings be condoned for the sake of potential medical benefit for all? Can the rights of some (*potential* terrorists?) be taken away for the sake of the general sense of security of the others? Can all moral issues be quantifiable? How do you measure desire or happiness? Is a happy slave a moral option? Amartya Sen, a winner of the Nobel Prize in economics, has shown convincingly in his work *Development as Freedom* how economic development cannot be measured adequately by the usual display of social and economic statistics. A deeper understanding of the notion of freedom and how to measure it is also critical. None of this however is to deny the validity of utilitarian thinking. Specifically, Sen lists two advantages: (1) the importance of taking account of the *results* of our actions; and (2) the need to pay attention to the *well-being* of the people involved.[9] In other words utilitarianism's greatest claim is that it forces us to take seriously the *consequences* of our actions. As long as it is not the only principle that is applied, it remains extremely valuable in making moral decisions.

2. Universal Principles

What is my duty? What is my obligation? What is the law? In other words, forget the consequences; you can't really know what they will be anyhow. What might help one person will hurt another. There has to be some more general principle for making moral decisions. How can I be sure that I am not acting merely out of my own needs and desires? Assurance doesn't come merely from looking at consequences because we hardly know what they will really be. More than just *my* desire is what can be generalized, what would apply to all, what would oblige me, despite the consequences. If that has the ring of the German philosopher Immanuel Kant (1724-1804), it is because no one has so systematically and thoroughly based morality on this principle as he has. "An action done from duty," he wrote, "has its moral worth, not in the purpose to be attained by it, but in the maxim in accordance with which it is to be decided upon."[10] Decisions about what is right must be based on broad abstract principles, such as honesty, promise keeping, fairness, rights, justice, respect for persons and property. It is the universality of these notions that makes the claim on the individual and grounds the rightness of the action. In the Judeo-Christian tradition, we find these broad moral principles in the Ten

---

[9] Amartya Sen, *Development as Freedom* (New York, Anchor Books, 2000; orig. published, New York: Knopf, 1999), 58-63.

[10] Kidder, *How Good People Make Tough Choices*, 157.

Commandments. While other religious traditions might verbalize these broad universal imperatives differently, every tradition will point to an ethical way of life that includes this type of generalized moral obligation.

Business is not a stranger to this type of moral thinking. While business tends to focus more on bottom-line, consequence-dominated thinking, it also recognizes the key role played by rules, procedures, and fairness. Hiring, firing, and promoting, for instance, will be based on merit and not on gender, race, or age. When company rules clearly state that any employee actively engaged in a physical fight will be immediately discharged, then all such persons must be discharged, never mind that one of the two has a general bad attitude and is believed to have started the fight while the other one has an excellent work record. A utilitarian approach would be to discharge the one and not the other. Yet a business with a strong ethical sense will apply its rules evenhandedly. Padding expense reports will no more be tolerated in a star salesperson than in a marginal one. At some point, the issue moves beyond immediate consequences to what is right and fair—as applied to all—regardless of consequences. The validity of this base for moral-decision making can hardly be questioned. Yet, what is one to do if two principles conflict? Which right or which duty takes precedence? Do not ethical dilemmas of conflicting values make this more than just a hypothetical question? How do you resolve the right of the privacy of the individual and the right of the company to control what its computers are being used for? How do you take account of the particular talent or particular weakness of any given employee? Is the adage "If I let you do it, I'd have to let everyone do it" really the final word in all circumstances? What about the exception? Does the universality of law, duty, and obligation really meet the moral reality of every situation? To demand that every moral decision must be able to be universalized is to overlook the unique individuality of each person as well as the claims of unique circumstances in an imperfect world.

This is not to say that there is no truth to this way of moral thinking. Duty, law, and obligation do call us to a moral rightness that goes beyond the mere consequences of our acts, which can easily enough be merely self-serving. The obvious limitations to this philosophy must also be recognized.

3. Virtues

If the basis our moral actions does not lie outside of ourselves, as we have explored in "consequences of our acts" or in "what can be universalized," then perhaps we need to turn inward. A pattern of moral thought based on virtue or care turns to the motivation, the intention, the character of the person. This approach does not mean that consequences, rules, and principles are not considered. Rather, they are all considered seriously, but in the context of the moral sensitivity, character, and integrity of the moral agent. It probably comes to a focus most clearly in the golden rule: "Do unto others as you would have others do unto you." It is a moral test that asks us to put ourselves in the other person's shoes. For most of us, it is probably the most important and most recognized principle of moral-decision making. It stands at the center of the moral teaching of all the world's great religions. Some variation on the theme is central to every culture. Parents first awaken a moral sense in their children by encouraging them to consider how an action would make the other person feel. As adults, we use the golden rule as a quick rule of thumb to settle ambiguous moral action. Its great strength is that it draws us out of ourselves by coaxing us out of our own restricted perspective in order to care about others.

But its very simplicity and universality can limit its usefulness in deciding moral issues. Most elements are merely assumed. How do we define the other? Is it my family, my tribe, my country, my business, my religion? And, if there is more than one other involved in the situation, which one do we consider? We generally identify the other in terms of ourselves, of our agenda, of what we want to accomplish, not the other as genuinely other. Then again, what is appropriate to want for ourselves? If we have a low opinion of ourselves, we would really expect others to treat us poorly. Drive-by shootings occur so arbitrarily because the one shooting has so little sense of his own worth. It is the person who already possesses a highly developed moral sense who will be able to benefit most from a virtue-based ethic.

The point here is not to declare a winner among the three philosophies. Nor is it to mechanically apply the three tests and come up with a correct score. They are not formulas that produce right answers. They are principles that can help us think through moral issues. They can help us see a problem from more than one perspective. They can clarify, enlighten, and deepen. Ultimately, we must think through the situation ourselves. To assist in this process—and process it—there is one more method for thinking through a moral decision. It can involve as many as nine separate activities.

NINE STEPS TO SOUND ETHICAL-DECISION MAKING

These steps are not a formula. They are not a linear walk to a conclusion that appears at the final step. Some steps will lead you back to earlier points. No particular order needs to be followed. Some steps will be harder than others, but none should simply be bypassed. The total momentum should lead to a more thorough understanding of the moral decision you are facing. This is a process that will only be used when a moral dilemma is extremely complex or when the final decision has grave implications.

1. Gather the Facts

As discussed in chapter 5, there is no more obvious, but also no more important, starting point than knowing the facts. This is also not the easiest step. It usually takes more time than we seem to have. It's much easier to jump to conclusions based on our own desires and fears, prejudices, and biases. To know how a situation unfolded, whether it is a singular occurrence or a repeating pattern, to determine who might not be telling the whole truth, who is being protected, who is being blamed, and what the future consequences might be—all require an impartial, painstaking, and time-consuming effort. Not to do so is to poison the conclusions from the outset.

2. Define the Ethical Issues

One must determine if it is really an ethical issue. Many of the dilemmas and tough choices in business have nothing to do with ethics as such. Is it a good marketing plan? How much can we reasonably charge and remain competitive? Should we develop a new product line or enhance our current one? What do our customers need? Can we produce the product cheaper, quicker, better? Do we make or buy? What is the cost/benefit ratio? Do we hire or contract labor? Do we strive to be at the high, middle, or low end of competitive salaries and why? Do we discount and how? Business is all about making decisions, most of which have to do with economic, technological, or market issues, as long as the facts are being presented honestly.

On the other hand, there are decisions that are clearly ethical. Do we really need to lay off personnel because of reduced demand or is this an opportunity to get rid of older employees who are not as productive as they once were? If it is, indeed, an ethical issue, is it a right vs. wrong or a right vs. right issue. We have already seen how we can distinguish one type from the other and how important that first step is. If the issue is really one of right vs. wrong, then the continuation of these nine steps is probably not much more than an attempt to justify an immoral decision. Another tendency in defining the ethical issue is to stop at the first cause that comes to mind. Mull over the whole situation. Look at it from different angles. I have long ago come to appreciate the wisdom of a simple philosophical principle: "When the effect is greater than the cause, there is another cause." When a supervisor overreacts to the behavior of one of her direct subordinates, the moral issue might not be what is appropriate disciplinary action but, rather, what is really going on between the two of them? When problems, each logical and reasonable enough in itself, continue to come from the same department, then it is time to start looking not at the individual problems but at the supervisor in the department. Usually the root problem lies there. An honest attempt to locate the ethical issue will often take you back to gathering more data. Is the problem one of poor workmanship on the production floor or a poorly engineered product or process? How you assemble the facts gives weight to an issue even before you begin the moral examination. Defining the ethical issue correctly goes a long way toward resolving the ethical conflict. A truly moral decision is always an informed decision.

3. Identify the Affected Parties

Who is being harmed and who is benefiting from the decision? An honest look at all the stakeholders will help clarify just what values are at work. We must be able to see the situation through the eyes of others. Identifying the stakeholders is critical to being able to see perspectives other than your own. It is not the same as feeling sorry for others but rather the exercise of the more significant moral quality of compassion. To feel sorry doesn't get you out of your own shoes, but "feeling with" demands a move outside of yourself. This kind of identification can get you beyond such generalizations as profit motive and market demands in order to appreciate the whole picture. Generalizations can easily become rationalizations for sloppy or immoral-decision making.

Current business practice is generally more sensitive to understanding the necessity of knowing the viewpoints of affected parties. Instead of just presuming to know what employees think about benefits or working conditions, for instance, more effort is given to actually identifying their thinking through discussions and surveys. In any case, the identification of *all* affected parties is bound to enlarge the true scope and implications of moral decisions.

4. Identify the Consequences

This is an application of the consequentialist philosophy identified earlier. It is a natural, in keeping with the realist, way of doing business. Don't get starry eyed. Keep your eye on results. Unless you identify the consequences of your actions as best you can, you are not ready to make a moral decision. The difficulty, however, is not in the fact of needing to look at consequences but in being able to identify as many of the consequences as possible. Although we can never determine all the consequences of an action, still we will achieve better moral clarity by identifying as many as reasonably possible.

It is precisely by first identifying the parties affected by a decision (step 3) that we are in a better moral position to determine all the consequences. By considering the consequences to each group we are forced to broaden our perspective. Serious decisions will probably affect more than one group, and in different ways. A company that invests the assets of its 401(k) plan in company stock, for instance, is looking at consequences such as boosting stock prices, finding economical ways of matching employee contributions, and creating employee buy-in. As good as these consequences might be, a failure also to consider the corresponding consequences to individual employees, such as the potential danger to an individual's retirement being totally dependent on one investment, is not to consider all the consequences of one's decision. Identifying consequences means to look both at the long-term and short-term consequences, both at the consequences for all employees and for each individual employee. What are the consequences not only to the shareholders but also to the other stakeholders? Even after all potential consequences are identified, there is the further need to establish the probability of each of the consequences. In making a decision to purchase expensive safety equipment, for instance, it is important to determine if the danger is extremely remote or highly probable.

Identifying consequences is not a process of arriving at logical conclusions. To some degree we all see the consequences we want to see. It's easy to maximize the importance of results we consider favorable to our desires and to minimize the consequences we really don't want to consider. The probability of consequences is another way of stating risk. If we have already made up our mind, we tend to ignore the risk factor for our own position and emphasize the risk for the opposite position. The famous explosion of the space shuttle Challenger as a result of questionable O-rings is a case in point. The need to get the shuttle launched and move the space program forward was weighed against the need for safety and avoidance of disaster. Consider how many possible consequences, along with what levels of probability they entailed, must have gone into that—and every—launch decision. Then think of how easy it would be to measure those consequences based on personal agenda and point of view. Identifying the consequences, *all* of them, together with an accurate assessment of their *probability*, is a difficult and necessary step on the way to tough moral decisions.

5. Identify the Obligations

As a salesperson, for instance, I have an obligation both to the customer and to the company. As a buyer, on the other hand, my obligation is to the company. I must identify, in a given case, just where my obligation lies. If I have promised someone that I will not reveal his identity as the source of some potentially damaging information, then I have an obligation that is different from merely not being a gossip. Trust builds on obligations being observed. Customers trust companies that meet their obligations to deliver goods and services as promised. Employees trust managers who meet their obligations to treat them fairly and reward them adequately. The obligation of the CEO for a company's profitability is different from the engineer's obligation in that regard. In making a moral decision, it is important to identify what my obligation is in this particular decision.

Particularly significant in this regard is the role of professional associations. Most professions have developed associations that set standards and provide legitimacy. These associations set principles of ethical conduct that transcend the individual business. In case of conflict, the standards of the profession should prevail over the business expediency of the moment, even though the business is paying the salary. We trust the nurse, for instance, not primarily because the hospital is ethical but because she is a member of a profession that sets the highest standards. More and more professions identify obligations that come not from a company but from the profession itself. Consider the following professions and begin to list the obligations that come right from the role itself: manager; auditor; lawyer; human resource director; engineer; reporter; trustee. Identifying your obligation is another factor that must be considered in coming to a moral decision.

6. Consider Your Character and Integrity

This is another version of the newspaper or Mom test. If your decision were broadcast in public or made known to someone important to you, how comfortable would you be? Is your reason for keeping a decision secret based on legitimate privacy needs, or is it just a rationalization for being ashamed or embarrassed if it came to light? I have found salary administration to be a good example. Obviously, an individual's salary is a confidential matter. Also, determining a salary commensurate with an individual's skill, knowledge, and effort is a very complex process. Secrecy, then, is a blessing or it can be a cop-out. It becomes a cop-out if it provides cover for sloppy determinations or favoritism. I find my own test of integrity in this regard to be the following hypothetical question: "Can I provide a realistic explanation for this person's salary if I had to explain it to the other employees?"

Another way of approaching this issue is to consider how you imagine a person of integrity or character would handle the decision. It's like practicing moral-decision making in your mind. Still another take on this step is to ask yourself how you would like to be remembered after you are gone, either from the company or from this life. Try imagining your tombstone and what you would like to write on it about yourself. This can help you clarify your own moral character.

7. Think Creatively about Potential Actions

Put negatively: don't box yourself into an either/or situation. Either/or thinking can be appropriate for right vs. wrong types of decisions—don't lie, cheat, or steal—but, as we have seen, at least as many moral decisions involve dilemmas of opposing values. Often, by thinking outside of the box, a more adequate solution can be found. Life cannot be adequately comprehended in concepts. Situations can coax us to think in bigger terms. Often the most helpful exercise to come to creative alternatives will be the thorough pursuit of the first six steps. Don't be pressured into a decision if you are uncomfortable with your options. Give yourself time to consider alternatives.

How do you deal with a nonperforming employee? Shape up or ship out? That may ultimately be the only viable alternative. If so, also recognize that it represents the failure at least of one if not of both parties. Failure, however, should be the last, not the first, option. Was it a poor hire to start with? Why? Is he being challenged? What about a different type of work? A different manager or department? A mentor? More direct confrontation? Add more responsibility? More recognition? Leave of absence? These questions and more might provide a better solution than the either/or of tolerate or terminate.

8. Check Your Gut

The prior seven steps have all been highly rational processes that lead us toward reasonable and responsive decisions. On the other hand, we know that an ethical dilemma involves a conflict among competing values. Furthermore, it is our feelings and emotions that put us most directly in touch with our personal values. Therefore, at some point in the decision-making process, particularly toward the end, we need to get in touch with those feelings. If our moral decision leaves us feeling uneasy, then we need to question further. Why are we uneasy? Is it because the consequences of the decision are fearful? That can be a good thing because it makes us aware of the dangers involved. Are we energized? That may let us know that the decision is in tune with our basic values.

Emotions alone cannot resolve moral decisions, but they can give us a sense of whether we are on the right track. Sometimes intuition, instinct, gut feeling, a hunch might be the only indication we have that something more is going on than meets the eye (or the mind!). It is not a coincidence that we tend to pace or move about when we are worried, uneasy, or enthused. Our whole body lets us know when something is up. But that is all it can do. We then need to pursue the issues further through the type of steps outlined here until we can find equilibrium. The practice of sleeping on an important decision is based on the realization that good decisions will find a resonance in our whole being while inadequate decisions will leave us uneasy. On the other hand, the rush to decision and action in the heat of the moment is also often ill fated, because it tends to be blind, without the aid of rational thought.

9. Talk It Out

There is something about externalizing our thoughts and potential decisions that allows us to see them more objectively. Talking out our decisions has a number of helpful aspects. First, there is the negative factor. If you find that you are unwilling to talk it over with anyone, you then need to ask why. Confidentiality is no excuse. Everyone needs to have a friend or confidant who can respect a confidence. The answer probably has more to do with something in the decision that makes you ashamed or uneasy. The second benefit of talking it out is just the fact of hearing yourself say it in front of someone else. How does it sound, out loud? It's almost like testing it in the real world. The third and most obvious advantage of talking it out is to test it against the reality of another person, especially if the other person is someone we respect and trust.

To explore the implications of a moral decision with a person we respect can open up a space that allows us the opportunity to test our assumptions. Our implicit assumptions and our moral philosophies, whether based on consequences, universal principles, or virtues, often operate beyond our own awareness. Our real agenda contained in the decision may well be hidden from us. Talking out our decision does more than only help us to identify our own motivation, to see consequences we have overlooked; it also allows for the possibility of entirely new alternatives to emerge. That area of true freedom where dialogue can take place without fear of repercussions is a gift, indeed a necessity, to anyone who must make serious decisions that can affect the lives of others.

These nine steps in their entirety ground many of the quicker, simpler tests that companies have developed to do a quick ethical take on an issue. Here is the one used by employees of Texas Instruments.[11]

- Is the action legal?
- Does it comply with your best understanding of our values and principles?
- If you do it, will you feel bad?
- How will it look in the newspaper?
- If you know it's wrong, don't do it, period!
- If you're not sure, ask.
- Keep asking until you get an answer.

CONCLUSION

We are bringing a long chapter to an end. A few summary points are in order.

1. Obviously these are not the types of exercises needed for every moral decision. Most are of the "don't cheat, lie, steal" variety. You just need the moral integrity to do it right.
2. In the real world of business, however, there are a significant number of decisions that are not that clear-cut. By looking at the paradigms of moral dilemmas, we can appreciate the tension of conflicting values. How these types of issues get resolved can tell you a lot about the real values a company and you yourself operate from.
3. Identifying dilemmas and using nine- or seven-step procedures are not magical formulas for getting answers.
4. The practice of these exercises—and that is what they are—can bring additional light to the situation. I have often seen how the use of these steps has brought resolution or creative alternatives to tough moral decisions that involve conflicting values.
5. Morality is not blind nor is understanding immoral. By exploring consequences, identifying affected parties, checking your heart, identifying obligations, etc., you are really trying to illuminate the full scope of the situation before you. Light and darkness are not just accidental images of good and evil. The Ten Commandments, for instance, are fittingly called light and life and gift.

---

[11] Treviño and Nelson, *Managing Business Ethics*, 94.

6. The moral person is the person with the greatest vision, who sees things and people for what they are, in their fullest dimensions.

QUESTIONS FOR REFLECTION

1. In terms of moral dilemmas, consider God as both vengeful/awesome and merciful/compassionate. How do you reconcile them?
2. Take an example from each of the four dilemma paradigms and have different people make the case for each side. Then bring it to a decision.
3. Consider how your own country's history and culture will tend to tip the scales toward one or the other pole of a dilemma: justice vs. mercy; short term vs. long term; loyalty vs. truth; the individual vs. the community. For example, how would very strong family identities in a culture impact the operation of a business? What about the significance of "saving face" within a culture?
4. Short term vs. long term: What happens when a culture does not have a long-term vision of change or progress? Is that a necessary condition for economic development?
5. Compare Kant's moral basis of "principle" with the Catholic understanding of "natural law."
6. Take the five stakeholders as laid out in chapter 1, and determine what moral obligation is specific to each role.
7. Systematically work through all "Nine Steps to Sound Ethical Decision Making" on a tough ethical decision you are faced with. Does it illuminate the situation to the point where a moral decision becomes clearer?
8. Why is it necessary to go through the different types of analysis presented here? If someone just loved God and neighbor, would that not be enough? Is the rest just rationalizations? Did not St. Augustine say, "Love God and do what you want"?

SUGGESTIONS FOR FURTHER READING AND STUDY

Caroselli, Marlene. *The Business Ethics Activity Book: 50 Exercises for Promoting Integrity at Work*. New York: AMACOM, American Management Association, 2003.

Kidder, Rushworth M. *How Good People Make Tough Choices: Resolving the Dilemmas of Ethical Living*. New York: Fireside, 1995. If you have time for only one book, this is it.

MacIntyre, Alasdair. *After Virtue*. Notre Dame, Ind.: University of Notre Dame Press, 1984. A serious, contemporary, philosophical study of morality.

Treviño, Linda Klebe, and Katherine A. Nelson. *Managing Business Ethics: Straight Talk about How to Do It Right*. Second edition. New York: John Wiley & Sons, 1999. Many good insights, suggestions, examples, and practical applications for business ethics.

8

Moral Development
in a Business Environment

A great many people think they are thinking when they are merely rearranging prejudices.

William James

This chapter grows out of two fundamental insights. The first is that growth in moral development is a *lifelong* task and a personal achievement. A moral life is never an either/or condition or a state of perfection. The second is that business decisions are human, hence moral, decisions. Both of these insights have been developed in previous chapters. The point of this chapter is to explore how business provides an important context and impetus for real moral development. It is not to say that business is the only, or necessarily the most important, context for moral development, but only that it is an increasingly significant locus of that development.

THE WORKPLACE AS AN OPPORTUNITY
FOR DEVELOPMENT

Instead of understanding our business activity as a kind of blunting or blurring of our moral resolve, something like "discharging our moral batteries," it might be considered more accurately as an important impetus to moral development. If business is about the concrete, about doing and making, and ethics is about doing the good, then there are definite parallels. Philosophically, our being is our becoming; we develop by doing; we become the person we are by the free choices we make. That process is never ending. What we are today is not what we always were, and, generally speaking, not what we need to be in the future. This process of making ourselves the person we become is the most fundamental personal and moral responsibility we undertake. That process is not the result of some esoteric navel gazing but of functioning in the world we live in. But along what lines, and in what ways will that development proceed? Just as we develop through functioning, so that development proceeds along the directions in which functioning succeeds. The results, however, can be ambivalent. The philosopher/theologian Bernard Lonergan, S.J., sums up the issue succinctly:

> Again, one develops through functioning and, until one has developed, one's functioning has the lack of poise, of economy, of effectiveness, that betrays as yet undifferentiated potentialities. Unless one is encouraged out of shyness, timidity, pretended indifference, to zest and risk and doing, to humility and laughter, one will not develop but merely foster the objective grounds for one's feeling of inferiority. Rather, one will not develop along a certain more common line; one will seek and find less common fields in which to excel; and there one will be apt to overcompensate for deficiencies elsewhere.[1]

There are a number of connections to business here. First, business provides a rich and diverse field of opportunities for developing our potential. If our development is along the lines in which our functioning succeeds, then it becomes important to discover that line of success. Most people gradually seem to find a niche in business in which they can genuinely develop. How often we observe people grow and flourish over the course of a business career. It may be a deepening within a specific discipline such as engineering or accounting or a move into management or entrepreneurship. A career may take a number of turns before finding the path of success. It may have nothing to do with one's formal academic degree—or lack of it! Business, in its almost infinite variety of possibilities, provides not only the opportunities but also the freedom to allow a person to find her potential. A wise manager once told me that there is a job suitable for everyone. It might mean a change of companies or of careers; you just have to find it.

Second, business can encourage us out of our "shyness, timidity, pretended indifference to zest and risk and doing." In a value-based business culture, it does so by recognizing talent, rewarding results, and holding out further career paths. To the degree that business is focused on a vision of producing goods and services and is based on integrity and rewarding merit, it continues to call out the best in us. The challenges of the work itself, evaluations, peer

---

[1] Bernard J. F. Lonergan, S.J., *Insight: A Study of Human Understanding*, ed. Frederick E. Crowe and Robert M. Doran, vol. 3 of *Collected Works of Bernard Lonergan* (Toronto: University of Toronto Press, 1992), 495-96. The notion of development is grounded philosophically in the section entitled "The Notion of Development," 476-507.

response, new responsibilities, promotions, merit increases are all ways of encouraging us out of our status quo. On the other hand, these same factors let us know when our development has stalled or regressed.

Third, business is the great reality check. Just as businesses fail when they are no longer able to provide the goods and services valued by others, so individuals who are all talk but no action will eventually be discredited. The temptation to excel in esoteric fields as a way to "overcompensate for deficiencies elsewhere" will be held in check. Our own peculiar quirks and oddities, our exaggerated notions of our own abilities, our grand schemes to change the world (or human nature!), our justifications of our own behavior are all brought up against the same dynamics in others, only to meet the need to find a way to get things done in the real world. While compromise is surely a part of this process, another part is the recognition of our own rationalizations and limitations. For real development to take place, it must be based on genuine self-knowledge, not on fantasy or wishful thinking, which is "apt to overcompensate for deficiencies elsewhere." To put it simply, the greater our sense of inferiority, for instance, the greater will be our need for illusions of grandeur in some way, perhaps even in moral superiority!

In addition to this introspective look at the relation of business to moral development, there is a new dimension to the issue. In the past, a person's neighborhood played a key role in moral development. Next to family, it was perhaps the greatest regulator of behavior. Children were known in the neighborhood. Adults were easily accessible and shared similar values. Standards of conduct were commonly accepted and enforced through group pressure. Who others were and what they did mattered. Who came and who went was duly noted. Neighbors were there for one another, whether the call was for an emergency, a quick ride, or a party. Someone was home during the day, and most everyone was around in the evenings. While the behavior may have been motivated by external expectations, it also would gradually become an integral part of a person's identity. That sense of neighborhood has disappeared, except perhaps in small towns. In its place is the anonymity of the city and the suburbs. Apartment dwellers hardly recognize one another. Yards are fenced in high to provide total privacy. Work is 24/7 and "out of town." The word "neighbor," and I would dare add the word "citizen," no longer carries the same meaning and value it once did. We are more and more defined by our economic status and our occupations.

I believe that in many ways the workplace has become the new neighborhood. Longer hours, the greater need for teamwork, greater personal identification with one's work, the sense of a community of people assembled around common values and objectives bring a closeness that is often lacking in the geographical neighborhood. Even the business reality of common standards and objectives stands in stark contrast to a physical neighborhood where everyone does her own thing. Business expectations of behavior in everything from codes of ethics and dress codes to respect for others and the public elimination of discrimination and harassment set standards of conduct that were once the function of the old neighborhood. As discussed earlier, there are the added professional standards that come from the associations and societies that have formed around every profession. Some businesses have extended the neighborhood concept even to the point of providing concierge services and discount shopping. Charity, car insurance, savings accounts, medical reimbursements can all be a function of payroll deductions. Employee assistance plans for counseling, legal advice, addiction recovery, and crisis intervention are becoming more common. Day care is an attractive benefit offered by some larger companies. "Best companies to work for" is beginning to sound a lot like "best neighborhoods to live in." The role played by this new neighborhood in the moral development of the individual can be at least as significant as that played by the geographical neighborhoods of the past. Our communities of value, communities of strong personal relationships grounded in common meanings, are no longer based on *place*. They do not link to neighborhoods, towns, and, I would add, in our day, not even to nations. We need to think differently about what community means in our own times.[2]

Work Works for People

When Amartya Sen says that "the freedom to participate in economic interchange has a basic role in social living," he is speaking of something more than just the promotion of general prosperity.[3] The other role of economic activity is the development of the individual person. Work works for people. It brings them up against the needs of others. The process of meeting human needs is not only the service of the human race; it is fundamentally the making of the human person. Negatively, work acquaints us with the workings of the reality principle. It teaches us about our own limitations and about the importance of domesticating our personalities to make ourselves tolerable to others. The nurturing cocoon of family and friends is broken open to the

---

    [2] Douglas K. Smith, *On Value and Values: Thinking Differently about We in an Age of Me* (Upper Saddle River, N.J.: Financial Times Prentice Hall, 2004). While surely not the last word, this book is an excellent exploration of how society itself will need to reinvent itself in a world dominated by organizations, markets, and global networks.
    [3] Amartya Sen, *Development as Freedom* (New York: Anchor Books, 2000; orig. published, New York: Knopf, 1999), 7.

larger world of strangers and distant purposes. I am constantly amazed how a group of people who not only would never choose one another for friends but would naturally avoid one another socially somehow come together on a daily basis and produce goods and services for the benefit of others. Business becomes a great crucible for dealing with differences by stretching one's own emotional and mental horizons and moving beyond natural limitations.

On a more positive note, the business world becomes the testing ground of our own potential and abilities, not in the fantasy of our private imaginations but in the give and take of daily responses to people and situations. Business helps persons discover what they are really good at by giving feedback in two ways. First, the constant stream of successes and failures that makes up each day points to a person's strengths and weaknesses. Business is always about results. Second, the praise and blame of others, whether of bosses, peers, or direct subordinates, help steer one's efforts, at least in the long run. As a result, business becomes an important arena for accomplishment and success. Everyone wants to be successful, no matter how someone determines what success looks like. That theme will be developed further in chapter 10. For now, it is enough to recognize how significant business is for a person's sense of achievement. While there is an obvious danger in overidentifying personal worth with one's job, the danger only points out that a personal sense of achievement is often realized through one's work. The fact of two-income families is the result not only of a perceived need for more money but also of a desire for greater personal achievement. It is interesting to note that people who become rich through successful business activity do not generally take early retirement and spend the rest of their lives in some form of idle hedonism. Many keep working hard and taking on new challenges. Work works for people!

That possibility is further enhanced by the vast array of professions and jobs developed by a market economy. In a basic agricultural society, careers are drastically limited. Apart from subsistence farmers or hunters, there are few other roles: leaders, elders, priests, healers, perhaps a dozen in all, depending on the level of development. Consider, then, the wide range of options open to someone entering a developed market economy. Apart from the trades in construction, manufacturing, and maintenance, there are the ever-widening specializations in health, finance, marketing, information technology, engineering, materials, counseling, law, etc. In addition, experts are saying that persons entering the workforce today can expect to have five or six careers over their lifetimes. New careers are being identified constantly. A list of twenty-eight emerging careers and job opportunities of the next ten to twenty-five years ranges from artificial-intelligence technician and computational linguist to relocation counselor and underwater archeologist. The disruption taking place currently in the United States is not because of the lack of job growth. Rather, there is a displacement of jobs from the *manufacturing* sector, which provided good jobs for people without formal education but who were willing to work hard, to jobs in the *information/service* sector, where education is critical.

THREE IMPORTANT PRINCIPLES OF GROWTH

Having set the general framework of growth within a business context, we need to look more specifically at just how growth and development really take place. Marcus Buckingham and Curt Coffman, in a controversial book called *First, Break All the Rules,*[4] reported on a survey they conducted for the Gallup Organization. What they discovered is that great managers universally understood the following:

- people don't change that much
- don't waste time trying to put in what was left out
- try to draw out what was left in

Let's take the challenge and try to understand these three principles of growth. Maybe then we will also comprehend why the authors also add a further observation to the effect that understanding these three principles is hard enough.

People Don't Change That Much

This principle is perhaps the most difficult of all to understand or, better, to accept. We are always ready to change others. We all know that the CEO, our manager, our co-workers need to change. We could probably write elaborate agendas detailing just what they need to do to become better persons, more effective leaders, and greater contributors to the success of the company. It doesn't stop there. The mayor, the pope, the president, my neighbor—all could use some changing. As we get closer to home, we could say the same about our spouse. And if we're really honest, we could say the same about ourselves! Intuitively we want to change people. The fact that none of us changes that much is indeed difficult to understand or accept. It is wisdom, for instance,

---

[4] Marcus Buckingham and Curt Coffman, *First Break All the Rules* (New York: Simon & Schuster Business Books, 1999).

that tells us not to marry someone in order to change them. It won't work. And it is usually even greater wisdom if, after years of marriage, we come to genuinely accept and love our spouse as truly other.

On occasion, managers will come to me complaining about one of their direct reports who is creating all sorts of difficulties, not getting along with others, neglecting some part of his job, etc. I will usually bring them up short with the comment, "then fire him." More often than not, there will be a response along the lines of "But he's really good with customers, knows the product," or some other admirable quality. From there the discussion can go to how much good does he bring to the table vs. the grief he causes, and how much turmoil can the manager live with. Indeed, termination may be the best answer. It all has to start, though, with an acceptance of the basic fact that people don't change that much. That basic fact is not simply the result of lack of effort or good will. As neurology is realizing with greater clarity, our brain develops circuits that expand along the lines of use. Synapses connect neurons together. Pathways in the brain are strengthened by use. On the other hand, synapses that are not used deteriorate. A teenager at sixteen has only half of the synapses she had at age three. "Use it or loose it" holds true here as it does in so many areas of life. Not only are there well-established psychological principles impeding real change, but, even more fundamentally, our physiology works against change. Yet every manager, co-worker, relative, spouse, secretly wants to change people so they do what he wants. A strategy of fixing people is usually fanciful daydreaming that goes nowhere in the long run. In fact, it can shortcircuit the process of meaningful change. And ultimately, it is doomed to intense frustration on all sides.

If this is the case, then why bother with ethics or anything else? Have we not preached a mantra of change and development over a lifetime only to be told now that "people don't change that much"! The real issue, though, is to focus the question more precisely along the lines of "How much of someone can you change?" and "Where can you realistically expect the most change?"

Don't Waste Time Trying to Put In What Was Left Out

This principle is a strong corollary to the first one. If people don't change that much, then all the effort to get them to change is mostly wasted, if by "change" is meant the elimination of weaknesses. Still, intuitively it is what we keep trying to do. The Gallup poll conducted a survey asking what will help you achieve greater success: building your strengths or fixing your weaknesses? Only 41 percent believed that focusing on their strengths was the key to

success.[5] Annual performance evaluations tend to focus potential development along the lines of getting rid of our weaknesses. Even when we look at
our own improvement, we focus on what we are not doing right. We are eager
to identify weaknesses and then to tell people, including ourselves, to go fix it.
Should it be any surprise that it doesn't work, that year after year we get more
or less the same reviews listing the same weaknesses! Is it not a commonplace
to peg people with statements like "There he goes again" or "Consider the
source"? Is that not what we had to struggle with in the first principle?

And yet we continue to spend time trying to change people or to solve problems by telling people to change. Witmer & Associates, a business consulting
firm, has taken this basic principle and applied it to very specific skills required
for business sales.[6] The first list identifies skills that are *not able to be developed:*

drive
integrity
conceptual thinking
conforming behavior

The second list identifies skills that have *low potential for development*:

aptitude for detail
problem-solving ability
confidence
analytical analysis
executive presence
independence

The next list indicates skills that have *average potential for development:*

profit priority
organization
service orientation
listening
persuasion
strategic thinking
relationship building
motivational ability

The final list is of skills that have a *high potential for development*:

business and technical skills

---

[5] Marcus Buckingham, "Bucking the System," *Fast Company* (August 2005): 89.
[6] Witmer & Associates can be reached at their Web site: witmerassociates.com.

While one can argue with the details, the fundamental point is that not all qualities can be developed. In fact, the qualities that are most at the core of a person are the ones least able to be developed. Some such recognition becomes critical in understanding the second principle: Don't waste time trying to put in what was left out.

Try to Draw Out What Was Left In

In other words, focus on a person's strength. Maximize what people bring to the table. In the language of philosophy and psychology, development progresses along the paths of successful functioning. In the language of neurology, brain circuits develop along paths of neurons and synapses that are activated. Here is the real opportunity for development and change. It is where our effort and goodwill can make a difference. For that reason we must devote much more reflection to this principle.

In chapter 4 we highlighted the fact that leadership develops as we come to a deeper level of discovering and embracing "what really matters" to us. In this chapter we can now appreciate a further dimension of that discovery. An understanding of what really matters to us will also give us a good indication of where our strength lies. There is a strong correlation between being in touch with ourselves in terms of what really matters to us and our development along the lines of our particular strengths. Since what matters to us is always a question of our values and morals, we are in a position to maximize a synergy that brings together our strengths, our morals, and our constant desire for further development. The person who is truly in touch with herself because she knows what matters to her and is open to a lifetime of moral development in the direction of her strength can be energized to the core. It is the best assurance for sustained development. Herb Kohler, of Kohler Industries, often identified with bathroom products, had this to say when he opened a new golf course to rave reviews, "I love the creative aspect of business . . . That's what energizes me. We're always out on the leading edge. Whether it's making toilets, engines or golf courses, we never try to vary the quality."[7]

In a similar vein, Jeff Immelt, who followed the highly acclaimed Jack Welsh as GE's CEO, had this to say about leadership, "Leadership is an intense journey into yourself. You can use your own style to get anything done. It's about being self-aware."[8]

---

[7] *Chicago Tribune* (August 8, 2004), section 3.
[8] "Top 10 Leadership Tips from Jeff Immelt," *Fast Company* (April 2004): 96.

While the above quotes may sound a bit romantic and idealistic, the process of getting in touch with oneself is often filled with anxiety and false starts. Early in our careers we probably have no more than a vague sense of our talents, motivations, and values. Even in college we may move through several majors before settling on something that gets us through. Our first jobs and organizations may be poor fits. Because we are not clear about who we are and what kind of jobs we are best suited for, we can be seduced more easily by the money, glamour, or prestige associated with a particular job. A good opportunity becomes simply what is considered popular at the time. This is where the type of personal introspection introduced in chapter 4 can be helpful, not in the sense of navel gazing but in the sense of reflecting on past experience, identifying what you enjoyed and what brought you success. Development occurs along the lines of successful functioning!

Goal setting/planning have become popular ways of encouraging development. Here is what works according to Daniel Goleman, Richard Boyatzis, and Annie McKee in their book *Primal Leadership: Realizing the Power of Emotional Intelligence*:

- Goals should build on one's strengths, not on one's weaknesses.
- Goals must be a person's own—not goals that someone else has imposed.
- Plans should flexibly allow people to prepare for the future in different ways.
- Plans must be feasible, with manageable steps; plans that don't fit smoothly into a person's life and work will likely be dropped within a few weeks or months.
- Plans that don't suit a person's learning style will prove demotivating and quickly lose his attention.[9]

All these points are further elaborations of the basic principle that our strengths are what we can develop, if we are to develop at all. It is where we already see growth that we can expect the most change.

As for our weaknesses, stop trying to eliminate them. But that sounds so defeatist! What about freedom and the ability to make ourselves the persons we become? Yes, there is something we can do, but it is not eliminating our weaknesses. Why then do we keep going back trying to do just that! No matter how much we might have grown, how much we have achieved, how much we have been praised and admired, we still go back to trying to eliminate our weaknesses. It's like trying to keep our tongues from a new cavity in our teeth!

---

[9] Daniel Goleman, Richard Boyatzis, and Annie McKee, *Primal Leadership: Realizing the Power of Emotional Intelligence* (Boston: Harvard Business School Press, 2002), 144.

When we get a performance review, we tend to fixate on the negatives. We judge the review by how negative it is. When we consider improvement, we tend to look at what's wrong rather than at how we can further develop our strengths. Why we tend to do this so instinctively is a profound question. At one level it is rather obvious. Business is about performance. Failure to perform is easily apparent. Nothing is so critically measured as business performance. If the culture of a company is such that it focuses primarily on what's wrong, if it constantly seeks to find someone to blame, then the tendency to look at the negative is reinforced. However, that is only the immediate picture.

At a deeper level, people tend to look at their negatives rather than their strengths because they have low self-confidence or self-esteem. They don't really believe they are quite capable. They have no word or deed of their own so they take on the words and deeds of others. Spontaneously, then, they look at what they don't have. At an even deeper level, there is the perennial question of What am I worth? In still other terms, If people knew me as I really am, with all of my weaknesses and skeletons of the past, would they (or anyone) still love me? Do I have a worth beyond my words and deeds, my talents and my earnings, my own power? What do I need to do to make myself worthwhile, loveable? As long as the questions are posed in these terms, there is no answer other than continuing to try to *do* something or *eliminate* some weakness that will make me worthwhile. At this level we are at the religious question, answered by Christians as "salvation"; by Jews as "Shalom"; by Buddhists as "enlightenment"; by all as some form of blessedness or graciousness. In other words, our worth is something given rather than self-created. Without it we will tend toward perpetual dominance or inferiority. We are all told to admit our failings, to ask forgiveness if we have offended others, not to blame others for our own mistakes. At one level that seems easy enough, unless it ties into a false sense of our own worth.

Once we accept the fact that our weaknesses will never be eliminated, and that is a key moment, then what is it that we *can* do about them? The most we will be able to do is to manage our limitations, and that is a hard thing to understand/accept. Here is what it can mean specifically:

- Focus your effort on developing your strengths and following your passion.
- Understand/accept what impact your limitations have on others. Understand why some others will always have difficulty with you, why you seem at times to be misunderstood, why your actions might be one-sided, why you are not always as effective as you might be.
- Ask for advice before making decisions. One company put it this way, If you don't seek advice, you're fired.

- Bring people around you who have *different* abilities from your own. That way you can compensate for your own limitations. This is especially true for managers, and critically important the higher you go in leadership. It is a sign of a poor manager who only brings on people less capable than herself or much like herself.
- Change careers, jobs, or companies if your limitations are keeping you from moving forward. In other words, pursue situations in which your strengths are really needed and where your important weaknesses are not a *serious* drawback.
- If you are the manager, try to help your people find positions where their strengths can grow and the effects of their weaknesses will be minimized. Sometimes it can be accomplished through discipline. Set out clear behavioral procedures that a person must follow. It might help a person accomplish what they cannot do from internal motivation.

Marcus Buckingham and Donald Clifton wrote a sequel to their original work which further developed their earlier insights. It could be summed up in their own words, *"You will excel only by maximizing your strengths, never by fixing your weaknesses. This is not the same as saying 'ignore your weaknesses.' The people we described did not ignore their weaknesses. Instead, they did something much more effective. They found ways to manage around their weaknesses, thereby, freeing them up to hone their strengths to a sharper point. Each of them did this a little differently."*[10] Does it sound a little Pollyannaish? In fact, it can mean anything from quitting jobs and turning down job offers to hiring people to work for you who are, in some ways, smarter than you.

To put the issue negatively, you might come to the realization that something is seriously wrong about your present job if you demonstrate a majority of the following symptoms:[11]

1. *Overload.* At a time of serious cutbacks, we are often called to perform double duty. We can do this on a temporary basis. If we find ourselves overstressed continuously, we need to take heed.
2. *Unsung hero.* Do you feel like the martyr, working extra hard but going unrecognized and unrewarded? We all need to speak up and share how our actions make a difference to the company.

---

[10] Marcus Buckingham and Donald Clifton, *Now Discover Your Strengths* (New York: Free Press, 2001), 26- 27.

[11] As presented by Sander Marcus, Ph.D., a professional career counselor with Friedland & Marcus in Chicago, Illinois. The points were outlined in "Dead-End Job? Seven Signs," on Career Builder.com (September 23, 2005). CareerBuilder.com is an excellent Web site not only for job searches but also for career development and change in the current business world.

3. *Out of the loop.* If you feel you are no longer in the know, being consulted, brought into the picture, it could be a sign that you are no longer valued.
4. *Looming dread.* Do you dread getting out of bed in the morning because it means facing another day at work? Are Sundays spoiled because you are already starting to dread Mondays?
5. *Is this all there is?* Have you started to lose interest in your job? Is your productivity slipping? Are you coasting?
6. *Temper, temper.* Do what you once considered "annoyances" now trigger anger? Are you often just at the edge? Have you lost your professionalism?
7. *Alienation.* Do you no longer feel emotionally invested in your co-workers? Have you lost interest in them? Do you no longer feel connected?

None of us is unaffected by some of these symptoms, at least some of the time. The point here is to recognize how many of them have become regular attitudes. If you say yes to five of them, then you need to take serious steps to change the situation. It may mean learning new skills, taking on new projects, changing jobs, or changing companies. Your present situation means that further growth or development has come to an end.

Feedback

There is another important lesson to be learned from the three principles of growth: good feedback is essential. Is it not through feedback that we come to recognize and appreciate our strengths as well as our weaknesses? Over time we learn what aspects of our work gets praised, what kind of things others come to us for help with, what kind of promotions we get, what type of assignments we are given, what is recognized in formal performance appraisals, what kind of awards we might have received. All of these are forms of feedback. They tell us much about where our strength lies. And that *is* the key point— feedback is, first of all, positive recognition. If we "develop along the path of successful functioning," then feedback is an important way of recognizing where we are successful. A company that is driven by value and merit provides an environment that supports growth. That environment is created not only or even primarily by formal award programs. It's the day-to-day recognition by others of work performed that sets the climate. A positive comment on work submitted for your review, seeking out someone for advice, calling attention to someone's successful though perhaps behind-the-scenes efforts, sincere thanks to the person who has helped you out, and recognizing the contribution of others in a job for which you have been praised are some of the varied ways that positive feedback continues to occur. Most people don't have a problem giving this kind of feedback, other than not doing enough of it.

On the other hand, feedback can also be critical and negative. The flipside of being aware of our strengths is the recognition of our limitations. Again, feedback plays a significant role. It occurs not only in what we get blamed for and in formal review items for improvement, but much more subtly in what we are not asked to do, in which project teams we are not asked to participate, in the promotions we don't get, at what level of responsibility we seem to be fixed, the people who never come to us for help or advice. Negative yet constructive feedback is very difficult to give. In a survey of four thousand Fortune 500 executives, five out of seven said they would rather lie to employees about performance than confront them about performance problems.[12] I knew of an executive, very bright and to all appearances cold and calculating, who was so incapable of giving negative feedback that he would have "economic" layoffs rather than confront poor performance directly. Nonetheless, we need to know our own limitations, not to change them but to manage them better, perhaps with the help a supervisor can give us.

Again, if we "develop along the path of successful functioning" we need to know when our successful functioning takes us into a fantasy world where "one will seek and find less common fields in which to excel; and there one will be apt to overcompensate for deficiencies elsewhere." If we have come to believe that our successful functioning has been in playing office politics, then we will continue in that course until it becomes "unsuccessful." If our success has been in talking a big game but coming up short on performance, then we will continue until it is no longer successful. If our success is trying to please everyone, then we will continue until we are confronted by the fact that there will always be some who will be unhappy with our actions. At some point only honest, critical feedback can help us get back to other paths of development. The reality checks that are integral to the very nature of business can be extremely important principles of our own growth and development.

Unfortunately, there are two groups of people who tend to get shut out of this healthy process— minorities and high-level executives! What could they have in common? Let's look at each group. Minorities, including racial minorities and women in a male-dominated business, often do not get hon-

---

[12] Linda Klebe Treviño, and Katherine A. Nelson, *Managing Business Ethics: Straight Talk about How to Do It Right*, 2nd ed. (New York: John Wiley & Sons, 1999), 130.

est feedback. The reasons are varied. There is, first, the general fear of saying something that could lead to a discrimination lawsuit. This is unfortunate especially since the intention of the law is to promote the welfare of minorities. Rather than work with a troubled person, it becomes easier to tolerate bad behavior for a period of time and then get rid of the person. But there is also a deeper reason. A white male giving feedback to another white male feels he is standing on common ground with common understandings and expectations, yet this is not necessarily true. But the white male who needs to confront a white female or an African American male tends not to be so sure of himself, shares less common ground, and can more easily be challenged on his own deep general presumptions about women or racial minorities. The easy way out is not to confront, to keep reviews very general and innocuous. Both parties are diminished in the process. The same would hold of the female or African American manager confronting the white male.

The situation is similar but a little different with the executive. High-level executives have huge egos. In itself, this is neither surprising nor disturbing. They have generally arrived at their positions through recognized successful functioning over a period of time. Their sense of self has become rather well defined. For a leader, this sense of his own values and vision is critical. In a study of CEOs of health-service companies, Eric Hartner found that "self-awareness of leadership abilities was greatest for CEOs of the best-performing companies and poorest for CEOs of the worst performers."[13] There is a tendency for leaders as they advance in an organization to inflate their abilities, to see themselves as better than they really are, and better than others see them. But who is going to give them appropriate feedback? Too much power is associated with the position for most people to want to risk that confrontation. In addition, most executives are not very receptive to personal change. Their strengths have gotten them to the top. Who is going to argue with success at that level? Yet Hartner's results showed that those at the highest levels had the least accurate perception of how they acted with others.

Corrective personal feedback is difficult to give. We don't want the confrontation. We rationalize our own hesitancy by saying we don't want to hurt people's feelings or we don't want to demotivate them. Yet, most of us really crave feedback. Even if no salary increase is in the works, we want to know how we are doing. Good, honest feedback is a gift and a source for growing our strengths and managing, not eliminating, our weaknesses. In summary, failure to provide critical feedback is a disservice to everyone:

---

[13] Goleman, Boyatzis, and McKee, *Primal Leadership*, 94.

- to the *individual* who becomes stuck in nonperformance;
- to *fellow workers* who want to believe that successful performance matters;
- to *other managers* who inherit the poor performer down the line;
- to the *company* that fails to excel as a result of the nonperformer.

Unfortunately, managers tend to ignore people's patterns until they can't stand it any longer. Then the quick answer is to fire the person. If someone is genuinely surprised at being fired, it is a sure sign that the feedback process had not taken place.

HINDRANCES TO GROWTH

Up to this point we have been considering the business world as a positive factor in human growth and development. We now need to look at some hindrances to growth. While most are not unique to business, they can definitely flourish there.

The Ubiquitous "They"

Everyone has a "they." "They" are whoever it is that won't let you accomplish what you want to do. At work, the assembler has her supervisor; the supervisor has his director; the director has her vice-president; the vice-president has his CEO; the CEO has the board of directors; the board has its amorphous shareholder. There is always someone to blame for the inability to get something done. If it is not someone, then it is something: the company is too large, too small, privately owned, a corporation, a not-for-profit. Whether it is academia, government, or private enterprise, there will always be resistance that must be dealt with. How many "theys" are there? Always one more! And if you want, you will always find one to blame for your failure to act. The important step in moving forward is to identify the "they" in question. "They" tends to remain invisible and unnamed. It's what gets blamed for everything we don't understand, agree with, or gets in our way; it represents the resistance. There is always resistance to change. Once the resistance is identified, the process of finding some commonality and moving forward becomes easier.

Buckminster Fuller uses an interesting analogy. How do you get a huge ocean liner like the Queen Mary to turn course? What kind of huge rudder and what tremendous pressure would it take to change the momentum of an ocean liner that large and powerful? The answer is what is called a trim tab.

On the huge rudder there is a much smaller tab/rudder that initiates the turn, which is then completed by the engagement of the complete rudder. In like manner, Fuller talks of about the 5 percent in an organization who can be considered a critical mass. Once that is established, another 15 percent will come on board. Twenty percent of an organization is enough to change it. Look for the 5 percent!

> Identify at least three "theys" in your own life—what keeps you from doing what you really want to do. Select one from your work, from your family life, and from your career. Now try to find a way of dealing with each of them in a way that will allow for at least some movement.

The subjective side of "they" is *blame*. Real leaders take responsibility for results, both good and bad, and don't try to look for excuses or a "they" to blame. Of course there are limits. No one has control of the universe. There are situations that are intractable. No matter what a person did, there could be no successful results. The point is not to spend one's energy looking for whose fault it is and whom to blame. For mature persons, the focus is always on what can be done to solve problems, to make things better.[14]

Change

When a group of retired persons were polled about what they wished they would have done differently in their lives, the second most frequently mentioned response was the wish that they would have taken more risks.

Change or die! What if you were given that ultimatum? What are your odds of changing? Surely they must be extremely high because the stakes are so high. Guess again. Experts are saying that the odds are against your changing![15] The medical profession has concluded that 90 percent of heart-bypass patients do not make the permanent lifestyle changes needed under the circumstances. It has also claimed that 80 percent of the health-care budget is consumed by five behavioral issues—excessive smoking, drinking, eating, stress, and not enough exercise. In other words, most of the enormous health-care budget is absorbed by the fact that people don't change their behaviors.

---

[14] See Henry Cloud, *Integrity: The Courage to Meet the Demands of Reality* (New York: Harper-Collins, 2006), 185-88, for further reflection on how real leaders take responsibility for results.

[15] Alan Deutschman, "Change," *Fast Company* (May 2005): 53-56.

In short, change is extremely difficult. Yet change is critical to human and moral development as well as to business success. Abraham Maslow claims that less than 1 percent of the population continues to develop, therefore change, for an entire lifetime. A major part of the problem is that change is a two-dimensional reality. There is the external element that catches our immediate attention in the use of the word "change." It is the new product, new procedure, new behavior, new location, new challenge. There is also, and more fundamentally, the psychological process involved in change, which we might better name "transitions." The real resistance to change lies not in the externals but in the losses and endings, the fear and uncertainty, the letting go to reembrace. While there are an army of gurus and a library of self-help books to assist us through the transitions, let us look at just one person who might help us appreciate some of the complexity involved. Elizabeth Kuebler-Ross, in her world-famous study *On Death and Dying*,[16] researched the experiences of others in dealing with the greatest change and transition that we will all face—death. She discovered a distinct pattern of emotional responses that needed to be dealt with in order to bring this momentous change of death to a satisfying conclusion. It is interesting to note that what she identified applies equally to all types of change, both individual and organizational. Examining what she calls the five stages of dying can be instructive to all of us in dealing with the fundamental reality of change.

First Stage: Denial

The quickest and easiest way to deal with change is to head it off at the pass. There are many forms that this denial can take. The most basic is to attack the credibility of the messenger—kill the messenger. She doesn't know what she's talking about. She's too young, too old, too emotional, not in the know—whatever it takes to discredit the messenger. In that way, no one has to take the message seriously. If that doesn't work, you can still deny the message. The data are false, one-sided, irrelevant, not of my concern. Indeed, denial is a first line of defense that can last a long time. The first step in moving beyond addiction of any kind—drug, alcohol, obsessive compulsiveness—is to stop denying the problem, to admit that something is wrong. Albert Einstein once said that the sign of real craziness is when a person continues to do the same thing but expects different results! Sometimes it takes a disaster to break through. A threatened divorce, for instance, is sometimes the only way through denial.

---

[16] Elizabeth Kuebler-Ross, *On Death and Dying* (New York: Collier Books, 1993).

In an organization, denial can be just as devastating. If we have developed through our past successful functioning, then we can reach a plateau, individually or collectively, where we use that very success to deny the need for further change. "It has always worked in the past" is a common rationalization both in our own lives and in an organization. When a business ignores the competitive signals that come from others in the same field, it is in a state of denial that can have disastrous consequences. When change is occurring faster in the general culture than in the company, the company is in a spiral of decline.

Second Stage: Anger
If the data and the messenger are strong enough to break through the denial, then the first emotional response is typically anger. We respond with anger because we have come to realize at least partially that something needs to change. We all live in some type of comfort zone. It is the place—physical, emotional, or intellectual—where we feel at home, where we feel safe and comfortable. It is the place where we have invested much effort, many dreams, much hope. To have it now attacked will undoubtedly make us angry. At the very least it will make us uncomfortable. We do not want to give up our former investments. The threat of that loss leads us to anger. Instinctively, together with all animals, anger is our first, and salutary, response to being threatened. The important issue here is not to deny the anger but to recognize how we are directing it. Anyone or anything can become its target.

In a business, the CEO can direct that anger at the employees who "just need to work harder." It can be aimed by sales and customer service at the customer who "should change or be educated." Clerks or assemblers can aim it at bosses who "don't know what they are doing." It can be aimed at the messenger who "doesn't really know what is going on." In the face of death or serious loss, it can be aimed at God. Anger always seeks the source of danger to one's comfort zone. While the anger is instinctive, understanding the real threat is a matter of greater discernment. Anger, or its milder version, discomfort and uneasiness, can provide the energy for facing the need to change.

Third Stage: Bargaining
When the need for change is unavoidable, the need to bargain or negotiate our way out of real change takes over. I'll be more religious, go to church, make a promise, if only I can have a few more years to live. When progressive discipline leads to the point of discharge for absenteeism, "Just give me one more chance." How often do we hear the familiar ring of "if I had more help," "if we just cut people," "if we reduce our expenses," "if we just work harder," "if we just have a little more time," as a way of dealing with adverse numbers in

our operations. Now there certainly are situations in which any or all of these responses are appropriate for the problem. But it must be recognized as well that these can also be ways of avoiding the real change that is required. An alcoholic will promise the world to his spouse, his family, his employer, as long as it doesn't require giving up alcohol. In other words we need to recognize when our bargaining is really rationalizing our desire to protect our original comfort zone. It is our time of "bargaining with the devil." Most of us have probably tried at least some form of this negotiating before finally moving ahead.

Fourth Stage: Despair

Bargaining may even bring some short-term relief. We want to believe that things will get better. Small changes for the better, in our health or in the performance numbers, can lead us to exaggerated projections. But if the situation really calls for fundamental change, then these minor changes will fail. When that reality hits, it can lead us to disorientation, deep sadness, and even despair. At that point we are at a watershed. We are caught between the realization that we can no longer go back but are unwilling to go forward. It may require grieving, a time to celebrate "the good old times"—some way to close this chapter on the past. We must allow ourselves some time for this process if we are to move forward as whole human beings without leaving something of ourselves in the past. At some point, however, we also need to be able to say "enough is enough." My much beloved boss is gone. The old technology doesn't work anymore. The market is no longer looking for buggy whips. We need genuinely to let go. Paradoxically, it is only as we are able to let go that we are able to make progress. The child will not walk until it is willing to let go of its mother's hand.

Fifth Stage: Resignation and Integration

As grieving comes to an end, new possibilities begin to emerge. Imagined obstacles begin to fade. We begin to experiment and explore. As we take new steps, halting and tentative as they might be, still other possibilities open before us. This is why authorities on change talk about celebrating small, yet distinct, victories. Hope starts to take over. It is based on the anticipation that our efforts can yield results. Hope is critical at this point. If we do not see that our efforts can make things better, we will fall back into our old patterns. Hope is driven by the vision of what we can become or what the business can become. It is important, however, that the small victories, as well as the greater vision, are based on reality. False hopes and imagined results will lead only to greater despair. Here again, integrity and a culture built on value is paramount. Gradually, the new ways of doing things and the new principles of operation become comfortable and part of the new routine. Integration gradually takes place without the drama of anger and despair.

This process of change or transformation is pervasive in nature and in human nature. At its most profound level, it takes place in birth and in death. Kuebler-Ross has identified its stages in the deep human drama of death. Every religion is based on some form of transformation. The Christian lives it out in the death and resurrection of Jesus Christ. Psychology explores its implications in the process of growth and development, in the cycles of letting go and moving on. History studies it in the rise and fall of civilizations. Successful business measures it in the bottom line of profit and loss. Change is no longer optional or merely a way of coping with crises. It is no longer just a way of adapting to changing circumstances in some evolutionary fashion. Rather, change is a new constant; it is our way of anticipating the future. Any business that is not changing is not just standing still; it is falling behind. From the dynamics of change that we have traced, it becomes obvious that genuine change must be driven by personal integrity and moral development. The ability to stay open to the questions that arise from the dynamism of the human spirit allows us to face change with integrity. Lack of openness will lead not only to business failure but also to moral atrophy. Our concern here has been to recognize that real change is, first of all, deeply emotional and demands moral integrity.[17]

Fear

Most cultures have some version of the myth of the person who goes out to slay the dragon. Reluctantly, and with great trepidation, he heads out to take on the Herculean task. Upon meeting the dragon, he realizes that the dragon represents his own personal fear. Once he faces that, he returns victorious. The story is universal precisely because our personal sense of fear is universal. It is also what makes change difficult. If change always involves some level of letting go of the familiar to head out of our comfort zone, then fear is a natural and salutary response to exploring the unknown. Fear is necessary; it heightens our sense of what can harm us and forces us to take things seriously. However it can also paralyze us. It can keep us from taking risks, one of the two

---

[17] John P. Kotter, a Harvard Business School professor, is recognized as an authority on organizational change in business. His bestseller, *Leading Change* (Boston: Harvard Business School Press, 1996), outlines eight steps for transforming an organization.

biggest regrets of older people as they reflect on their past life. Risk taking, however, is not the same as gambling. Both involve some movement into the unknown. For the gambler, it is strictly a "crap shoot." For the mature person there is more calculation involved. Accordingly, a closer look at how fear operates in our lives becomes critical for sustained development.

First and foremost, as is true of all emotional responses, there is the need to recognize the feeling of fear. We talk about the "grip of fear." It often feels like a tightening or a squeezing. Another common symptom of fear is the racing of the heart. We want to run, to get away from danger. Once we have recognized the feeling of fear, we are in a better position to explore just what it is we are afraid of. It is most likely some version of fear of failure. Why don't we take risks? The spontaneous answer comes back: because we might fail. Failure, whatever that might mean in a particular situation, stands behind every risk. Karl Wallenda was known worldwide as the greatest tightrope walker that ever lived. He walked every expanse you could tie a rope across until he plunged to his death in Puerto Rico. What his wife had to say is most instructive: "All Karl thought about for three straight months prior to it [his fatal fall] was *falling*. It was the first time he'd ever thought about that, and it seemed to me that he put all his energies into *not falling* rather than walking the tightrope."[18] Concentrate on winning, not on *not losing*.

It is not so much failure, as such, that keeps us from taking risks, but the *fear* that potential failure stirs up in us that holds us captive. Perhaps the best summary of this experience that we all face, if we are moving forward in our own lives, comes from the guru on leadership development, Warren Bennis:

> Our adult view of failure blocks our ability to take risks, to stand up for what we know is true, and respond to situations that demand leadership . . .
>
> Each of us makes many mistakes in the course of each day. Some we notice because we are sensitive to a particular mistake or because someone has called attention to it . . . We can consider each mistake a natural part of life from which we can learn and grow, or we can use failure as evidence of our lack of self-worth.[19]

A number of points are worth noting: First, fear of failure is a natural part of taking a risk. It's what makes risk risky. The fact of fear is common to every-

---

[18] Warren Bennis and Joan Goldsmith, *Learning to Lead: A Workbook on Becoming a Leader* (Reading, Mass.: Perseus Books, 1997), 83. The authors recount other examples as well.

[19] Bennis and Goldsmith, *Learning to Lead*, 84, 87.

one. If we have never felt that fear, then we have never really taken any risks. If we have always allowed that fear to turn us away from taking the risk, we have stopped growing. When was the last time you volunteered to do something you didn't have to, to take on a new project, to speak out on a potentially touchy subject? Any specific fear taps into our elemental and undifferentiated fear and reminds us of our basic fragility, of the fact that we really don't have complete control of our lives. It is that resonance that makes any fear so frightening.

Second, while we are all aware of our own particular minefield of potential mistakes or failures, we need to remember that it is really our own perception of what constitutes failure. We actually make many mistakes every day. However, there are only self-selected ones that make their way to our consciousness. It is always interesting to observe how a person defines the job responsibilities or challenges of her particular job. It reflects not only what she consciously identifies as the scope of the job but also what is, usually unconsciously, excluded. What is excluded tends to be what the person considers to be his world of potential failure, his limitations and weaknesses. If an accountant, for instance, sees his job to be merely the proper recording of data and the proper monitoring of procedures, then failure is narrowed to that challenge. Neglected issues of company integrity, potential losses, and cost-saving opportunities are simply not recognized as personal mistakes or failure. It removes the risk factor of looking at other issues, but at the expense of restricting further personal development.

Third, our fear of failure is something learned. While fear is a natural response to the unknown—for example, the child's fear of the dark—it takes its particular form from our own experiences. It can be very helpful, then, to reflect on the elements of our own fear of failure. Often our nightmares, or dreams of impending failure, can give us a good clue. Even more significant can be the exercise of reflecting on a past situation when we took a risk and succeeded. Perhaps it was giving a presentation to a group, starting a new job, taking on an additional assignment, or speaking out on an issue that was important to you. Try to remember how you felt before taking the action: were you nervous and fearful, did you start to regret taking on the task? What was it you really feared? Were you going to make a fool of yourself, or be put down? Then recall how you actually carried out the challenge. How did it go? Did you feel OK while doing it, even though you were nervous? The real payoff though occurred when you finished. Remember how glad you were that you took the risk—the sense of achievement, the doors it opened for you, the positive response of others, the heightened sense of confidence. Just remembering that sequence can help you overcome some of your fear and consequent reluctance the next time you confront another risk situation. The fear of failure or the risk factor will return, most likely in the face of even greater risks. Only by overcoming your fears in smaller matters do the larger risks and potential rewards open up to you. You have to stand before you can walk. By identifying the fear and the particular form it takes for you, as well as by remembering that prior successes came from accepting the risk of failure, you will be able to take major steps in your path to continual development.

Fourth, how failure and mistakes are treated in your company is a good indicator of company culture. If mistakes are occasions for blame and recrimination, then we will avoid them at all cost, and the greatest cost is the failure to risk and grow. If mistakes are viewed as learning situations, then we can proceed with confidence, even daring.

Fifth, the courageous person is not the one who doesn't sense fear. Rather, it is the one who recognizes his fear yet wants something that is more important. That's why we talk about love conquering fear. It's not that it takes away fear, but it allows us to overcome our fear. There is something more worthwhile than our fear.

There are some practical applications to career development coming from the above considerations of change and fear or risk. In making decisions about job opportunities, two factors need to be considered. The first is obvious: How good is the fit between who the person is and the position (including the organizational values of the culture)? The second is more far reaching: How good is the fit between who they are and who they want to be (or who you are and want to be)? In other words, what are the learning opportunities and the developmental possibilities of the job? From a developmental perspective, the best assignments are the ones in which the fit is imperfect, that there is a "stretch" in terms of talent (not values) to do the job. This is surely a riskier and more subjective judgment, but the risk can be tempered. The job should be one where one's strengths are really needed and the weaknesses are not a *serious* drawback. Core values, of course, must always be consistent with the organization. One rule of thumb is that the risk is probably too great if it will take more than six months to produce some meaningful results in the new position. Another danger to career development is that the very strengths that initiated a career (e.g., strong technical skills or strong tendencies to control) can actually become fatal flaws at a higher level of management. As discussed throughout this chapter, the continued reliance on the initial strengths that proved so successful can be inadequate or inappropriate in the face of new and different challenges.

SUMMARY

This is a lengthy and perhaps rambling chapter, but then human development is the same. It does not follow a straight line and cannot be completely controlled. Sometimes the things that happen to us are much more significant than things we have deliberately chosen. Much more could be added to this chapter. The following general principles can stand us in good stead.

- Moral growth is a lifelong process and is always concrete.
- We develop along the lines of successful functioning.
- We grow by developing our strengths rather than by eliminating weakness.
- Business is becoming our new neighborhood, the place where we live and share common values.
- Development implies change and change has definite patterns.
- Primary obstacles to change include resistance (they) and fear.

QUESTIONS FOR REFLECTION

1. Religion tends to see life as a journey or pilgrimage and assumes that we have no final home in this life. How does that tie into the notion that our life calls us to a never-ending process of self-constitution?
2. How will different cultural understandings of life as a journey into another life affect attitudes about business?
3. Is human development as pursued in this chapter a moral issue? Do we have a *moral* responsibility to develop our talents? Consider the parable of the talents and the fate of the one who buried his talent.
4. Has the dominance of business in human living actually undermined the traditional communities of family and neighborhoods?
5. Does business as a new possibility of personal identity, meaning, and community actually free a person from the dominance of family, religion, and nation? Does it limit the control that these traditional communities exercise over the individual? Is this a positive or negative development?
6. The recognition of sin and weakness for what they are is fundamental to religious belief. Forgiveness is an integral part of our relation to God as it is to every human being. Is this not also fundamental to business in the sense that we need to face the truth about ourselves and about the functioning of business? Is this not an aspect of business transparency?

7. List the most significant changes you have made in your life. Think through the process that you used to navigate each change. What were the most helpful factors? How can you help others through the process?

SUGGESTIONS FOR FURTHER READING AND STUDY

Bennis, Warren, and Joan Goldsmith. *Learning to Lead: A Workbook on Becoming a Leader*. Reading, Mass.: Perseus Books, 1997.

Buckingham, Marcus. *Now, Discover Your Strengths*. New York: Free Press, 2001. See also www.marcusbuckingham.com for free resources on strengths.

Clawson, James G. *Level Three Leadership: Getting Below the Surface*. Upper Saddle River, N.J.: Prentice Hall, 1999.

Kotter, John P. *Leading Change*. Boston: Harvard Business School, 1999. The classical handbook on organizational change.

9

Globalization

Of the hundred largest economies of the world,
more than half are not now nations at all,
but corporations such as Mitsubishi and Ford
N. Boyle, *Who Are We Now?*

Perhaps nothing so polarizes popular opinion as the notion of globalization. For some it conjures up superrich, multinational corporations raping and exploiting the poor of the world. For others it is the single most significant factor that has lifted millions of the world's population out of economic poverty to new levels of material prosperity. Or, on a more individual basis, for some it has become dreaded in America and western Europe as the cause of lost jobs and reductions in wages. For others, it has been warmly embraced as the source of cheap TVs and shirts as well as the impetus to explore peoples, foods, and cultures other than one's own. In any case, there is no doubt that it is the particular challenge of our age. We have reached a point in history that no other civilization has ever realized. We are global citizens; our neighbor lives everywhere on the planet Earth; we have the technology and know-how to feed and shelter everyone without exception. What are we to do? There is no going back, and the way forward is uncharted, filled with dangers, real and imagined. No doubt, political, business, and religious leaders have played on those fears and hopes to promote their own agendas. Political activists and moral crusaders have found in globalization a fertile ground for polarizing emotional responses. Reactions tend to be spontaneous and ideological. Our own approach must be more tentative. Since globalization is a *developing* reality, we are faced with the insecurities of a future that is not yet defined. At the same time, we are confronted daily with the consequences of that new reality. It affects us politically, socially, culturally, economically, religiously. Thus, it becomes even more important to try to understand what is really happening. What we have come to understand about the nature of business as such should be helpful.

Business, after all, is probably the most concrete symbol of this emerging phenomenon. Not only has it been deeply impacted by the forces of global-ization, but it is, to a large degree, driving the transformation. This is all the more reason for business to try to understand what is going forward, even if the steps must be modest. Our self-imposed limitation is to focus our atten-tion not on the total phenomenon of globalization but on how that reality plays out in the world of business. Perhaps, in this way, it can add a little light to the larger mosaic of global interconnectedness.[1]

WHAT IS GLOBALIZATION?

Some examples might be a good place to start. Chicago was once the meat packer of the Midwest. Cattle were driven to railway yards for a final ride to the slaughterhouses of Chicago for processing and distribution. With the invention of refrigeration the processed meat itself, rather than the much bulkier cattle, could be transported more effectively and cheaply. The meat processors could be located closer to the grazing land of the cattle, and places such as Omaha and Kansas City replaced the more distant Chicago as the meat butchers of the Midwest. Through the utilization of a new technology, mobile refrigeration, vast distances could be joined more efficiently. Chicago lost jobs as well as whole industries, but the country had cheaper meat. Glob-alization writ small!

Another example is from the history of manufacturing PCBs (printed cir-cuit boards) for the electronics company where I work. In the 1950s, all PC boards for TVs were manufactured in Chicago, which, at that time, was the TV capital of the world. Gradually that manufacturing moved to Japan, where it could be done cheaper. But after a period of ten years or so, manufacturing in Japan became too expensive, so PC board manufacturing was moved to Taiwan. After a while, rising manufacturing costs there led to relocation in Korea. Again, the same cycle repeated itself so manufacturing was moved to Malaysia. Presently, not only the PC boards but also the CRTs and LCDs are being manufactured in China. A few things become evident. Globalization is not a static process. An advantage at one time is no guarantee for a later period. Also, advances in globalization are always associated with gains in technology. Most importantly, the seminal question needs to be asked about

---

[1] For a broader and penetrating assessment of the positive and negative dimensions of globaliza-tion together with a process for moving forward, see Robert J. Schreiter, C.P.P.S, "A New Modernity: Living and Believing in an Unstable World," presented at the 2005 Anthony Jordan Lectures, New-man Theological College, Edmonton, Alberta, Canada, March 18-19, 2005 (unpublished).

why the manufacturing process gradually becomes more expensive in a given location over a period of time. These are just a few of the issues that globalization brings to the surface.

Globalization Is Not Something New

At first glance, globalization is nothing new. The ongoing passion of business for better, quicker, cheaper has been driving business since the beginning of commerce and exchange. It is interesting to note that even the voyages of Christopher Columbus to the New World were stimulated by the quest to find a *better trade* route to the East! The basic issue was identified by Aristotle when he distinguished three natural and fundamental types of association[2] in a way that is still enlightening today. The first is the *household*—obvious from the fundamental association of male and female to propagate the species. The second is the *village*, a number of households necessary for the satisfaction of something more than daily needs. Aristotle refers to "sons and grandsons" as natural larger extensions of the basic household into villages. And the final association, formed of several villages, is the state. As he goes on to say, "For all practical purposes the process is now complete." Most significant is the justification he gives for the need and the nature of this larger association— "self-sufficiency has been reached" to secure the good life.[3] Throughout history there has been an evolution of various forms of this third level of association—the tribe, the city-state, the empire, the nation. All reflect some altered understanding of what is needed to maintain self-sufficiency. We now no longer live in ancient republics, medieval kingdoms, or even autonomous nation states. Because of the avalanche of innovations in technology and communication that have become embedded in daily living, self-sufficiency for securing the good life cannot be achieved other than on a global basis. There is no more dramatic instance than the fact that even the most powerful economy in the world, the U.S. economy, is not self-sufficient. The real change, then, at least at first glance, is simply extending the boundaries of what is required for self-sufficiency. Globalization, from an economic perspective,

---

[2] Aristotle, *The Politics* 1257b25, trans. T. A. Sinclair; revised and re-presented by Trevor J. Saunders, in *Aristotle: The Politics* (London: Penguin Books, 1981), 57-59.

[3] See Robert G. Kennedy, *The Good That Business Does* (Christian Social Thought Series 9; Grand Rapids, Mich.: Acton Institute, 2006), 56-61, who approaches the same issue but focuses on Aristotle's reflection that business pursues specific goods while political and family associations pursue the good of general well-being.

describes the expansion of goods, services, labor, and capital across borders that were once considered impregnable.

But what about the interesting fact that production continues to move because of the gradual increase in cost at each location? This remains a puzzle as long as we continue to view economic globalization from the perspective of a fixed economic pie that must now be divided into more pieces—or, technically, zero-sum economics. It assumes that there is some determined amount of wealth in the world and the only issue is who is greedy, tricky, or smart enough to get a bigger part of it. Conversely, it assumes that a richer nation got that way by taking it from the now-poorer nations. What is overlooked is the fact that the world did not start rich. All peoples started poor in economic terms. The basic argument of this entire book is that business increases wealth. In other words, it enlarges the pie. In the last 100 years, we have created more wealth than in the previous 100,000 years. In the last century, work hours have been halved in the Western world.

And yet the belief persists widely that someone who has more of the pie is either lucky or immoral. Why does this run so deep? Perhaps it has to do with survival. For most of the history of the human race, life was indeed a zero-sum game. What other tribes hunted or gathered, you lost. If someone gained, you had reason to be suspicious. Resources were limited. Water, food, territory were vital to existence. If you had more, it had to be at someone else's expense. Someone had to lose! The instinct is still alive and well. With Karl Marx, capital increased at the expense of labor; the rich at the expense of the poor; rich nations at the expense of the poor nations; everyone at the expense of the environment. Someone has to be blamed. Forget that forty million children in poor nonmarket economies die each year from lack of adequate nutrition.[4] The other option is that some countries are just lucky. They happen to have an abundance of natural resources such as oil, or minerals, or fertile land. Forget that Japan has no natural resources and yet has prospered in a free-market economy. Forget that India and China had the same natural resources both before and after their transition from socialist to market economies. Unless one believes in the resourcefulness of people actually to *create* wealth, there will always be the condemnation that, whenever greater prosperity appears, someone, somewhere, somehow, is being victimized.

Beyond all ideological speculation, there stands the fact that globalization itself and the attendant reduction of global poverty have been the product of a wide-ranging market economy. *The very nature of business is to create and*

---

[4] John J. Macionis, *Society: The Basics*. (Upper Saddle River, N.J.: Pearson Education, 2002), 228-29.

spread wealth. That statement, grounded as it is in free-market practice, runs counter to socialist tendencies. To polarize the positions is to make caricatures of each and allows for easy dismissal of uncomfortable truths. The cry of the poor and the suffering, especially when faced in person, touches the deepest part of our soul. Our humanity calls for instant response. We want to find a reason for the tragedy, someone or something to blame—a harsh environment, a corrupt government, a greedy multinational corporation. Many a book has been written out of compassion, guilt, or outrage at these conditions. Orbis Books, the publishers of this book, has long provided a forum that brings that cry home to us.[5] We need to hear the pain, whether it comes as a result of a subsistence farming enslaved to the harsh rhythms of nature or from a harsh political or economic system that victimizes its people. Our response, however, must seek not only to alleviate immediate pain but to enable long-term solutions. Our personal response probably has less to do with the accuracy of the numbers or the depth of our compassion than with our basic understanding of the human person, and, even more immediately, of ourselves. After all, if one side points to the misery of sweatshops, the other side notes that the dramatic increase in world population is not initially the result of increased birthrates but of a decrease in early-death rates![6]

While the debate and the demonstrations continue, it is hard to gainsay the results of a global market economy. In 1970, for instance, 11 percent of the world's poor were in Africa and 76 percent were in Asia; but by 1998 Africa had 66 percent of the world's poor and Asia only 15 percent. The obvious explanation lies in the fact that Asia has made immense progress in reducing poverty through economic growth. Our earlier observation that manufacturing costs continue to rise in an initial low-wage population only exemplifies the proposition. Wages rise not because of unions or government but because of productivity gains—people get more money when they produce more value for other people. I have been told that cost estimates for manufactured goods from China at this time include almost nothing for the cost of labor. Labor is that cheap. If nothing changed, there would be no change in wages. However, as some individuals become more efficient and the use of technology becomes more pervasive, and as individuals are able to produce more in the same time, they can also demand a higher wage. As demand increases, skills become scarce. Competition for effective labor sets in; expectations and demands

---

[5] See, among many others, the following publications: John Neafsey, *A Sacred Voice Is Calling: Personal Vocation and Social Conscience* (Maryknoll, N.Y.: Orbis Books, 2006); and Vincent A. Gallagher, *The True Cost of Low Prices, The Violence of Globalization* (Maryknoll, N.Y.: Orbis Books, 2006).

[6] Macionis, *Society*, 405-12.

continue to rise; skills become more critical; education needs to meet the increasing demands for higher-level and more effective operations. Paying higher wages and benefits for the higher skill and efficiency levels becomes cost effective. In other words, rising prosperity begins to set in, and other countries are sought out for low-skilled and low-cost labor. In the meantime, the countries that were once paying low wages have now developed skill and expertise levels that allow them to engage in higher-level production efforts. In fact, they often play important roles in moving basic manufacturing to the new low-wage countries. In the example above about the change of location of the manufacturing of PC boards, it is Taiwanese engineers and Malaysian managers who are working with mainland China to support the manufacturing effort there. It is interesting to note that as of this writing the Chinese are beginning to take manufacturing to its next logical destination, Africa.

On first blush, then, globalization is essentially nothing new. Business reaches out into the ever-expanding boundaries of commerce and exchange in order to increase efficiencies. Aristotle explained the basic rationale for exchange by saying that it adjusts inequalities due to nature in the distribution of goods.[7] For example, people living by the sea exchange fish for wine produced in the hills. The process allows everyone to have access to a greater range of goods useful for living. The fact that this promotes the prosperity of all has been explored in earlier chapters. The only new thing is the amazing technology and resourcefulness that allows that exchange to take place not only from the seashore to the hills but from one corner of the world to every other place.

Globalization Is Something Completely New

A further analysis is not only possible but necessary. It begins with a return to Aristotle and the definition of the state as the association large enough to maintain self-sufficiency. What happens when no state, not even economic powerhouses like China or the United States, is large enough or strong enough to be truly self-sufficient? Or again, why is it that, at a time of rapid globalization and unification, there is an inverse movement to smaller units of association, such as ethnic groups (and devastating ethnic cleansings), renewed religious communities, such as the growth of evangelical churches, as well as the breakup of larger nations into smaller political units, as is happening in the Balkan Peninsula and the former Soviet Union? Is not the global-

---

[7] Aristotle, *The Politics*, 1256b40-1258a18.

ization of economic exchange also undermining the self-sufficiency of the *nation*? That fact, in itself, need not be devastating. After all, the independent nation is a rather recent creation. Older forms of self-sufficient organizations included the tribe, the Greek city-state, the Roman Republic, the kingdoms of medieval Europe and the vast empires from China and the Middle East to the British Empire, on which the sun never set. On the other hand, Germany only became a unified nation in 1871; France became a democracy at the time of the French Revolution in 1789; Indonesia became an independent nation in 1949; Italy became a republic in 1946; and the United States started its slow journey from colony to nation in 1776.

What makes globalization something completely new is the realization that a global economy undermines the criterion of the self-sufficiency of the nation. The nation is assumed to provide not only economic self-sufficiency but also a total identity that is social, cultural, historical, religious, and political. "I am an American" (or any other nationality) had a resonance that echoed through the whole person. It summed up in shorthand "who I am." Nationalism, of course, had its limitations. Cultural relativism has become a permanent dimension of contemporary consciousness. Two world wars, a cold war, and continuing national military actions around the globe have made us less sanguine about the possibilities of the nation. Nonetheless, one's nationality still runs deep in the psyche of most people.

For an increasing number of people, however, "what I do for a living" is becoming more important than nationality. Computer technicians, for instance, can find a greater affinity with computer people in other nations than to farmers in their own country. Centers of business activity are being less defined by nation and more by a specific geographical location, like Silicon Valley in California, the Indian call center in Bangalore, and Hong Kong. The shopping mall, fast-food chains, and the superstore are becoming global icons, often more significant than local enterprises. Centuries of suspicion and hostility between the French and the Germans are suspended in the collaboration demanded to build Airbus. McDonald's and Coca-Cola are more recognizable worldwide than most national or religious leaders. My own sobering experience occurred in Italy when an Italian asked me if we have Coca-Cola in America too! Doctors Without Borders is another example of a new kind of reality. Nongovernmental organizations (NGOs) are proliferating. These are just a few indications that something profoundly new is taking place, something that, if not initiated by globalization, is certainly radically accelerated by it.

What is happening, I believe, is a deep transformation of the sources of our personal identity. The city of the classical world, the ancient *polis*, from which we derive the word "politics," was primarily the site for the practice of politics or the art of living together to foster the good life. The city of the medieval world was the gathering place for the public worship of God, a place where the church was the highest edifice in the city. Early American cities centered on the courthouse, the symbol of rule by law. In contrast, the modern city is identified as a center of commerce and economic exchange. It is not by accident that the tallest buildings in this new city are no longer the cathedrals or the courthouses but the skyscrapers, those monuments to economic activity. As long as politics or religion prevailed as a source of identity, then one's humanity was rooted in and protected by the broad values of the nation or the church, mosque, and temple.

Globalization, however, is rooted primarily in economic values, in short, in the marketplace. What allows globalization to expand at such a rapid pace is the fact that everything can be given a universal monetary value. By means of international trade and currency exchange, for example, it is possible to put an hourly wage to the efforts of a basket weaver in the Highlands of New Guinea as well as to the CEO in Stockholm, Sweden. The following quote has a sobering tone:

> What is it that allows us to interact globally? The technologies of communication and transportation is the quick and easy answer. But what really allows us to cross cultural, religious, political divides? What is it that gives us a common base from which we move forward? Our common humanity seems like a reasonable answer. But it is exactly our humanity that has created the cultural, religious and political differences that have kept us apart. I suggest that the single common unit that has translated all differences is *money*. If that seems crass and demeaning then we need to look deeper into the meaning of money. We have always been concerned about possessing money, not for itself, but for what it can buy. It has always been important as the universal means for obtaining whatever we needed or wanted. But a market economy, and even more a global market economy, does not esteem a monetary unit as a unit of *possession* but rather as a unit of *accounting*, as a way of keeping track of costs and benefits. By way of double-entry bookkeeping (cost-profit analysis), international stock and currency exchanges, and a host of other accounting and banking practices, the flow of goods and services are defined in globally recognized monetary units commonly referred to as a form of money such as the dollar or the euro. Money translates the value of everything into economic units.[8]

---

[8] Craig M. Gay, *Cash Values: Money and the Erosion of Meaning in Today's Society* (Grand Rapids,

If this is a fairly accurate assessment of the role of money in our globalized society, then globalization does indeed bring something entirely new into history. It is not surprising that the common expression 24/7 has its origins in the business community. In effect, everything is reduced to an economic unit measured in terms of productivity. An open-ended twenty-four hours separates us from the Earth with its natural rhythms of day and night. A continuous seven days a week separates us from the common cultural and religious celebrations embodied in Sundays and national holidays.

The point here is not to decry present development for the sake of some imagined and idyllic "good old days." Rather, the fact of globalization calls us to proceed forward with as much understanding, ingenuity, and integrity as we can possibly command. We are all aware of the benefits of globalization. The reduction of global poverty and the enhancement of prosperity around the world can hardly be denied. The bridging of historic national and cultural divides is without precedent. The rise of democratic institutions of government to parallel growth in market economies is no accident. Economics creates a stability that can overcome the capricious acts of politicians. In fact, the Cold War can be seen as a victory of economic strength over political and military might. Religious condemnations give place to dialogue and open respect. Racial and gender discriminations are yielding to "whoever can best do the job." These are no mean accomplishments. But they also come at a price. That price is a certain reduction of the full range of human activities and values to quantifiable units of production. The danger is that our identity becomes increasingly defined as consumer-producer. Nicholas Boyle, in his work *Who Are We Now?*, gives a profound insight into this new identity. It is worth quoting in full:

> Anyone had the right to be able to do anything. But the freedom we are encouraged to have today is the freedom merely to choose, as consumers, from whatever the market offers—while a veil is drawn over what is in a closed system the necessary symmetrical complement of this freedom: our enslavement, as producers, to the demands set us by the market, for the more choice we give ourselves as consumers the heavier the chains we forge for ourselves as workers. In the modern, post-revolutionary world there are no longer any pure consumers, there is no longer a leisured aristocracy—we are now virtually all consumers *and* producers, proletarians, who live by selling our labor.[9]

Mich.: William B. Eerdmans, 2004; first published as part of the New College Lecture Series (Sydney: University of New South Wales Press, 2003), 35-45.

[9] Nicholas Boyle, *Who Are We Now? Christian Humanism and the Global Market from Hegel to Heaney* (Notre Dame, Ind.: University of Notre Dame Press, 1998), 116.

And later he says,

> For the market seeks to conceal from us—lest it inhibit the arbitrariness and frequency of our choices in it, that is, of our purchases—that it has another, a shadow, side. It is not only the place where needs are satisfied; it is the place where orders for work are given. The market not only serves consumers; it disciplines producers. And in the contemporary world, where we are all—more or less—equally both consumers and producers, the market has to conceal from us that we shall eventually come to feel the consequences of our consumer choices in the form of constraints on our productive activity.[10]

In other words, the reverse side of the ability to freely choose from the constant parade of goods that a free-market economy can produce is to accept the constrictions put on a person to produce, as a wage earner, in that same economy. There is no free lunch! As a result, even more of our identity becomes defined by being a consumer-producer. When nationality, religion, or political persuasion is no longer the source of identity, then culture, religion, and political assembly are themselves measured in terms of a monetary unit that quantifies the value of all things. Our global unity becomes a one-dimensional economic unity. The monetary unit, as the universal measure, judges the effectiveness of the state, the vitality of religion, and the usefulness of culture. Before globalization, the nation maintained a self-sufficiency that provided an identity richer and deeper than that of consumer-producer. What institution can now protect the values of the human? Who can champion the person as something more than a consumer-producer? The price we are paying for global unity can be the reduction of the individual to a quantifiable economic unit. A new set of philosophical assumptions or prejudices about the nature of the human person are beginning to come to the fore.

These issues are raised here not to condemn a market economy that has become global but to become aware of some of the issues that must be addressed when we talk about globalization. Globalization is not just business now conducted on a worldwide scale. It is a new reality that needs to be understood more completely. Briefly, if a global market economy has relativized other commonly accepted sources of identity such as race, gender, political party and nationality, then how do we move beyond finding our identity in the market as a consumer-producer?

---

[10] Boyle, *Who Are We Now?* 154.

Greatest Challenge of Our Age

This new reality emerging in our midst, which we identify as globalization, poses the greatest challenge to our generation. I believe it will be the agenda for several generations. Just as the movement from tribe to state, to kingdom and empire, and more recently to nation did not happen overnight but was the result of many false starts and deliberate excesses, so, too, the movement of globalization will need to mature over time. If we have looked to government to protect its citizens in the pursuit of "life, liberty, and happiness," where do we look when government itself is no longer capable of controlling its own destiny in the face of a global economy? To speak of rights and duties without the reality of organizations and institutions that support those rights and duties is to speak of an abstraction similar to speaking of education without families, schools, and systems of control. Where do we look for our identity when the global marketplace speaks the final word? Is it even possible to be simply a global citizen? What kind of "loyalty to" or "responsibility for" can one give to an abstraction like humanity? Does it really come down to finding our global unity in the increasingly common denominator of consumer-producer?

It is clear that we are gradually losing our identity based on place. We may still call ourselves Koreans, African Americans, Brazilians, but we don't *live* the active part of our lives there. Yes, we still live as friends and family, but more and more people are living in *markets, networks, and organizations* that are truly worldwide—www—World Wide Web! More and more we find ourselves sharing fates, not because of the place where we live but because of the roles and relationships we form.[11] One of the problems arising from this situation is that the determining forces of our lives are truly global but the institutions of support that protect and nurture human values are still local.

The creation and development, then, of mediating institutions and associations that can support this new global reality are key tasks of our times. The United Nations comes to mind immediately. Much can be said about its weaknesses and inefficiencies, but the world cannot return to a condition of the absolute supremacy of the *nation*. Globalization plainly demonstrates that no organization smaller than global can be self-sufficient. Something like the

---

[11] Douglas K. Smith, *On Value and Values: Thinking Differently about We in an Age of Me* (Upper Saddle River, N.J.: Financial Times Prentice Hall, 2004), 4-7. Douglas Smith's work is a serious in-depth attempt to explore the possibilities of new levels of community in a digital age when the geography of neighborhoods and nations no longer provides that base.

United Nations is now a part of our consciousness, even if we are completely unhappy with its present form. Unfortunately, the deep controversy initiated by the recent war in Iraq can perhaps best be seen as the result of well-meaning persons attempting to resolve conflicts stemming from the effects of globalization by means of national supremacy. Even the notion of fighting a war on terrorism contains its own ambiguity. Terrorism is not a nation, but war is historically the concerted effort of states.

Other institutions specifically oriented to a global economy are also trying to establish themselves. We can think of the World Bank, GATT (General Agreement on Tariffs and Trade, now merged into the World Trade Organization [WTO]), as well as regional agreements such as the OAS (Organization of American States), NAFTA (North American Free Trade Agreement), EU (European Union), and ASEAN (Association of Southeast Asian Nations) as attempts to stabilize and unify commerce and exchange beyond the national level. All of these institutions can be easily criticized for their inadequacies. But they are a start in establishing mediating institutions comparable in scope to the global supply chains that ring the world. Until such regulatory agencies can be established to cross national boundaries and enforce standards of fair play, there is nothing to protect the larger human aspects of globalization. Until there are some common norms governing international exchange there will be no standards to which business can be held accountable. And until there is some transparency through global reporting, there will be no way to monitor compliance. Is there any wonder that the task is specifically for our times but will take several generations to mature? In a word, globalization is about creating new forms of *interdependence*. To focus on independence and self-sufficiency is foolhardy. The problem needs to be reframed along the lines of C. K. Prahalad's suggestion, "If global firms have to compete effectively for global markets as well as retain their position in established markets, they must have the ability to improve their cost, quality, time-to-market and capacity to innovate."[12] This requires a constant search for talent, production capabilities and new markets, wherever they may be found.[13]

BUSINESS ETHICS IN A GLOBAL ECONOMY

The first section of this chapter has been an attempt to outline, admittedly in very broad strokes, some of the dimensions of this new phenomenon of glob-

---

[12] C. K. Prahalad, "The Art of Outsourcing," *Wall Street Journal*, June 8, 2005, A14.

[13] Jeffrey Hollender and Stephen Fenichell, *What Matters Most: How a Small Group of Pioneers Is Teaching Social Responsibility to Big Business and Why Big Business Is Listening* (New York: Basic Books, 2004), 112-13.

alization. While that analysis is tentative and partial, it can help us appreciate some of the large historical issues that face us today. It is important to keep in mind that globalization is not an "ism," that is, it is not a unified theory that dictates future direction, similar to what one expects from social theories such as capitalism, socialism, and communism. Since globalization is market driven, it is really constituted by the billions of choices and exchanges that take place daily, exchanges of labor, information, technology, expertise, raw material, money, products, and services, truly a worldwide web that is constantly changing.

This section will attempt to deal specifically with some of the practical ethical business decisions that have to be faced in a global market economy. A first realization is that globalization tends to make ethical business decisions even more complex and at times more ambiguous. We will look at some common problems, try to define the issues at stake, and attempt to move toward some solutions.

Cultural Relativism

"When in Rome, do as the Romans do" sums up the traditional wisdom of dealing with differences. But what if a person encounters business practices that appear unethical but are commonly accepted in the culture? Child labor? Bribes? Unsafe working conditions? Do we move on merrily with a glib word about "it's the culture" or do we take an absolutist position insisting on the ethical norms we are accustomed to, regardless of how they apply? This much is clear: business cannot renounce its own driving principles: elemental prosperity for all, the rule of law and ethics, the practice of freely given consent. A further refinement and development might follow the distinction made by Thomas Donaldson between *core human values* and *gray zones*.[14] Core human values can never be compromised. They are the right vs. wrong decisions discussed in chapter 7. While there are important differences between Western and non-Western cultural and religious traditions, there is a level of agreement that centers on these three qualities: respect for human dignity, respect for basic rights, and good citizenship. *Respect for human dignity* means, first of all, that people are never treated as mere tools, as means to an end. A human being has an absolute value that is different from everything else. *Respect for basic rights* finds common expression in the UN Charter of

---

[14] Thomas Donaldson, "Values in Tension: Ethics Away from Home," *Harvard Business Review on Corporate Ethics* (Boston: Harvard Business School, 2003), 114-38.

Human Rights. Those rights must be safeguarded. *Good citizenship* means, first of all, the observance of the established law of the land. In addition, it means supporting and even improving the institutions on which the community depends.

These values are absolute. A business that disregards these core human values is not being culturally sensitive or remaining neutral to local practices but is acting immorally. While there remains the issue of determining just how a company actually promotes these core values, there can be no doubt about the obligation to do so. At this level, a corporation has the duty to challenge the culture in which it operates.

There is, however, a second area of moral decision making that is definitely more relative, the gray zone identified by Donaldson. What is a fair wage? What is an acceptable level of quality? What is a safe working environment? What constitutes child labor? What is a bribe? These and a host of other questions can have relatively different answers depending on cultural values and the level of economic development. A sense of the potential conflict of competing cultural values can be appreciated from the following short comparison.[15]

Non-Western Values	Western Values
kyosei (Japanese): living and working together for the common good	individual liberty
dharma (Hindu): the fulfillment of inherited duty	egalitarianism
santutthi (Buddhist): the importance of limited desires	political participation
zakat (Muslim): the duty to give alms to the Muslim poor	human rights

Of course, the ability of business to connect with the deep cultural values of a people can be a dynamic impetus for genuine business growth.

---

[15] Donaldson, "Values in Tension," 122.

The Level of Economic Development

The gray zone is complicated by differences in cultural values, as indicated above. Ethical standards can also conflict, however, simply because nations are at different levels of economic development. A standard of quality for medical cleanliness in the United States and in the Congo would look quite different. To insist on the same level for both would be to halt the development of medical care in the Congo or downgrade protection in the United States. Yet some specific level of cleanliness and sterilization would be judged appropriate for each. What that level is cannot be determined in the abstract. Only the considerations of responsible and ethical practitioners can determine what it should be in each case.

Donaldson uses the following question to help resolve the conflict of relative development: "Would the practice be acceptable at home if my country were in a similar stage of economic development?"[16] Regulatory standards will vary dramatically depending on stages of economic development. Let us consider an example. A drug company in the United States develops and produces a food supplement that provides additional nutrition and vitamins that enhance the general health of its users. It is manufactured in the United States under the highest quality standards for purity and consistency. It is a product that could also enhance the health of the people of Angola, Africa, for example. To maintain the highest quality standards, the product must be imported to Angola. Cost, obviously, would be high. Few would be able to afford it. What if the drug company considered producing the product in Angola? No amount of surveillance could generate the quality level required in the United States. The infrastructure that supports the supply chain of materials and processes involved in production are simply not at the required quality level, nor can the drug company simply recreate the total economy of the country. Yet there are obvious benefits to producing the supplement in Angola. Cost would be dramatically reduced, which would allow for the wider use of a beneficial product. Jobs would be created up and down the supply chain. Potential export to neighboring countries could be envisioned. Yet the quality level would not be acceptable in the United States. In fact, the drug company would be sued for the sale of a product of that quality level in the United States. Should the company proceed with production plans in Angola? What are the issues that need to be addressed? Are there any safeguards to be installed? What about future developments. Should it then also

---

[16] Donaldson, "Values in Tension," 129.

be exported to the United States? Spell out these considerations. Any solution that implies a U.S. quality level is simply to avoid the question. Variations on these types of considerations are commonplace in a global economy. A similar scenario could be drawn up around environmental, safety, or just-wage considerations. Unfortunately, these objections are often raised not from serious moral concerns but from a fear of job loss or wage reductions in Western advanced economies. These issues often have no absolute, one-size-fits-all answer, yet they do have an ethical answer that needs to be discerned with the help of a clear understanding of the current level of economic development. Business is starting to pay more attention to the world's poor not primarily as a source of cheap labor but as a viable market for new goods and services. The private sector has always been about the creation of value, as we have argued extensively. The challenge here is to see what form the creation of value might take among the four billion poor of the world with less than five dollars a day in disposable income. The Harvard Business School is now offering courses on operating businesses with legitimate profit goals in that context. It can be done, but it calls for new understandings and strategies.[17]

> **Three Challenges for a Business Operating in Globally Poor Markets**[18]
>
> 1. *Cultural distance between corporate decision makers and local poor.* Need to find novel ways to integrate the preferences, constraints, and habits of the poor into business development
> 2. *Serious lack of infrastructure and formal institutions.* Companies must rely on local leaders and community agents to bring people together and build incentives for everyone to play by the rules.
> 3. *Investment must be for the long term.* Profit driver lies in volume rather than in profit margins to justify high start-up costs.

---

[17] V. Kasturi Rangan, John Quelch, Gustavo Herrero, and Brooke Barton eds., *Business Solutions for the Global Poor* (San Francisco: Jossey-Bass, 2007). See also the review by Sean Silverthorne, "Business and the Global Poor," at the Harvard Business School Web site: working knowledge@hbs.edu.

[18] "Business and the Global Poor," review by Sean Silverthorne, in *Working Knowledge* (February 2007).

Loss of Jobs

The great specter that haunts every recess of globalization from a Euro-American perspective and casts its pall on what must be considered one of the greatest achievements of our generation is the fear of losing jobs, or, at least, of well-paying jobs. Jobs touch on survival issues. And a threat to survival will produce the most radical type of self-defense. For that reason, it becomes more difficult to consider this issue openly. In times of risk, an openness to the unknown becomes simply too dangerous.[19] We are unwilling to explore the full range of what is happening. We become schizophrenic. When we can buy inexpensive electronic products, we are *for* globalization. When it threatens our good jobs, we are *against* it. We are unwilling to deal with the contradiction of wanting high-paying jobs and cheap goods and services.

Let us consider some issues that can help put the problem in perspective. There is no doubt that some jobs will be lost. The economy is changing in ways that will not allow for a reversal to the "good old days." For those caught in the change, there must be transitional assistance. The safety net of unemployment compensation and training as well as aid in starting new businesses must be made available. At the same time, let us not forget that job transition is nothing new. Miners from the depleting mines of the Upper Peninsula of Michigan were lured to the automotive assembly plants of Detroit. Farmers have left the land to find work in factories and finance. Automation has cost jobs in manufacturing but created new ones in information technology. The difference today is that job transition is not national but global.

"More Work Is Outsourced to U.S. Than Away From It, Data Show" is the heading of an article in the *Wall Street Journal*.[20] The second paragraph is worth quoting in full:

> The value of U.S. exports of legal work, computer programming, telecommunications, banking, engineering, management consulting and other private services jumped to $131.01 billion in 2003, up $8.42 billion from the previous year, the Commerce Department reported Friday. Imports of such private services—a category that encompasses U.S. outsourcing of call centers and data entry to developing nations, among other things—hit $77.38 billion for the year, up $7.94 billion from

---

[19] Schreiter, "A New Modernity," 12, for a further exploration of the problem.
[20] Michael M. Phillips, "More Work Is Outsourced to U.S. Than Away From It, Data Show," *Wall Street Journal*, March 15, 2004, A2.

2002. Measuring imports against exports, the U.S. posted a $53.64 billion surplus last year in trade in private services with the rest of the world.

Not only does globalization create jobs to serve the global economy, but foreign companies build plants and open offices in the United States. These are staffed by American workers. Examples abound. Honda continues to expand its U.S. facilities in order to export cars to other nations. Daimler-Chrysler decided to locate its manufacturing facility in the United States. Novartis is moving its huge worldwide research and development operations from Switzerland to Massachusetts. Samsung is building a $500 million semiconductor plant in Texas. Ironically, Mexico, which was once likened to a "great sucking sound" absorbing North American jobs is now investing in the United States. A *Wall Street Journal* article explored how some failing American businesses are being bought up by Mexican entrepreneurs and returned to profitability.[21] An article in 2006, unobtrusively buried in the mountains of newsprint in the *Wall Street Journal*, started with "Japanese auto makers produced more vehicles overseas than they did at home for the first time ever in the year ended March 31. . . ."[22] Is this not another stage in globalization that makes us revisit the standard lament about job loss?

All of the above is not meant to simplify a complex situation by saying there is no problem. It is meant to say that much more analysis of the *whole* picture is needed. Businesses must be able to think locally and globally at the same time if they are to survive. They must be able to adjust, negotiate, recalculate on a continuous basis. Those activities must be based not on some ideology but on the competitive demands of the market. International attempts to control the market must be based on business needs for transparency, for a stable money supply, as argued in the danger of ultracapitalism, and for a level playing field which does not favor certain groups over others.

Just Wages and Human Working Conditions

The words "sweatshops," "child labor," "10 cents per hour wages" have at times become rallying cries for protesters of globalization. Multinational corporations, on the other hand, can rightly claim that no local law is being

---

[21] Joel Millman, "Go North: In Castoffs of U.S. Industry, Mexico Finds Some Bargains," *Wall Street Journal*, May 10, 2004, A1.

[22] Associated Press, "Japanese Makers of Cars Produce More Overseas," *Wall Street Journal*, August 1, 2006, A2.

broken. Again, almost as a corollary to job loss, the issue becomes polarized. Laborers will decry the fact that foreign companies pay poverty wages, accept unsafe and inhuman working conditions, disregard reasonable working hours. Moralists will be caught up in declaring that offshore manufacturing inevitably hurts the poor worker to the degree that it helps rich consumers. It becomes hard to distinguish between what is justifiable outrage at inhuman conditions and what is a self-serving interest disguised as moral posturing.

Rol Fessenden, head of global procurement for L. L. Bean, whose legendary rubber-soled hunting boot and reputation for customer service helped it grow into a $1 billion-a-year catalog retailer, might give us a way forward.[23] In his position, he was responsible for selecting the factories that supply L. L. Bean with all the products in its catalog. That network extends to sixty countries. Price, he points out, is not the same as cost. Cost is a concept that includes the whole spectrum of value: the quality of the merchandise, the reliability of the supplier, the success of the product in the marketplace. The lowest price is not the real measure of cost. Considerations other than the lowest wages add to the cost. The dichotomy of price vs. quality is a false starting point. When the factors of quality, reliability, adaptability are taken into account, then the lowest wage no longer represents the lowest cost. Other countries, including high-wage countries such as the United States, may still represent low cost. Outsourcing help-desk functions, for instance, to low-wage countries is not necessarily proving to be a low-cost solution. Unfortunately, U.S. factories can take a defeatist attitude about outsourcing and fold up rather than take on the challenge of beating the competition on the basis of real cost rather than only price. There is still much to be learned here. In general, multinational corporations pay higher wages than local industries.

On another front, Fessenden again takes a broader perspective. What about the absurdly low wages of foreign workers? Despite the protestations of many, he points out that a ten- or fifteen-cents-per-hour pay rate can be a middle-class wage in a place like Bangladesh. "It means clean clothes, absence of disease, food on the table all the time, kids who survive," he says. But that does not justify subhuman working conditions that counter the core human values we discussed above. Fessenden has a group of factory inspectors who continuously survey working conditions. They will spy on factories through binoculars, conduct surprise wage audits, and make sure that foreign factory

---

[23] Thomas Petzinger, Jr., "A Humanist Executive Leads by Thinking in Broader Terms," *Wall Street Journal*, April 16, 2000, B1.

bosses are willing to use the same bathrooms as the workers. He does so because he is convinced that good working conditions invariably go hand in hand with high quality, high reliability, and, in the broad view, lower costs. The final words of the interview with Fessenden are worth quoting: "Where people mistreat employees, you tend to see reliability problems, too . . . More often than not economic and social performance align." In other words, profitability and humanism are not mutually exclusive. If fair wages and working conditions are set in a broad perspective, polarization of the issue is a false problem. The issue of a fair wage will always be a challenge, but it will not be solved by some magic formula. Cultural differences and levels of economic development are significant factors, as is the type of industry involved. On the other hand, a minimally subsistence wage is self-defeating. Put succinctly, "free trade fails when workers in poor countries do not have sufficient spendable income over bare subsistence to make the reciprocal purchases upon which free trade depends. . . ."[24]

Perhaps the best argument comes from practice. The following chart provides a sample selection of budgeted salary increases for employees of technology companies across twenty-four countries in a survey conducted by Culpepper and Associates, Inc.[25] Executives did not necessarily get the highest percentage of increases, nor did the employees in Western industrialized economies do the best. Draw your own conclusions.

Country	Executive Wage Increases	Salespeople Wage Increases	Technician Wage Increases
China	2.7%	3.8%	4.3%
India	5.8%	7.3%	7.1%
Canada	3.0%	3.0%	3.3%
Mexico	4.4%	3.7%	3.6%
U. S.	3.9%	3.2%	4.1%

[24] Ray Carey, *Democratic Capitalism: The Way to a World of Peace and Plenty* (Bloomington, Ind.: AuthorHouse, 2004), 200.

[25] Eric Van Cleven, "Hot Topic: Global Base Pay Increases," The Management Association of Illinois, www.hrsource.org, August 24, 2006.

Bribes and Corruption

This is another arena made more complicated by globalization. Many countries consider bribery and payoffs as a way of doing business. It has been part of the culture for centuries, even if it is against the law in those same countries. What is a multinational company to do? What is the individual businessperson to do? Am I not at an unfair disadvantage if my competitor is willing to pay expected bribes, and I am not? How can I do business in a country where payoffs are a necessary cost of business transactions? Many Asian, African, Latin American, and Middle Eastern cultures require bribes to expedite any transaction. While I may personally consider bribery as immoral and be repulsed by the practice, I may not have a choice in the matter. Refusing to go along with the traditional practices of the country is merely to give a wide-open playing field to unscrupulous companies. How is ethics to be served? There is seldom a good solution. Take this example. What would you do?

> A company paid a $350,000 "consulting" fee to an official of a foreign country. In return, the official promised assistance in obtaining a contract that would produce a $10 million profit for the contracting company.[26]

An initial distinction, however, needs to be made. There is one type of bribe, often to lower-level bureaucrats, whose sole purpose is to facilitate the performance of normal clerical or ministerial duties. We might consider these payments as "tips" given for better service. A distinguishing mark of such payments is that they do not significantly change the final decision or result. Even the Foreign Corrupt Practices Act (FCPA), passed by the U.S. Congress in 1977 in response to the growing problem of bribery in the global market, recognizes that this type of facilitating payment is not bribery in the sense outlawed by the act.

The law focuses on the real meaning of bribery and payoffs, namely, payments made to directly influence the outcome of the business contract. It is against the law if money is paid to sway high-level people to make decisions they would not otherwise make. Is this too harsh? Will not an unethical competitor step up to the plate, make the payoff, and deliver a product that is perhaps inferior to your own. What about the notion of "do as the Romans do" with the hope of gradually changing the culture? Is bribery not merely inci-

[26] Linda Klebe Treviño and Katherine A. Nelson, *Managing Business Ethics: Straight Talk about How to Do It Right*, 2nd ed. (New York: John Wiley & Sons, 1999), 297.

dental to business? It is precisely here that the real dynamics of business is challenged. The heart of the free-market economy is grounded in the free exchange of values. When bribery and its resulting corruption reign, then it is no longer the quality of the product that is the basis of free-market exchange. Ordinary people suffer. When people are paid off under the table, the benefits of competing on quality and cost are destroyed. The results are higher prices or shoddy products or most likely both. Corruption and business are diametrically opposed. This is really just another version of the basic premise of this book that long-term business success and ethics are essential partners.

There is another aspect to bribery that is not as obvious. When bribery is rampant, the start-up of a new business becomes problematic. An astonishing number of rules and regulations, each protected by someone with an out-stretched hand, makes the process of starting a business both expensive and prolonged. In countries with high bribery cultures, it will take an average of four months to comply with all the regulations for launching a legal business. By contrast, it takes a mere two days to open a business legally in Canada. As a result, many small businesses sidestep the process and open illegally. As a result they are vulnerable to extortion, blackmail, and the caprice of lower-level government bureaucrats. Their ability to get legitimate loans and credit is also seriously jeopardized. In this way, bribery and corruption not only skim money right off the top but also inhibit capital formation and job development. It is claimed that only one in ten Africans works in a legally recognized enterprise and lives in a house that has legally recognized property rights. How does one get credit to start a business?

The challenge of business in the face of bribery and corruption is to work toward convincing locals of the benefits of playing by the rules of good business. Perhaps there is a special role here for multi-national corporations who have greater resources, more power, and easier access to independent credit. Some degree of ethical commitment to fair exchange is the basis for a free-market economy to prosper. In some markets there is no way of avoiding payment of bribes, except by exiting the market. In fact, many companies will not even attempt to do business in a country ruled by corruption and bribery. Again, it is the common people who suffer most. On the other hand, the example of Hong Kong is also illustrative. It has become a center of finance and commerce precisely because of its reputation for honesty. Corruption is kept in check by a powerful local law enforcement agency with broad powers.

Free Trade vs. Protectionism

Sugar beet farmers in the southern states were in trouble. Their livelihood was being threatened by the importing of cheaper cane sugar from Central America. What to do? An appeal to government was effective. A large tariff was imposed on imported cane sugar, a move that made the sugar from beets competitive. A moral victory? Jobs were preserved together with a way of life. Several years later candy makers in Chicago started to shut down. Plants started to relocate out of the country. Jobs were lost. What happened? One of the determining factors was that the high cost of sugar in the United States made it impossible to compete in manufacturing candy in Chicago, which was once a major candy producer for the nation. Who wins?

The mere mention of NAFTA (North American Free Trade Agreement) once put fear into the hearts of hard-working U.S. workers afraid of losing jobs. The fact is that, since the passage of NAFTA in 1993, farm exports to Mexico have doubled. Again, a recent agreement between Canada and Chile removed duties on the sale of wheat and potatoes to Chile. Farmers in Nebraska and Idaho, on the other hand, continue to pay an 8 percent tariff on anything they try to sell in Chile. Who benefits?

Anecdotal evidence is no basis for understanding something as complex as free trade, but it can give some insight into the dynamics of protectionism and free trade. Trade restrictions and long-term government support of specific industries are short sighted solutions. Protectionist measures to save jobs will actually kill them. Jim Owens, CEO of Caterpillar Corporation, comments that the flourishing of the U.S. economy could be "endangered if our policy-makers implement wrongheaded protectionism—or if American companies refuse to engage constructively with the world." The same observation could be made of business anywhere. Free-trade critics seem more intent on bashing the idea of free trade than on coming up with constructive solutions to the problems they identify. No doubt there is much work to be done in the ongoing task of developing genuinely open and free global markets. No doubt there are interests to be protected, at least in the short run. No doubt nations will jockey for a more favorable advantage. But there is also no doubt that only the increased productivity that results from free trade is capable of increasing economic prosperity. If that is still in doubt, then the following figures might help. The overall rate of inflation in recent years has stayed around 2 percent, obviously something to be desired. How has that been accomplished? Here is a clue. The figures reflect increases and decreases since 1997.[27]

Heavily traded goods have *decreased* in price:

- computers and peripherals -86 percent
- video equipment -68 percent
- toys -36 percent

---

[27] Richard W. Fisher, "Protect Us from Protectionists," *Wall Street Journal*, April 25, 2005, A14.

- women's outerwear -20 percent
- men's shirts and sweaters -17 percent

Goods and services not subject to foreign competition have *increased* in price:

- college tuition and fees +53 percent
- cable and satellite TV +41 percent
- dental services +38 percent
- prescription drugs and medical supplies +37 percent

The argument about free trade, its benefits and dangers, will no doubt continue.[28] Here we can only advert to the issue and recognize that free trade and not protectionism will generate prosperity and, consequently, the jobs we count on for living well. It is interesting to note that our focus is now on China as the behemoth that threatens our lifestyle. What has happened to our prior dragons, once feared for their ability to devour U.S. jobs—Japan and other East Asian countries (called "tigers" to identify their potential danger to the U.S. way of life)? Obviously, our fears have not materialized. But we seem condemned to repeat the cycle with a new tiger, China. It is difficult to stay open and face the unknown when we feel threatened. To realize that trade actually increases prosperity on all sides is not easy to understand. What could really threaten our lifestyles would be a full retreat into protectionism.

The National Association of Manufacturers (NAM), a group that might be most intrigued by some form of protectionism since they stand most to lose through globalization, is calling for a quite different public-policy agenda which includes the following fundamental principles:

- We must lower government-related production costs in the United States.
- We must level the international playing field with our trading partners.
- We must do a better job preparing our twenty-first century workforce.
- We must promote public policy that encourages and rewards innovation, investment, and productivity.

That's a far cry from the response to the sugar beet farmer we met at the beginning of this section. In fact, John Engler, president and CEO of NAM, firmly believes that "the U.S. can compete with anyone on a level playing field" and is consequently urging a crackdown on product counterfeiting, currency manipulation, and intellectual property theft. The most important

---

[28] See references to works on trade, especially Jagdish Bhagwati, *Free Trade Today* (Princeton, N.J.: Princeton University Press, 2003), in Vivjav Joshi and Robert Skidelsky, "One World?" *New York Review of Books*, 51, no. 5 (March 25, 2004).

natural resource of any country is a people who are educated, skilled, honest, creative, and not afraid of the work it takes to be competitive in a global economy.

Free Trade vs. Aid

In 1945 the World Bank was established to finance economic development. Since then it has poured billions of dollars into "developing nations."

Thirty years ago China and India were among the world's poorest countries. Both are now growing at a fast clip but not because of billions in foreign aid.

The previous two statements are helpful in trying to understand what is happening in a world of very disproportionate economies. The problem with aid from multinational development banks and national aid grants is that they are government entities and so, by convention, work directly through other governments. The aid, then, is only as effective as the government it passes through. Unfortunately, most of those governments operated from some sort of socialist ideology. The aid was often harmful because it helped to prop up socialist regimes that stifled entrepreneurship and tried, unsuccessfully, to manage the economy from the top down. Economies are built from the ground up, by entrepreneurs who have ideas, are willing to take some risks to start a business and make it grow. What China and then India did, without billions in aid, was to invite foreign investors and guarantee their property rights. From there, the creativity and initiative of local people could take over. Countries that started with billions in governmental aid are now often saddled with huge debt and without a growing economy to pay it down. What happened to the aid? Whether it was siphoned off by corrupt officials, used to build a military machine, or to showcase public works that did little to grow an economy, the final result was huge debt. Is it right, or even possible in some cases, for the people now saddled with that debt to be forced to pay even the annual interest, an amount greater than the total expenditure of the country on education or medicine? The international community needs to find some way to forgive burdensome debt without undermining a basic market-driven economy.

In the long run, it is the opening of markets and the free exchange of goods and services that will most benefit a developing nation. It becomes hypocritical for a nation to profess its commitment to aiding poorer nations, even by donating large amounts of aid to those nations, while maintaining high protectionist tariffs on goods and services that would promote the economy of that country. Of course, every nation is also trying to protect the well-being and livelihood of its own citizens. If the importing of cheap food or shirts threatens the farmers or textile workers of their own country, how does a nation maintain its responsibility to these particular citizens yet still promote the greater well-being of all its citizens through the greater benefits of global trade? These and many issues like it are the hard choices and compromises that need to be faced if we are to move forward. There are no automatic answers other than, in the long run, trade is the best form of aid.

The ongoing struggle between the short-term interests of protection and the long-term benefits of free markets is played out by governments in the constant debates and compromises of the World Trade Organization. Unfortunately, the WTO tends to function on the mercantilist view of trade; namely, exports are good, imports are bad. On this basis, any opening of markets is viewed as a "concession" for which some type of "compensation" or reciprocity is required. It tends to protect the interests of the producer at the expense of all others, specifically the importers and the consumer at large. Remember the sugar beet farmer![29]

In "More Trade, Less Poverty,"[30] Susan Schwab, the U.S. trade representative, makes the following four observations: First, in the 1990s, per-capita real income grew three times faster for developing countries that significantly lowered trade barriers (5 percent) than other developing countries that lowered barriers less (1.4 percent). Just as important, the income gains were enjoyed by people at all income levels

Second, Schwab notes, the Organization for Economic Cooperation and Development (OECD) considered the impact of 50 percent cuts in tariffs, agricultural export subsidies, and domestic support programs and concluded that it would account for a 59 percent increase in potential global economic gains.

Third, the World Bank estimates that eliminating trade barriers in goods alone could boost incomes in developing countries by at least $142 billion a year. That exceeds the combined total of $80 billion in foreign economic assistance by G-7 countries.

Finally, the problem is not only between developed and developing economies. Presently, around 70 percent of the duties on goods that developing countries pay go to other developing countries.

---

[29] "Globalisation and Its Critics: A Survey of Globalisation," *The Economist* (September 29, 2001): 3-30, is a dense, closely reasoned and documented attempt to answer the common objections raised against trade and a worldwide market economy. It also describes how a global institution such as the WTO struggles to mediate among governments and a global marketplace.

[30] Susan Schwab, "More Trade, Less Poverty," *Wall Street Journal*, June 29, 2006, A14.

Gordon Brown, the former U.K. chancellor of the Exchequer and now prime minister, makes similar observations in "The Protectionist Backlash."[31] He notes that the World Bank suggests that further trade liberalization could lift up to 95 million people out of extreme poverty; and since 1975 world trade has grown at 6 percent a year, the main motor for 3 percent world economic growth. Of course, there will always be a place for aid, but not as a substitute for trade. Aid will always have a role as the response to natural disasters. Droughts, earthquakes, tsunamis, epidemics call for global answers. Nor is disaster aid only an altruistic response. Our global interconnectedness not only promotes the benefits of a global market but also threatens us with global dangers. Communicable diseases such as AIDS, SARS, and avian flu show us how vulnerable our interconnectedness makes us. Terrorism is not restricted to local gangs but extends to global networks. No single nation can deal with the potential threat of global warming, the destruction of the environment, or the depletion of the world's oil supply. If globalization brings us together, it does so for both good and evil.

A Market Economy and Forms of Government

Again, we are faced with an issue that merits a book—many have been written on the subject—but we are forced to introduce it in a few pages. To ignore this issue at a time of increasing globalization would be to simply ignore a critical dimension of that process. Peter Berger, a distinguished sociologist and director of the Institute for the Study of Economic Culture at Boston University, has laid out the scope of the issue as clearly and comprehensively as anything I have seen. I will follow it closely here.[32] While there is precious little real hard-core socialism left (one thinks of North Korea and Cuba; will Venezuela follow?), the enticements of socialist-type governments continue to lure many. Its proponents continue to expound its merits: economic performance, political liberation, social equality, and quality of life. History has been the greatest refutation of socialist claims. Not one of the four claims made in its defense has come to realization. Yet its allure continues. Excuses are plentiful: it wasn't tried seriously enough; it wasn't given enough time; it was enforced by a corrupt regime; it wasn't "real" socialism. The list goes on but the results are the same. It has never delivered on its promise. At some point, one must suspect the theory.

---

[31] Gordon Brown, "The Protectionist Backlash," *Wall Street Journal*, September 6, 2006, A20.
[32] Peter L. Berger, "Social Ethics in a Post-Socialist World," *First Things* (February 1993): 9-14.

On the other hand, market economies have contributed greatly to all four claims. They have delivered abundant economic prosperity and lifted masses of people from abject poverty to decent levels of material life. They have created political liberation by establishing institutions of business and finance that are not simply subject to the capriciousness of government decisions and that establish respect for elementary human rights. In addition, market economies have led to greater social equality, at least in the sense that they have created greater mobility in allowing people to move from class to class through individual initiative and achievement. Finally, they have created the possibility for a quality of life that used to be the exclusive domain of kings and landed gentry.

Yet who is to say that socialism is dead. Its allure continues to this day. Berger finds its source in the deeply rooted impulse to create a perfect community on earth. Utopia has been the dream of peoples through history. It appeals to many social ethicists and social engineers because it is a concrete blueprint, based on an allegedly scientific understanding of history, and open to control along clear guidelines for action. A market economy, on the other hand, is, by its nature, uncontrolled. It is constituted by billions and billions of random individual choices and decisions and exchanges every day of the year—a rather messy alternative to the clear command and control of a socialist agenda!

The historical achievements boldly announced above are the result not only of the workings of a market economy but of a market economy joined with some type of democratic governance. What is put in place is not some theory of utopia but two institutional mechanisms that, with a little luck and a lot of hard work, can facilitate the creation of wealth and the protection of basic human rights. Even when both institutions are working well, there are still many problems that will not be solved automatically. Racial and ethnic hatred, the male/female divide, the relation of technology to the environment, the limitations of human beings, the inequalities of wealth and talent are problems of all societies and are not simply eliminated by instituting a democratic market economy. Meantime, in the wings, there will be a socialist answer ready to solve each problem. A left-leaning socialist utopia is not to be replaced by a right-wing capitalist one. The two institutions establish a tension that finds no permanent solution. Berger establishes three such fault lines that go a long way to defining the ongoing conflict in every democratic market economy.

1. A Market Economy or a Democratic Polity—Which Comes First?
For some, the issue may seem like two sides of the same coin. In fact, they are not. It can be shown empirically how a successful market economy releases

pressures in favor of democracy. The free choices of individual entrepreneurs and consumers presuppose a level of freedom that is incompatible with monolithic government. It can also be empirically demonstrated that a market economy is a necessary though not sufficient condition for democracy. While a market economy eventually tends to generate a democracy, there is no need to have a democracy in place *before* a market economy can take off. Generally the two do not happen at the same time. England, France, and Germany, some of the earliest instances of market economies, could hardly have been described as democracies when market economies first began to flourish in those countries. On a whole, there is enough evidence to show that generally a market economy will precede a democracy. The reason is clear. The transition to a market economy will cause disruption and pain. That pain will not be equally distributed among all. Some will benefit immediately; others will be aggrieved. A full-blown democracy can more easily block initiatives that include short-term pain for long-term gains. Vested interests can slow down and even abort market efforts. To put the issue bluntly, it might be better to put up with a benevolent autocrat in order to introduce market economics than to insist on honest elections before moving to a market economy. At best, however, this can only be an interim position and an interim ethics that can only be justified by the empirical situation at hand.

Having said this, however, there is still the concrete issue of limits. Does the goal of general prosperity through a market economy justify any type of action? Using tanks against unarmed civilians? Imprisonment of large numbers of dissenters? Military crackdowns? Torture? False hopes and broken promises? Regularly? Occasionally? These can present moral dilemmas that demand hard answers. But the real questions get lost when both sides—human rights and market economy—are each idealized as the answer to all problems.

2. How Much Redistribution of Income Can a Market Economy Sustain?

There is no doubt that a market economy can tolerate a fair amount of government redistribution of wealth. It is only when the issue is polarized into a matter of a socialist/welfare state vs. laissez-faire capitalism that there is no resolution. There are no current governments that actually represent these two extremes (with the possible exception of Cuba and North Korea). It is true that most actual governments lean a little more to one or the other side. But that is exactly the issue here; just what is the right mix of free market and government intervention to best promote the common good? Let us not think that the United States represents an extreme of laissez-faire capitalism with a minimum redistribution of wealth. Without exploring all aspects of this important issue, one fact should help put the matter in perspective. IRS statistics show that the richest 50 percent of taxpayers contribute 96 percent of the total tax revenue. These numbers remain rather consistent over a ten-year period. This represents a huge income redistribution when you consider that it is tax revenue that funds Social Security, Medicare, education, military, welfare, agriculture, regulatory agencies, as well as all judicial, legislative, and executive functions.

Now it would be easy if some wise king, social scientist, or economist could give us a formula that would generate the optimum redistribution. There is no such thing. It is clear that excessive movement to either pole will bring diminishing returns for all. At what point does a welfare state start to strangle a market economy? At what point does well-meaning political intervention become tyrannical? This applies not only to the actual redistribution of wealth but also to the enactment of laws that meet specific societal needs. How can the needs of society be met without bloating government bureaucracy to a point where it deprives people of more and more control over their personal lives, especially when the road to economic disaster is frequently paved with good intentions? Consider again the sugar beet farmer. On the other hand, at what point does a runaway market economy need some governmental restraint to protect the weak, the young, the old, the sick, those disadvantaged in some way? To revert to a rugged individualism waving the flag of "pull yourself up by your bootstraps" ignores the fact that we are a collective, that none of us begins or ends life in isolation, and that what we become is deeply influenced by the society in which we live. To isolate ourselves, physically and morally, in gated communities, high-rises, and affluent suburbs does not make the problems go away.

There is a natural tension here that has no fixed resolution. For a poor society, the main issue is going to be how to meet the most pressing social needs without strangling a young and still fragile economy with high taxes and social regulations. For a richer society, the issue is how to maintain adequate services to the weak and disenfranchised without starting a process of slow deterioration of market dynamics. A strong democracy is probably the best way to keep the tension healthy.

3. What Is the Relation between Economic Development and Cultural Values?

Max Weber may not have hit it exactly right when he fingered the Protestant ethic as the strategic factor leading to modern capitalism. It is true that there is a relationship between certain virtues, particularly those of self-denial, discipline, and hard work, and our modern economy. The ability to delay gratification for the sake of some higher value, whether that be personal betterment, the future of one's children, or the kingdom of God, was a hallmark not only of past immigrants to America but of recent ones as well. The same values can be witnessed in the economic miracles of Asia. Some form of what Weber called inner-worldly asceticism is essential to getting a market economy growing.

How that is going to play out in Western societies, where the values of instant gratification and unrestrained individual freedom dominate, is still to be seen. From one perspective, these values might be seen as expressing greed, selfishness, and irresponsibility. From a different perspective, they could be seen as liberating, joyful, and humanistic. How will this change in cultural values affect the economic vitality of richer nations? An even larger issue is, Does it really matter? There is the old story of an American tourist vacationing in Mexico who came upon a fisherman bringing in his boat with his daily catch early in the afternoon. Upon being asked what he planned to do now, the fisherman said he was going to the local bar, meet up with his friends, have a drink, play on his guitar, and watch the sunset. The American informed him that if he fished longer he could catch even more fish. "And then what?" asked the fisherman. "Well, you could buy another boat and have others also fish for you." "And then what?" continued the fisherman. "Well, you could process your own fish and so eliminate the middle man." "And then what?" the fisherman asked again. "Well, you would be able to retire with wealth." "And then what?" the fisherman persisted. "Well, you could go the local bar, meet up with friends, have a drink, play the guitar, and watch the sunset!" Somewhere along the line we all have to make those choices. If government or religion is capable of controlling our lives, so is business. Is it really even true that the supposedly "softer" cultures of the West are not hard working and lacking in discipline? Are the 24/7 demands of the global market economy creating a modern version of the sweatshop?

Even if one were to grant that the market economy demands the "tough" virtues, there is a further question of whether we indeed want to pay the price for that level of economic success. Do we want people to submerge their aspirations for self-realization to the demands of total loyalty and dedication to the corporation? Are we not saying that our concerns for family and personal time are carrying us beyond the constrictions of earlier generations that made our economic well-being possible? To put the issue bluntly, how much of an economic price are we willing to pay to develop a more rounded and indeed fuller realization of who we are? Where is the magic divide between economic development, both personal and global, and other cultural values?

Amartya Sen, winner of the 1998 Nobel Prize in Economic Science, addresses this issue particularly as it applies to developing countries. What happens, he asks, when some part of the tradition/culture of a people cannot be maintained along with needed economic or social change?[33] A glib answer of both/and will not do. On the one hand, economics does make some relentless demands. A two-hour siesta in the middle of the day will not create an efficient production line! On the other hand, losing part of one's tradition is not like exchanging old tools for new ones. When traditions are lost, they are gone forever. Sen's answer is to insist that the people themselves must have the freedom to choose what they value. The real conflict, he insists, is between (1) the basic value that allows people to choose the traditions and values they wish to follow, and (2) the insistence that established traditions must be followed as those traditions are decided by religious authorities (the ayatollahs and clergies) or by the political rulers (bureaucrats and dictators) or by cultural "experts" (moralists and social engineers). In other words, it is a freedom that can be preserved only in some form of democracy. We come back to Berger's insight that only a combination of free markets and strong democracies will ultimately lead to the general prosperity of the largest number of people.

There is still another critical aspect of culture that affects a market economy. If a particular culture does not see improvement as a distinct possibility or as a worthwhile goal, then change becomes meaningless. There is nothing new under the sun, and one's fate in life comes down to living out one's allotted role in one's allotted time. The ancient caste system in India used to be a social and religious rationalization for the stability of the permanent status quo. Similar social setups are evident in Africa. A market economy, on the other hand, is grounded in a deep belief that individually and collectively we can improve our condition in life. People came to the United States because they wanted to better their lives in some way. The vast current migration of people around the globe is driven largely by that same desire.

If this section on market economy and democratic polity has been elaborated at some length, it is because a market economy is now a global issue. The three tensions will play a larger role as we move forward, whether we are a fragile new entry into the global economy or one of the current eight major economies of the world. There is no magic resolve or happy medium to these polarities. They are moral issues that each culture and each person must balance as best as possible. To repeat A. Sen, the creation of wealth gives us "the freedom to lead the kind of lives we have reason to value."[34] What we value, and not sheer necessity, can now be the stuff of our lives.

---

[33] Amartya Sen, *Development as Freedom* (New York: Anchor Books, 2000; orig. published, New York: Knopf, 1999), 31.

[34] Sen, *Development as Freedom*, 14.

CONCLUSION

This chapter has tried to deal with some of the greatest challenges of our age. In the course of that effort much has been left unsaid. Major issues (market economy and political order) are opened but not brought to resolution. Extremely complex and nuanced problems (trade and economic development) are outlined in a few broad strokes. Some considerations (enculturation and values) are hardly addressed at all. In addition, it might be asked just what do these broad issues have to do with the basic morality of the individual person who is just trying to do a good job?

Despite these legitimate concerns, I believe it is essential to include this chapter in a book dealing with business ethics. The reasons are considerable.

1. We no longer live in local or national economies. How one acts morally and responsibly in a global economy when people are being laid off because of foreign competition and outsourcing affects our outlook on business.
2. The defensive reactions of self-preservation under the threat of personal loss or unidentified, yet vividly imagined, demons can be very short-sighted and self destructive in the long run. Protectionism would be a good example.
3. The need to "act locally but think globally" will be one of the greatest challenges of anyone who hopes to be a leader in our times.
4. The ability to understand the moral implications of our actions demands the greatest breadth and insight that we can bring to the task.
5. The polarizations that globalization tend to foment need to be seen as false dichotomies.
6. The dimensions and implications of globalization are beyond the horizon of any one person at any time or of all of us at this time. Yet we live in its reality. Any attempt to understand its meaning more fully has to begin somewhere, however haltingly and piecemeal.
7. The development of a world economy calls for the development of a world community. Further, the development of a world community calls for the development of the spiritual powers of the human race to embrace all as our brothers and sisters.
8. The positive benefits of globalization, however, do not give any of us an excuse to ignore the cry of pain, of hunger, of need on the part of the world's poor.

I hope that the attempt to delineate some of the issues of globalization will help provide a framework for moving forward on the billions of words and choices that will make us truly think and act like global citizens. The realization of that hope will most likely be the accomplishment more of our children and grandchildren than of ourselves.

QUESTIONS FOR REFLECTION

1. Put yourself into a chat room where you know absolutely nothing about the other person. If you could know only one thing about that person, what would be the *one* thing you would want to know that would give you the most comprehensive understanding of that person? Would it be, for instance, nationality, religion, age, gender or, rather, what the person does for a living, what is the person's profession?
2. Come up with as many examples as possible of the controlling role business has exercised on our political, religious, and cultural lives, for example, holidays scheduled around weekends, the use of cell phones, being on call 24/7.
3. Consider the role of the Internet in creating a new place and new time in which to live. Are we creating a new culture that is no longer linked to neighborhoods and concrete communities? What are the implications for human living?
4. Identify job losses and job gains within your business or community owing to globalization.
5. Make the case, either individually or as groups, for free trade vs. aid as the most important factor in increasing prosperity.
6. Is democracy necessary for a full-blown market economy? Explain.
7. Consider the role of the multinational corporation in the global economy. Make the case for both sides of the argument, for example, more powerful than local/national governments vs. pays higher wages and can draw on international credit and skills.
8. What is the role of the Christian, and of religion in general, in the phenomenon of globalization?
9. Is not the fact of globalization just a further advance on our religious understanding that all human beings are our brothers and sisters?
10. Compare Eastern and Western values. Are they really as diametrically opposed as they are sometimes made out to be? Amartya Sen (*Development as Freedom*, 231-40) makes the case that they are not really irreconcilable.

SUGGESTIONS FOR FURTHER READING AND STUDY

Boyle, Nicholas. *Who Are We Now? Christian Humanism and the Global Market from Hegel to Heaney*. Notre Dame, Ind.: University of Notre Dame Press, 1998. An in-depth exploration of personal identity in a global economy.

Falk, Richard. *Predatory Globalization: A Critique.* University Park: Pennsylvania State University Press, 1999. The negative dimensions of globalization.

Friedman, Thomas L. *The World Is Flat: A Brief History of the Twenty-First Century.* New York: Farrar, Straus and Giroux, 2005. An interesting, if somewhat sanguine, description of global business possibilities as reflected in the Indian IT economic boom.

"Globalisation and Its Critics: A Survey of Globalisation." *The Economist.* September 29, 2001. An important discussion of the global market economy.

Joshi, Vivjav, and Robert Skidelsky. "One World?" *New York Review of Books.* Vol. 51, no. 5. March 25, 2004. A review of four wide-ranging works on the global economy, including evaluations of the writings of Peter Singer and Jagdish Bhagwati.

Sen, Amartya. *Development as Freedom.* New York, Anchor Books, 2000. Originally published in hardcover, New York: Alfred A. Knopf, 1999. An insightful study of how economic activity is really a dimension of human activity and contributes not only to economic but also to human development.

Wolf, Martin. *Why Globalization Works.* New Haven, Conn.: Yale University Press, 2004. An assessment of the positive dimensions of globalization.

10

When More Is Not Enough

If you look to lead,
invest at least 40 percent of your time
managing yourself—
your ethics, character, principles,
purpose, motivation and conduct.
Dee Hock, CEO, Visa

Let us summarize the path that has brought us to this point. We began with the statement that business and the larger market economy can only be successful in the long run if it is ethical. We have tried to reach that understanding by showing that business is primarily a *human* activity rather than a mechanical formula for making money. Being rooted in the human, it is by that fact grounded in the moral. All the other consequences follow from that basis:

- Business is about producing goods and services that increase general prosperity.
- Producing goods and services that are valued is dependent on a community of persons who embody those values (core values).
- Leadership and integrity are indispensable moral qualities for sustaining those values.
- Ethical performance is as much a group (or cultural) effort as it is individual.
- Business provides a rich context for both ethical choices and for moral development.
- Business takes on a greater significance as a result of globalization.

The critical role of ethics in a market economy is highlighted by Amartya Sen, winner of the Nobel Prize in Economics, in his classic work, *Development as Freedom*:

> While capitalism is often seen as an arrangement that works only on the basis of the greed of everyone, the efficient working of the capitalist

economy is, in fact, dependent on powerful systems of values and norms. Indeed, to see capitalism as nothing other than a system based on a conglomeration of greedy behavior is to underestimate vastly the ethics of capitalism, which has richly contributed to its redoubtable achievements.[1]

He goes on to say that a solid grounding in such virtues as honesty, trust, truthfulness, and regard for the other is much like the oxygen we breathe. We take it for granted until it isn't there. A market economy cannot exist in a void; it requires an underlying moral edifice. Without a strong humanistic ethics, business will flounder in a swamp of corruption and deceit—a fact well documented in the collapse of high visibility companies such as Enron and WorldCom.

In this chapter we need to reverse the perspective. We will consider not how ethics affects business but rather how business affects ethics. This is not some moralism about how wealth can corrupt. Poverty can corrupt just as readily. The issue of corruption must be settled on the more personal basis of moral integrity and spiritual transformation. Our concern here is to focus on the dangers and ambiguities peculiar to the dynamics of a market economy that must be attended to if we are to flourish as persons in a world order increasingly distinguished by business and markets. The benefits of a market economy have become obvious: the increase in general prosperity, the reduction of poverty, the enlarged freedom to choose what one values, the loosening of the ability of politics or religion to control one's living, and the development of science and technology as well as of individual skills and talents. Are there corresponding areas of concern that must be examined if we are to nurture the ethical grounding so important to long-term business success as well as promote the full richness of what it means to be human? To do so, we need a more careful exploration of (1) the specific dynamics that makes business effective; (2) the development of personal identity; (3) the meaning of the common good; (4) the impact of a market economy on religion; and (5) Catholic social teaching.

THE DYNAMICS OF THE BUSINESS PROCESS

A professor of accounting recently asked me a provocative question: "Why is it that the whole world can be so united in economic matters and yet so frag-

---

[1] Amartya Sen, *Development as Freedom* (New York: Anchor Books, 2000; orig. published, New York: Knopf, 1999), 262.

mented in matters of religion, race, and culture?" The answer, I believe, lies in the way business looks at the world. Business is about systems and recurring cycles that can produce better pornography just as effectively as better cell phones. It is driven by "means to ends," or what is classically called "instrumental" reasoning. Economic analysis does not evaluate the content of production but the efficiency and success of its rhythms. Consider the reasoning of the following steps:

- If something is to be translated into a recognizable unit, it must be able to be measured.
- If something is to be measured, it must be objectified, that is, it must be externalized. It must become a commodity, stripped of all relations to time, space, or people.
- In effect, qualities must be converted to quantities. The complex must be simplified because attention can be given only to what can be measured and counted—the bottom line.
- Nonetheless, a market economy deals not only with the world of things but of the values implicit in the choices made in the marketplace. It is this objectification of values that enables economic agents to test and evaluate every business endeavor.
- Money is the common means for objectifying values. It is sheer instrumentality. It objectifies every relationship and every value.
- Money is an abstraction that converts all of reality into measurable, quantifiable units that allow us to precisely assess and calculate the relation of economic means to ends.
- Money, then, "embodies and sublimates the practical relation of man to the objects of his will, his power and his impotence."[2] Money makes it possible for us precisely to "contract" our relations to others and to be connected to them only insofar as we desire to be connected.

In effect, everything becomes a commodity whose value can be measured by money. Consider the example of a chicken breast—pure pink meat, no fat, bones, or tissue—individually wrapped, quick frozen, ready for use at anyone's request. It is a commodity, pure and simple, with a monetary value—abstracted even from the fact that it was once part of a chicken, a living animal raised by someone, somewhere, then slaughtered and cut from the bone

---

[2] Craig M. Gay, *Cash Values: Money and the Erosion of Meaning in Today's Society* (Grand Rapids, Mich.: William B. Eerdmans, 2004; first published as part of the New College Lecture Series [Sydney: University of New South Wales Press, 2003]), 37. This short work of some ninety pages illumines the meaning of money that goes far beyond the customary understanding of money as a medium of exchange.

by someone, packaged and shipped by someone else to somewhere else. Every relationship of that chicken breast to anything else—to its existence as a chicken, the work and skill, the hopes and fears of the many other persons involved in the process of making this chicken breast available to me—has been severed. It is simply a commodity to be consumed. Money is the one thing that interconnects the whole process. This is not a criticism but rather a call to reflect on what effect this "commoditization" that is so essential to a market economy might be having on us personally as consumers living in a consumer society.

One also begins to understand more profoundly the significance of money. Our preoccupation with it probably has less to do with greed, at least as traditionally understood, and more to do with the all-encompassing role it plays in society. Everything and, to some extent at least, everyone has a monetary exchange. Our work, our skills, our interests, our security, our ambitions, and even our deepest relationships to spouse and to children—all have a price tag. The role of money has expanded far beyond what it can buy. It is a way of *measuring* everything that can be objectified. Even more subtly, there is a reverse movement that wants to objectify everything precisely so it can be measured. There is, then, a consequent tendency of the money metric to limit the world of substance and meaning to its economic significance, that is, to the kind of results that can be quantified and measured. Reason and understanding themselves become truncated at the means-to-ends level. The full range of the innate dynamism of intelligence moving us forward to what is true in itself and what is worthwhile in itself gets lost in the incessant calculation of means to ends.

The basic symbol of means-to-ends thinking is money. It has become the most basic unit, the least common denominator, and it has become global. It is "the first and so far the only utterly successful universal language, expressing in terms everyone can recognize truths no one can fathom."[3] It can equate to anyone and anywhere in the world. It measures every human want and desire. It can measure the value of every activity, including waiting in a line. It can even measure relationships—the cost of a child, of a spouse in a divorce settlement, of a business partnership, of waging a war, of an offended person in a lawsuit, of feeding the hungry and clothing the naked. In summary, Nicholas Boyle states,

> The truth is that money is the most extraordinarily subtle and accurate invention for defining what people really want—by contrast with what

---

[3] Nicholas Boyle, *Who Are We Now? Christian Humanism and the Global Market from Hegel to Heaney* (Notre Dame, Ind.: University of Notre Dame Press, 1998), 105.

they say they want—and for expressing those wants in terms of other people's wants, even though the other people may be completely unknown to one and stand in no explicit political relation to one. Money is the visible expression of all the social relations of which we are unconscious.[4]

It is this absolute instrumentality of money, having no value in itself, that allows an economy to flourish globally. It focuses us on what serves our personal values. It does not question or challenge those values other than insisting the piper must be paid. All our consumption must be paid for by our production. Those values that drive our choices, however, are what are nourished and supported and challenged, not by the economy, but by our families, our culture, our tribe or nation, our religion. It is these values that lead us out of ourselves into the larger world of human living. Our values and relationships give us our identity. There is nothing more basic. The reason, then, why globalization is much more fragmented on the level of cultures, nations, and religion is that it is about something so much more personal than the flow of goods and services.

THE DEVELOPMENT OF PERSONAL IDENTITY

The ability to quantify all activity via a common unit that we call money is only the beginning of the story. It is only a slight, and mostly unconscious, move to go from calculating all human activity in monetary units to considering the individual person himself as an economic unit. Nicholas Boyle states the issue, perhaps too negatively, but certainly strongly enough to get our attention:

> But the freedom we are encouraged to have today is the freedom merely to choose, as consumers, from whatever the market offers—while a veil is drawn over what is in a closed system the necessary symmetrical complement of this freedom: our enslavement, as the producers, to the demands set us by the market, for the more choice we give ourselves as consumers the heavier the chains we forge for ourselves as workers. In the modern, post-revolutionary world there are no longer any pure consumers, there is no longer a leisured aristocracy—we are now virtually all consumers *and* producers, proletarians, who live by selling our labor.[5]

---

[4] Boyle, *Who Are We Now?* 104.
[5] Boyle, *Who Are We Now?* 116.

And to emphasize the point further, he continues in another passage:

> For the market seeks to conceal from us—lest it inhibit the arbitrariness and frequency of our choices in it, that is, of our purchases—that it has another, a shadow, side. It is not only the place where needs are satisfied; it is the place where orders for work are given. The market not only serves consumers; it disciplines producers. And in the contemporary world, where we are all—more or less—equally both consumers and producers, the market has to conceal from us that we shall eventually come to feel the consequences of our consumer choices in the form of constraints on our productive activity.[6]

What is clear is that there is a close link, if not an iron chain, between being a consumer and a producer. While we all have some sense of this in our awareness of mortgages, car loans, credit card debt, health insurance costs, pension provisions, we are not always as conscious of how our consumptions bind us to our jobs. It is much easier to see the parade of immediate goods and services than the debt to be paid by being a dutiful producer in the same marketplace. What kind of pressure (or, in Boyle's words, "discipline") does the market put on us to "perform," to "go along to get along," to cut corners in order to meet "quotas," to not rock the boat or blow the whistle in order to keep a job. Do we not become trapped financially? How many of us have achieved a personal level of freedom that allows us to make moral choices when we have a mortgage payment, car note(s), credit card bill(s) that demand their monthly dues? While we might not quite fit the caricature of a brainwashed automaton buying what the market says to buy and then dutifully trudging off to work in some impersonal corporation, we have probably not entirely escaped that dynamic either. Even more damaging, we may hardly be aware of the link. The credit card is probably its most dramatic symbol. It's our immediate ticket to the dazzling world of consumer goods and services, but then ties us to slow, and sometimes painful, repayment of consumer debt. Is it any wonder that the young and undisciplined become its earliest victims!

There is yet a more fundamental level to the issue. It is the question of self-identity. In a culture where the rhythms of consuming and producing dominate, finding one's identity within that rhythm can easily become an almost unconscious assumption. Its implications are dramatic, since making ourselves the persons we become is the most fundamental dynamism of our existence. If our identity is defined in economic terms, then success becomes measured in how *much* we produce or, more tellingly, how much we *consume*. But more

---

[6] Boyle, *Who Are We Now?* 154.

is not enough. The never-ending drama of making ourselves the persons we become is an open-ended call to greater self-transcendence. It calls us to imagine alternatives, to raise more questions, to reassert our freedom in the capacity to redefine what might be humanly possible. If that drama has already been defined for us in terms of production and consumption, then houses are not just homes and cars are not just means of transportation. They make a statement! Clothes are identified by brand and relationships are judged on their prestige factor. A child's education is determined by the potential it offers for a good job. Consumption is still based on need, but the need is no longer for goods and services in themselves but for their ability to provide identity. No one understands this better than the markets. Advertising promotes a steady stream of products that will identify the buyer as successful, sophisticated, intelligent, sexy, beautiful, or whatever other identity one wishes to achieve. That identity can be bought and sold, consumed and produced. The disappointment comes when one begins to realize that the deepest human desires are not material. More is not enough!

Perhaps the biggest threat of a market economy to personal identity is its capacity to manipulate our life of desire. Consumer desire, in its deepest fulfillment, is not oriented to any particular object of desire but to the desire itself. It is the hunt, the search itself that gives fulfillment. It is the desire for "the more" that brings the satisfaction. Any acquisition of a particular object of desire only feeds the endless desire. The particular object loses interest in a hurry, and we are fired up again by the search itself. It has been generally noted that when people are asked what salary level would satisfy them, their usual answer is about 20 percent more than they currently make—no matter what their current level is! Thomas Aquinas, long before the dominance of a consumer culture, noted this aspect of desire for temporal goods. Before material goods are "possessed, they are highly regarded and thought satisfying; but after they are possessed, they are found to be neither so great as thought nor sufficient to satisfy our desires, and so our desires are not satisfied but move on to something else."[7] We regret not the restless desires but their fulfillment. It is the desire that intoxicates, not the particular object. It is here that the desire for goods (the "bigger, better, cheaper") crosses over, taps into, is confused with the deeper dynamism of an open-ended transcendence that finds its fulfillment only in what is true in itself and what is worthwhile, or loveable, in itself. The desire to simply meet a human want—for food, shelter, pleasure, intimacy—is no longer at stake. The issue is not some type of crass materialism but the confounding of a desire that has no earthly term with the desire for needed goods that is incited and fanned in a consumer cul-

---

[7] Thomas Aquinas, *Commentary on the Gospel of John* (Albany: Magi Books, 1980).

ture. The desire takes a strange form. It is "fixated on consumption but not attached to things."[8] Few are caught up completely in this distortion; however, most of us are not completely free of its implications.

Religion in general and the Christian Gospels in particular do not disdain money; it is the *love* of money that is rebuked. When money is no longer a vehicle of exchange but becomes a substitute for identity and relationships and security, it becomes a false god. It is unable to deliver what it seems to promise. When the dialectic of consumer-producer becomes one's identity, then money and business take on a harshness and a competitiveness bordering on brutality, a devouring relentlessness and utter restlessness that characterize the negative images that stereotype business activity. In short, if you can be a consumer only to the degree that you submit to the disciplines of being a producer, and if being a consumer (having) is the measure of your identity (being), then being a consumer-producer is the most serious and all-consuming passion of life. By the same token, then, more will never be enough. Identity, or "who we are" and consequently "what we are worth," is fundamental. Former sources of identity—male/female, German, Mexican, black, Japanese, Catholic, Buddhist, Jew—have been undercut by the market economy. Skill, ability, productivity easily trump the old categories of identity. While we rightly laud this advance over old prejudices, we also are taking one more step toward confirming the notion that one's real identity is to be found in the marketplace. If gender, for instance, is neutralized in the marketplace, being a vice-president, engineer, accountant, as opposed to a clerk, homemaker, laborer, is not.

The young are particularly susceptible to looking for identity in the rhythms of production and consumption. Identity itself is particularly fragile in the young because establishing identity is a critical challenge of that stage of life. Consuming and producing can seem like a quick fix to the uncertainties involved in genuine self-realization. In addition, when starting out in a career it's easier to confuse what you do with who you are. Youth is a time when there is naturally a greater focus on *doing*; energy and activity are directed outward to test oneself against the world. If consuming and producing are the cultural standards, then the invitation to excel in the race is hard to resist—until one discovers that more is not enough.[9] Probably none of us

---

[8] Vincent J. Miller, *Consuming Religion: Christian Faith and Practice in a Consumer Culture* (New York: Continuum International, 2005), 127. Pages 126-45 give a perceptive analysis of how the confusing of the desire for goods and the desire for God lead to various aberrations in attitude and behavior.

[9] Martha Irvine, "U.S. Youth's Priority: Strike It Rich," *Chicago Tribune*, January 23, 2007, 1-3. This is borne out in a recent Pew Research Center poll which found that 81 percent of eighteen- to twenty-five-year-olds see getting rich as the most important goal in life. In UCLA's annual survey of college freshmen of 2006, 73 percent thought it was essential or very important to be "very well off financially." That compares to 63 percent in 1980 and 42 percent in 1966.

is completely free of this compulsion. The following exercise might help you identify some of its elements.

IS THIS YOU? Traits of a Workaholic[10]	
Workaholic	**Hard Worker**
Can't stop working without feeling anxious	Can choose to stop working without ill effects
Works to satisfy a compulsive need for approval	Work is just one part of life
Becomes self-absorbed and self-centered	Able to be loving and intimate
Loses touch with feelings	Stays in touch with feelings
Perfectionist and controlling	Tolerant of own mistakes and others
Loses control over schedule	Remains in charge of work schedule

When producing and consuming define the central rhythms of life, then everything changes:

- *Politics* becomes the art of ensuring the greatest range of economic and commercial freedom so that individuals can achieve their goal of self-fulfillment or self-constitution.
- *Leisure, evenings, weekends* are less a time to nurture other dimensions of one's person and more a time to rest and relax *in order to* go back to work with renewed vigor.

---

[10] Barbara Killinger, "Workaholics: The Respectable Addicts," as quoted in Sue Shallenbarger, "Working for a Living or Living to Work? Some Help for the Workaholic Spouse," *Wall Street Journal*, November 21, 2002, D1.

- *Success* is measured by one's ability to consume or acquire "the latest and greatest" that the market can produce.
- *Relationships* are not spared. Spouses become business assets; children are judged by their potential for successful careers, friends are nurtured for their prestige or good connections.

Some pursue these goals with a sharply focused and clear-headed intensity (those of this world are wiser than the children of God). Many of us, however, will drift into these patterns simply because they reflect the unexamined values of a life carried by a culture captivated by the rhythms of production and consumption. The shopping mall has become an American icon, and going shopping has mutated from a chore to a favorite form of recreation and enjoyment. Even vacations are highlighted by going shopping, enhanced with the enticement of different locations and unique shops. We come head-on against the limits of the market economy when we desperately try to find something new to buy as Christmas gifts. The simpler alternative becomes a gift card, which is really a pass to do more shopping.

The objective here is not to decry the market economy that we have tried to support in the prior nine chapters. It is not an attempt to replace the market system with a better system. No system as system will ever encompass or surpass the personal demands of human living. Any system, be it political, religious, or economic, will have its limits. The more perceptive one is to those limits and to the internal assumptions of its dynamic, the more one will be in a position to navigate a truly human life. How does a market economy make sense of delight and suffering, laughter and tears, joy and sorrow, the cry of the poor, lonely, and enfeebled?

An important step in answering that question is to deepen our understanding of the meaning of the human person. On one level, we all know what a person is. It's obvious, because we are all persons. On another level, as Socrates says, the unexamined life is not worth living. The faith of Jews, Christians, and Muslims is based on a profound belief that the deepest meaning of the human person is found in relationship to an infinite God. The study of the humanities is based on the conviction that there is a profundity to the human person that has given birth to the disciplines of art and literature, history and law, philosophy and psychology, anthropology and sociology, religion and morality—each driven by the yearning to explore some dimensions of what it means to be human. Obviously, the human person is not obvious.

The issue is further complicated by the nature of business thinking that has been explored above. Business is successful precisely because it can quantify and calculate means to established ends. To measure is to quantify and objectify. Even persons become units of production and consumption. How much greater awareness is required to see both ourselves and others differently! And the difference is not quantitative—not just more—but qualitatively different from all other interactions that make up so much of our life. In effect, there is a dimension to the human person that can never be quantified. More is not enough. In general, there is something intrinsically chilling about violating the absolute worth of another human being. A person's value cannot be measured; it cannot be earned and cannot be lost. It is *qualitatively* different from everything else. Even in the most extreme situations of human experience, such as war or servitude, there remains an absolute preciousness to the human person that must always be respected.

In other words, strictly business thinking which is characterized by instrumental reasoning about means to ends reaches its limit when the issue is no longer about means but about the end itself. And that end is ultimately the human person. A market economy posits no moral end for the human person. Business has no competence and no expertise to determine what is the end, the purpose, or the meaning of being human, unless of course the human person is also reduced to a commodity. While very few would explicitly hold such a notion, such thinking has a way of coloring our decisions.

If the divide between being and having, or identity and market economy, is to be bridged, then a new synthesis of the economist and the humanist is needed. That effort requires change on both sides. The effort becomes even more urgent as business occupies a more central role in every person's life. A first step is to locate business and a market economy within the fundamental dynamics of human activity and human community. The very renewal of a concern for ethics in business and for balance between work and life is another way of saying that business again needs to find its roots in the human. Why, for instance, should business schools not be located within the humanities? At the very least, a business curriculum needs to include more than accounting, sales, and marketing as the big three. Business is more than a profit-and-loss statement coupled with a balance sheet. It is not some mechanistic formula that, if followed mindlessly, will lead to success. As Ray Carey said, "As long as the prime goal of most new (business) graduates is to make a million dollars by age thirty, then a first-year course on Business Ethics is tokenism."[11]

On the one hand, the humanities must also make a major move. Humanities have traditionally erected an ivory tower of disinterest in what easily

---

[11] Ray Carey, *Democratic Capitalism: The Way to a World of Peace and Plenty* (Bloomington, Ind.: AuthorHouse, 2004), 26.

becomes viewed as the crass and messy activity called business. There is an assumption that it is the role of the intellectual few to develop and pass on the wisdom of the community. On the other hand, it is the role of the many to cultivate the land, carry on commerce, initiate and support families. Philosophy and art remain the idyllic or prophetic domain of an elite, and, to this day, there is an elitism in the academy that tends to distance itself from the everyday messiness of the buying and selling, the bargaining and compromising of the marketplace.

There is, however, a deeper dimension to this intellectual stance. The Western cultural tradition, so deeply influenced by Plato (427-347 B.C.) and Aristotle (384-322 B.C.), viewed the *state* as the agent of social change. According to them, the state is prior to the individual and the family because the whole is prior to its parts. Consequently, the state is naturally superior to and responsible for the individual and the family. Politics (from *polis*, the city-state), they concluded, was the most skilled art, and, of course, the philosopher guides the politician. All of this high-mindedness, however, had a seamy underside. Not only were slaves considered vital to domestic well-being but women were definitely second-class, with no intrinsic rights, just a step above slaves. The good life was the domain of the select few. The extent of this bias toward the common and ordinary comes home dramatically in the following excerpt from Plato's *Laws*:

> First, [it is important] for the state first to keep its trading class as small as possible; second, trade should be made over to a class of people whose corruption will not harm the state unduly; third, some means must be found to prevent those engaging in such activities from slipping too easily into an utterly shameless and small-minded way of life.[12]

This bias of the intellectual, articulated in Plato and Aristotle, has been pervasive in succeeding stages of Western culture. Instead of trying to find a higher synthesis of humanism and economics, intellectuals and religious people alike took the disparities of rich and poor as further evidence of the inherent greediness of rich businesspeople. Marx looked to class conflict to solve the problem, while intellectuals and liberals tended to look to the state to right the wrongs. Very little energy was expended to try to understand economics and promote other options of commerce. To this day, most colleges and universities do not insist on an understanding of market economics as a requirement for graduation, yet very few other subjects will probably have a greater impact on the graduate's future living than economics. Both

---

[12] Carey, *Democratic Capitalism*, 90.

class warfare and government control are based on an assumption that is hard to shake.

Without an adequate understanding of a market economy, the humanities tend to reside in an ivory tower playing the fiddle while the economy burns out of control. Without an adequate understanding of human nature, business focuses exclusively on highly selective numbers to the detriment of its own long-term welfare. Peter Drucker, the guru of business management, believed that "to transcend this dichotomy (of economics and the humanities) in a new synthesis will be a central philosophical and educational challenge for the post-capitalist society."[13] And, I would add, the same challenge applies to religious people everywhere. The unifying point of reference for any synthesis is the human person, understood in the fullness of who that is.

THE MEANING OF THE COMMON GOOD

In the classical framework of Greece and Rome, people gathered in the city *agora,* or public square, to discuss the politics of how to live the good life together. The good life is by its nature a collaborative achievement. A wholly self-sufficient person, Aristotle remarked long ago, is either a beast or a god. In the medieval period, people gathered as a community of believers around the cathedral to worship God. In our times, people come together in city skyscrapers to conduct business. In each case, there is the recognition of some level of a common world shared by all, a realization that life cannot be lived alone and that what we do and who we are is some function of a larger world. The recognition of that larger world and how it affects ourselves and others is what we call the common good, in contrast, not in opposition, to our personal well-being. Each has a profound influence on the other. The fact that commerce, and more dramatically worldwide commerce, has become the common ground or common good that we share needs to be explored more thoroughly.

Just as we have come to a deeper realization that the very success of a market economy, grounded in the dynamics of consumption and production, has influenced our understanding of the human person, so we now need to investigate the role of a market economy in shaping our present understanding of the common good.[14] If the meaning of our identity as a person can be thinned

---

[13] Peter Drucker, *Post Capitalist Society* (New York: Harper Business, 1993), 8. The same point is made very persuasively by Ray Carey throughout *Democratic Capitalism.*

[14] The use of the term "common good" has its danger. It can easily become an abstraction that becomes manipulated as a pretense for one's personal agenda, as in "I know what's good for you."

out to a primarily economic component, something similar can occur even more easily to our notion of the common good. In fact, can we not already observe some disturbing trends, not necessarily full-blown realities, in our Western understanding of the common good?[15] Among the trends are the following:

1. The basis of all human association beyond the family is economic. The most important reason human beings join together in cooperative activity is for the production, distribution, and consumption of material goods. All other associations are subordinate to that purpose.

2. Economic interest is always defined as self-interest. The pursuit of material advantage drives the behavior of individuals, groups, and social classes. Appeals to disinterested and principled action are either hypocritical or naive. Such appeals usually veil some self-serving interest.

3. What ultimately drives human progress is not the free responsible actions of citizens and statesmen but impersonal economic laws, the laws of the market, or the dialectical law of class struggle.

4. All human activities are measured by their productive potential. All non-productive forms of existence become suspect. Philosophical and theological speculation is useless. Art, literature, and music are useful to the degree that they can provide entertainment for purposes of relaxation.

5. The classical understanding of leisure is overturned by the new economic understanding of human existence. Leisure was considered essential for human culture. Freed *from* the demands of utility and necessity, people were free *for* the liberal and liberating activities of disinterested contemplation, prayer, speculation, political exchange, searching for truth and beauty in song and dance, in reading and discussion. While the economic understanding of human existence still approves of these activities, their *justification* lies elsewhere. Traditionally, these activities were considered the highest human achievements because they were critical to the discovery and elaboration of the human values and meanings embodied in one's culture. On the contrary, contemporary justification for leisure lies in its ability to provide relaxation, entertainment, and physical replenishment in order to get back to the *serious* business of economic life. Even the monuments to the classical sense of leisure, the cathedrals and public buildings, the rituals and dances of ethnic

---

Something like the "human good" might be more adequate because the way we interact with one another unfolds historically and dynamically. This can be an important distinction in reaching across cultures and cultural values.

[15] These thoughts are largely dependent on an unpublished lecture by Michael McCarthy at the Lonergan Conference in Toronto, August 2004.

peoples, are now "redeemed" by their economic consideration as tourist attractions for generating income!

6. Political life is also subject to the same upheaval. Political life was once considered the highest calling of the citizen, and the art of politics as the most difficult science. It was the practice of searching for the common good, for the good life that can only be achieved in common. The new political philosophy initiated by Thomas Hobbes and John Locke restricts the purposes of government to the protection of individual rights and liberties. As the understanding of human existence becomes more restricted to the economic, then the role of government becomes more and more associated with protecting economic interests—a sort of massive stock exchange that regulates the commerce and industry of individual interests. There is perhaps some basis here for our current cynicism about and lack of interest in politics as simply an arena of conflicting economic interests.

7. National governments can no longer control the economic health of their countries. There is an additional undermining of national governments that comes from the fact that, as the market economy becomes global, local and national governments, by their geographical limitations, are less able to effectively determine their own destinies. As a result, governments often find themselves either cozying up to business interests or fragmented and ineffective in resisting the inexorable onslaught of economic demands.

Without a concerted effort to resist these seven trends and to retrieve and deepen a richer understanding of the common good, there is a very real danger that citizens will think and speak of politics on the model of economic activity. More is not enough. As Michael McCarthy summed up so succinctly at the Lonergan Conference:

> When that happens [politics modeled on economic activity], citizens become private consumers, lobbyists become marketing and public relations experts, and elected officials become rhetorical peddlers whose political services are available to organized interest groups at the right price. Today's demoralizing political culture constantly obscures the vital distinctions between economic and civic agents in ways that injure us all ... It is hard to resist the conviction that the commonality defining us as Americans today is primarily commercial in nature. We are individual producers, merchants, and consumers, who meet, when we do meet, in places of commerce and entertainment. We are rarely cooperative citizens joining together in the work of collective self-government. For most Americans today, the government is *they* not *we*, for we are independent individuals, defined by narrower identities, and we must be about our private or group centered business.

If the notion of common good has really become so thin within the United States, consider how difficult it will be to develop an adequate notion of the global common good. It is new territory, calling for careful yet courageous steps. It is a new search for the whole (the common good). The whole, within which individual thought and action make sense, is no longer the confines of family, tribe, race, or nation but all the peoples of the earth. That whole human community is not monolithic; it is composed of diverse communities and cultures. A global society, then, must be attentive to cultural pluralism while reaching for the ever-deeper transcultural desires and norms that reside within every human being. The easier, but potentially more damaging, alternative is to reduce that common good to its economic dimension. To further complicate the issue, the *whole* is not only peoples but our planet and our place in the universe. Action by its nature is always local, at a specific time and place for a specific object, yet the awareness and purpose must be global.

Meanwhile a global economy sets up at least four fault lines or contradictions that will continue to undermine the effort to realize a genuine global society.[16] They are

1. As central governments attempt to exercise tighter control over economic activity, human activity is defined increasingly in economic terms. On the other hand, governments are faced with diminishing power and relevancy as economies continue to become global and create a sense of cosmopolitan identity. Even the U.S. economy, the largest in the world, does not control its own destiny and cannot halt, for instance, the worldwide movement of jobs.

2. As the ideal of freedom and personal identity, based on the supposition that anyone can do anything, continues to grow, the market continues to offer limited options that are the product of standardization, economies of scale and efficiencies. Consider the shopping mall, fast-food restaurants and the main streets leading into any city. Although one may have traveled thousands of miles to get there, they all have commonly recognized stores and brands.

3. As the global economy promises to all the ability to achieve unlimited potential, our planet is not unlimited.

4. As the range of consumption expands, servitude to the rhythms of production deepens. Perhaps the *credit card* is its icon. It can both liberate and enslave.

---

[16] Boyle, *Who Are We Now?* 118.

At this point it is perhaps more important to recognize these contradictions than to find easy answers to the dilemma they pose. It will take all the resources of a deepening realization of the human person and an expanding notion of the common good to work through these issues. Nicholas Boyle puts the central issue as directly as possible: "Recognizing ourselves as self-constraining consumer-producers we recognize not only our own finitude but that of the world we inhabit. There is one world and it is not endless and we have to work out among ourselves how we are to live in it together or we shall die in it separately."[17]

THE IMPACT OF A MARKET ECONOMY ON RELIGION

The very success of the market economy and its pervasive influence in contemporary living leaves no aspect of life unaffected. We have considered its influence on personal identity, the common good, culture, and the human community. Religion is integral to each of these elements and so is impacted as well. The nature of that influence needs to be examined carefully. The market economy and religion are not two competing institutions locked in a struggle for dominance. If we have argued strongly for the necessity of ethics if business is to be successful, we would argue just as strongly that mixing business and formal religious practice is a dangerous combination that has nothing to do with assuring business success. The real issue is much more nuanced. If religion exists within individual believers and their culture, then how can we know if the impact of the same rhythm of production and consumption that affects culture does not already predetermine our understanding of religion? While the issue calls for more extensive exploration under other rubrics, such as the role of culture in religion and the meaning of religious beliefs, some recognition of the issue must be noted in a work that purports to explore the moral dimensions of a market economy.

While we have considered some of the consequences of a market-oriented culture that focuses attention on *having* over *being* and can misdirect the struggle for identity to the marketplace of goods and services, there is a more subtle dynamic that results from a culture that is absorbed with production and consumption. Recall how a market economy quantifies all aspects of production through instrumental reasoning that focuses on means to predetermined ends. Instrumental reasoning abstracts from every relationship other than the product becoming an item of exchange in the consumer-producer

---

[17] Boyle, *Who Are We Now?* 119.

cycle. Everything becomes a commodity, pure and simple. For our part, we grow up learning how to be consumers. Money doesn't grow on trees, but it surely comes from a cash machine or a credit card. We are trained from infancy to be consumers, to be better consumers, to learn from our mistakes, and we practice, practice, practice. Everything becomes a content to be commoditized, distributed, consumed—music, culture, learning, sports, even war and natural tragedies. We become so accustomed to approaching everything, and often everyone, as a commodity to be consumed that it becomes our spontaneous approach to the world.

Do we not then, without reflection or hesitation, approach religion the same way? Religion itself becomes the ultimate commodity. A market economy has no ideology. It is an infrastructure capable of absorbing all cultures and all religions as "content to be commoditized." Religious beliefs and practices from around the world can be brought to anyone's living room. Icons and mosaics, prayer wheels and crucifixes, from any and all religious tradition can be reproduced and elaborately, even piously, explained. Gregorian chant, born and nurtured in religious community, can be heard on CDs or in commercials, if you prefer. Bibles, encyclopedias of world religions, explanations of everything from Wicca to New Age spirituality are available for consumption. The difficulty is not in the availability but in the consumption. More is not enough! To approach religion as a commodity to be consumed is to destroy the heart of religion. We need to understand this further if religious belief and practice are not to be increasingly deprived of their ability to influence and shape life.

As stated, a commodity by its nature must be abstracted from its original context and from any reference to other relationships. It must be removed from any particular practice that brought it into existence, remember our infamous chicken breast. It is ready for consumption. True religious belief, on the other hand, only makes sense as an understanding of a totality that is larger than we are. As long as it remains a commodity that we *choose*, then we remain in control. The whole that is the characteristic of religion is the larger reality within which we choose. It is the something greater that determines us rather than us determining it. It is why religious belief is always in the context of religious practice and a community of believers. It is a *response to* and not a *creation of* the wholeness of life. It is a *way* of life; it is a letting go, in love, to something, someone larger than oneself. There can be no commitment to a commodity, even if it is to a person unconsciously seen as a commodity. Some of our current religious climate, I believe, has its roots in the commoditization of religion. Consider the following indications.

- the shift from a world in which beliefs held believers to one in which believers hold beliefs

- searching for a religion or a parish that fits my personality and beliefs
- cafeteria-type selection of doctrines I believe or moral precepts I follow
- emphasis on personal spiritualities rather than on a religious community of believers
- religion as a therapeutic concern for personal well-being
- generalized nonspecific religiosity focused on something like "angels"
- intense emotional response to suffering without practical action
- religious call for self-transcendence and transformation confused with self-fulfillment—and not in the paradoxical sense of "he who loses his life will find it"
- the transformation of outstanding religious persons such as the Dalai Lama, Mother Teresa, Pope John Paul II into celebrities to be tracked, marketed, and consumed

There is another aspect of the consumer culture that needs attention, not because it is so different from religious desire but precisely because it is so much like it. Religious traditions are all grounded in some way in the human capacity for the infinite in a world of finite realizations. St. Augustine has given it the most recognized expression in his classical opening lines of the *Confessions*, "You have made us for yourself and our hearts are restless until they rest in Thee." The human spirit cannot be satisfied by any finite thing. Vincent Miller in *Consuming Religion* makes a very perceptive observation: "Close examination of the texture of desire in consumer culture reveals that [it] is not simply about fixing one's heart on material things or sensual pleasure. Indeed, it is about never being satisfied with them ... We are trained from infancy to never cease desiring. Does this lead to God?"[18] His discerning answer is that it leads to greater and greater desire to consume in the marketplace. Consumer desire, in its deepest fulfillment, is not oriented to any particular object of desire but to the desire itself, as has been explored earlier. Consider the following examples:

- going shopping as entertainment, even without buying anything
- reading the ads, even though we don't particularly need anything
- massing a collection of whatever: shirts, books, shoes, CDs, gadgets, jewelry, without ever using most of it
- up-scaling—whatever we buy has a more expensive version that feeds into the desire. Even wedding rings have starter models that can be upgraded later. TVs, houses, stereo systems, computers, cars—all have their higher versions on the ladder of desire.

---

[18] Miller, *Consuming Religion*, 110.

- the proliferation of self-help books built on the assumption that the individual has or should have complete control over his or her life.

The danger to religion is that the ongoing array of goods can easily mask a realization that is critical to spiritual development: the desire of the human person can ultimately be realized only in communion with God. More is not enough. Even union with God can present a problem. God becomes the final object to be consumed. Then what? "Rest in peace" could seem rather boring!

Toward a Solution

These observations on a market economy and its tendency to create a consumer culture are not a negation of what was said in chaps. 1 through 9. They are a critique of some of the limitations of that culture. One of the critical roles of religion will always be to provide a critique of culture. But if religion helps shape a culture, culture also shapes religion. How can the potential danger of religion being coopted by the culture be minimized so as to allow religion its proper function? Following the lead of Miller, here are some suggestions.

Greater Awareness of the Dynamics of a Consumer Culture
While an awareness of the dynamics of a consumer culture will not of itself resolve the problem, it is a necessary first step. The commodity fetish needs to be unveiled. When we consume food from nowhere and wear clothes made by no one, then we effectively dissociate ourselves from the human family that has become so interdependent. There needs to be a conscious effort to move beyond the commoditization of everything and, almost inevitably, everyone. Perhaps even labels of origin can help us become more aware of the places and faces connected to our purchase. With a little reflection, we might come to appreciate our global interconnectedness as we put on our shirt or cook our chicken breast.

Participation in a Community of Believers
Commoditization is the result of complete abstraction—from time, place, people, raw material. Merely proclaiming or debating religious ideas and doctrines feeds into the same pattern of abstraction. They can easily be understood as simply more commodities. Only the concrete interaction with other people can begin to break the pattern, especially when those relationships involve action. Doctrines and symbols and practices are again embedded within the context of a community of believers in which commitments are possible and the structural supports for commitments are present.

Time Out

Doing things differently is often the most important step to thinking about things differently. Time removed from the rhythms of production and consumption can help us break the cycle. Whether it is vacations without cell phones or else personal retreats and prayer, there is a need to do different things.

Hear the Cry of the Poor

What will be powerful enough to shake our identity? If the dynamics of production/consumption/commoditization have played an important role in forming us into who we are, then the issue is not primarily a change in thinking as much as a change in deep-rooted emotions. Classrooms and books have rarely changed anyone. Opening our hearts and minds to the pain of the other, particularly the marginalized, can evoke a deeper experience. As Brendan Lovett says, "if our problem is that our emotional life, our life of desire, is constrained, constricted and controlled, then only an experience that enables a more powerful emotion or desire to be experienced by us helps us to break out of the whole pattern."[19]

To endorse the preferential option for the poor is to recognize the subjective dimension in the search for truth. It is to recognize the correlation between knowing and loving. While we generally acknowledge that we can only love what we know, there is another sense in which we only know what we love.[20]

A Further Christian Reflection

Fundamental to the Christian experience is the realization that who we are has taken on a new dimension. We no longer take our deepest sense of self from being man or woman, rich or poor, Greek or Jew, American or Chinese, Catholic or Protestant but from our experience of God as *Abba*, Father, and creator, of Jesus as the incarnation of the truth of God, and of the Spirit as the love of God present in the universe. The exploration of that conversion experience is not the theme of this work. However, some additional reflections in light of that new identity are in order.

---

[19] Brendan Lovett, *A Dragon Not for the Killing* (Quezon City, Philippines: Claretian Publications, 1998), 179.

[20] Lovett, *A Dragon Not for the Killing*, 113; see also 109-12 for a critique of Michael Novak's work on the market economy.

Our Christian identity allows us a deeper sense of self than the identity so quickly and unreflectively thrust on us as consumers and producers. Larger territorial and cultural differences, even sexual differences, are gradually being obliterated as sources of identity, only to be replaced by what we can produce (our skills and professions) or consume (our possessions). Our belief that our identity and ultimate destiny is in our relationship as creatures to a God who, even when known, remains a mystery should help safeguard us from self-worship and maintain us in the conviction that nothing we know in this world is ultimate.[21]

At the same time, we will need to see God in the human world we have made through the rhythms of commerce and industry, technology and discovery, communication and innovation. We need to see God not just in some golden past, whether that be the Christianity of the catacombs, the Christendom of the high Middle Ages, or the dialectic of the Reformation. Our new level of global awareness and our ability to manage and control so much of our destiny and prosperity calls us to a new sense of what it means to be created in the image and likeness of God, the ultimate creator of all that is true and good. We take our rightful place in that process as co-creators with a responsibility for our world and all our fellow human beings. Our work is an indispensable part of creation.

Most genuinely religious people have great compassion and sensitivity to the human condition and resonate with the sentiments of human solidarity with the poor. Unfortunately, they are often illiterate about the economy and markets. In many ways it is a bad combination. Compassion wants to help, but understanding is required to avoid misinformation and misdirection. The quick and easy solution, then, becomes wealth redistribution through collectivist means—the state, social agencies, international organizations. Of course, there are times and places when there is nothing better that can be done, or should be done. But the long-term solution, as has been argued in this book, is not for wealth redistribution but for wealth creation. Religion's role in business, then, is not only to ground and safeguard a morality that is critical for long-term business success but also to provide a perspective that allows a businessperson to see her profession as a vocation as much as traditional "helping professions" such as nursing, teaching, and preaching. Business is not just about making money to then take care of the important things in life, but it is, in itself, the way to increase general prosperity, eliminate material scarcity, and develop human potential. Nor is this perspective the final capitulation of religion to the relentless imperialism of market economics. By now it should

---

[21] Boyle, *Who Are We Now?* 93.

be clear that there are limits to the market economy, and religion will always have a role in identifying those limits and calling people to the fuller meaning of human life. Market economics has given us the capability to feed, clothe, shelter, and collaborate with all the peoples of the earth. What shall we do? There is no one simple answer. Individually and collectively we will have to find our word and our deed. Perhaps some attention to the experience of the Catholic Church as reflected in its social teaching could be a good start. After all, the church has been an intimate partner in the development of peoples for the past two thousand years.

CATHOLIC SOCIAL TEACHING

The key issues that we have been pursuing in this chapter; namely, the meaning of the human person and the common good, are also anchored in the social teachings of the Catholic Church, most dramatically and vividly in two encyclicals of Pope John Paul II.[22] I believe they can help enrich and enlarge our discussion on these two themes. In *Globalization and Catholic Social Thought,* John Coleman, S.J., summarizes the core social principles under eight separate headings.[23] I will use those eight headings to group the following reflections. These eight topics could make for fruitful points of dialogue and research across political, cultural, and religious divides.

Human Dignity

This is absolute bedrock for any further reflection. The human person is created in the image of God and so has a worth that cannot be measured in any other terms. It is the foundation of a moral vision of society. That worth is inherent, not earned, and never lost. It is qualitatively different from any other type of measurement. To the contrary, the measure of every institution and every society is whether it threatens or enhances the life and dignity of the human person. Human dignity grounds inherent rights to satisfy basic needs in addition to the rights of freedom from coercion. In economic terms: *no person should be bought or sold.* Any question of deepening our understanding

---

[22] Pope John Paul II, encyclical letter, *Laborem Exercens*, On Human Work, 1981; and idem, encyclical letter, *Centesimus Annus*, On the Hundredth Anniversary of *Rerum Novarum*, 1991.

[23] John A. Coleman, S.J., and William F. Ryan, S.J., *Globalization and Catholic Social Thought: Present Crisis, Future Hope* (Maryknoll, N.Y.: Orbis Books, 2005), 15-18. The whole section is worth reading as a summary of Catholic teaching on the issue.

of the human person must be grounded in the absolute worth and dignity of the individual, which is rooted in the person's openness to transcendence. Not even the church mediates the total reality of the individual person, as is clearly stated in church teaching: "Conscience is the most secret core and sanctuary of a person. There he is alone with God, whose voice echoes in his depths."[24]

The Social Nature of the Human Person

Just as we have, by nature, an absolute worth as an individual so we are, by nature, interdependent. The person is not only sacred but also social. To be social means that the person is essentially embedded in a family and in those organizations, civil, cultural, and economic, that either promote or threaten the well-being of all. The same emphasis on common good also says that a person not only has rights but also responsibilities, to one another, to family, and to the larger society. A one-sided emphasis on personal rights is a distortion of the nature of the human person, who is essentially relational. That nature is ultimately grounded in the Trinity, where God himself is revealed as relational. The diversity of culture and language, symbol and art is a legitimate consequence of the social nature of the human person and must therefore be respected. The leveling effect of a market economy does not have an automatic right to eliminate everything that stands in the way of economic progress.

The Common Good

This is a critical principle, as we have discussed at length above. It is based in a moral order that promotes the flourishing of all people in the full human dimensions of personal living and self-constitution. It is central to the good society, to a well-functioning state, and to international order. It is not an abstraction but rather it is embodied in the sum total of institutions and organizations that safeguard, promote, and preserve the essential social nature of the human person. It is also a necessary corrective to a highly individualistic notion of human living. For instance, while the church has always defended the right of private property as important for personal growth and responsibility, it has also insisted that the right is not absolute. Some goods are public and therefore have a priority of common possession to which pri-

---

[24] Vatican Council II, *Gaudium et Spes*, Pastoral Constitution on the Church in the Modern World, 16.

vate property is subordinate. Air, the seas, the earth, family, and friendship are common goods that can be shared but not owned. *Not everything should be bought and sold.*

The question remains about who decides what should remain public or common and what is legitimately private. Yes, we need a dump, a highway, a prison—but not in my backyard! Do we keep our old traditions or join the new economy? Do we keep our view of the lake or build condos? Amartya Sen comes to our aid again with his interesting way of focusing the issue. He talks about "having the freedom to lead the kind of lives we have reason to value."[25] This decision should be made by the people themselves in some type of democratic fashion. It is not to be made by political or religious authorities or by cultural or academic experts either from within or outside the community. "The kind of lives we have reason to value" can be a liberating notion. The common good is then truly human and based on values.

Subsidiarity

Put negatively, the principle of subsidiarity states that "a community of a higher order should not interfere in the internal life of a community of a lower order, depriving the latter of its functions, but rather should support it in case of need and help to coordinate its activity with the activities of the rest of society. . . ."[26] This rather abstract sounding principle is rooted ultimately in the essential worth of the human person. Except in need or to coordinate activity with society at large, the family should not do what the individual should do; the state should not do what the family should do; government should not do what business should do; business should not do what private associations should do, and so on up and down the line. Each level of societal organization has its own competence that must be respected. Globalization does not necessarily mean mega-international corporations nor does interdependence mean mega-government or welfare states. There is no such thing as a global mind. A global perspective is never more than a horizon toward which a particular local standpoint expands.

From that realization, a number of considerations follow that can be summed up by the term *subsidiarity*. There is first the notion of societal pluralism. There is no overarching power, whether derived from the government, the corporation, the media, the intellectual establishment, or the church that

---

[25] Sen, *Development as Freedom*, 14, 56.
[26] Pope John Paul II, *Laborem Exercens*, On Human Work, 48.

can coopt or dissipate the role of the local unit. No bureaucracy or ideology or notion of political correctness has the final word. In a global society and a global economy there is a real danger of swallowing up or minimizing the local. Nothing that can adequately be done on the local level should be transferred to the universal level. Subsidiarity reinforces the fact that each level of society has its own competency and legitimacy. Authority ultimately comes directly from God; every other type of sovereignty is limited ("Render to Caesar, render to God"). To override that reality is to destroy something essentially human. Business itself is becoming more cognizant of that principle. This realization is expressed in such directives as "Drive down decision making to the level that has to deal with the consequences," and "Go to the expert—the person doing the job." It will only enhance the worth of every individual and help create a more meaningful workplace.

Solidarity

If the local is essential, it is not absolute. Fundamental to Catholic social teaching and to the belief of all major religions is the affirmation of the ultimate unity of the whole human race. Solidarity creates a *dynamism* toward unity that operates on many levels. There is the solidarity of man and woman, child and adult, labor and management, citizen and country, the individual and the human community, the past with the present, the present with the future. All of these are neatly summed up in the words of Pope John Paul II, "A person must work out of regard for others, especially his own family, but also for the society he belongs to, the country of which he is a child, and the whole human family of which he is a member, since he is the heir to the work of generations and at the same time a sharer in building the future of those who will come after him in the succession of history."[27]

The Preferential Option for the Poor

While a preferential option for the poor might be seen as simply an extension of the principle of solidarity, it has its own distinct focus. It means to give priority of care to the victims of history, to give a voice to the voiceless and the invisible of society, to respond to the "poor" in every dimension of that word. But in a world dominated and defined in economic terms, the gap between

---

[27] Pope John Paul II, *Laborem Exercens*, On Human Work, 16.

the rich and the poor, between the secure and the vulnerable, between the healthy and the sick, becomes even more dramatic. While there are legitimate differences as to how such needs are to be met, there is no doubt about the distinct and necessary role played by those who give voice to the voiceless of society and walk in the shoes of the vulnerable. A basic test of the morality of any society is how it treats its most vulnerable members. A twenty-four-hour-a-day, seven-day-a-week global productivity can easily develop a harshness and relentlessness that simply overwhelms and ignores whatever and whoever cannot accommodate to its rigors and discipline.

At the same time, the call is not to eliminate poverty but to defend the poor, to be a voice for the voiceless, and to come to the aid of the victim. Economic equality of everyone (or wealth redistribution) has never been a goal of Catholic social teaching.

Catholic Theories of Justice

Justice is not one-dimensional. Merely fulfilling a contract or having a vote does not exhaust the claims of justice. Justice makes a total moral claim arising from the multidimensional relations of persons to one another. Following the classical division of justice, Catholic thought distinguishes up to five senses of justice:

- *commutative justice*—based on fulfilling promises and contracts
- *distributive justice*—based on a fair allocation of burdens and benefits in society
- *social justice*—the establishment and viability of institutional arrangements that guarantee and enable the first two
- *participative justice*—a more recent realization that each person must have some genuine voice in determining the arrangements of the society that shape and determine her life
- *restorative justice*—an attempt to explore how amends can be made for past injustice.

An Integral Humanism

An integral humanistic view sees the person as a whole and refuses to allow the person to be reduced to any single dimension. Pope John Paul II spoke of six factors that must be taken seriously in any reflection on the human person: politics, society, economics, culture, the state, and the environment.

Authentic human development, then, must consider all these dimensions in judging the well-being of the person. It makes for a more ambiguous and messy situation, but it refuses to allow for a one-sided, facile, and slick definition of the human person.

In summary, there are three clear moral limits to the range of a market economy:[28]

1. *Many human needs are not met by the market but lie beyond it.* This is fundamental to all else—the ever-transcending dynamism of the human person.
2. *Some goods cannot and must not be bought and sold.* A clear priority of labor over capital. Labor is the source of wealth. All means of production are instrumental.
3. *Whole groups of people are without the resources to enter the market and need nonmarket assistance.* The assistance called for is not a handout but help to enter the circle of exchange.[29]

CONCLUSION

Let us bring this work full circle by returning to its beginnings, where we reflected on the fact that moral life is itself a journey. We either continue to grow in caring about a larger and larger world or we find our world contracting into ever smaller circles until it revolves only around ourselves. Morality is never static because it expresses the orientation of one's personal identity. To become more and more conscious of the full moral implications of "making a living"—something that consumes so much of our time and talent—is itself a significant achievement on the road to moral maturity and to a vision of what our world can possibly become.

QUESTIONS FOR REFLECTION

1. Explore the meaning of "what does it profit a person to gain the whole world and lose his soul" in light of one's identity as a consumer-producer.
2. Explore what it means to live humanly in a society of abundance and

---

[28] Pope John Paul II, *Centesimus Annus,* On the Hundredth Anniversary of *Rerum Novarum,* 4.
[29] Pope John Paul II, *Centesimus Annus,* 26.

prosperity. This is the first time in history that the issue arises on such a large scale. A new kind of creativity and lifestyle is called for.

3. Discuss the following: What does success look like to me? Will I know it when I see it? What are the key elements to those answers?
4. Does the Catholic Church's structure of "communion" offer a paradigm for world unity? That structure begins with the local community gathered at Eucharist. The local community is in communion with all other local communities through unity with the local bishop. Bishops are in communion with every other local church through their communion with all other bishops, expressed in their unity with the pope. This communion (community) of the local church in communion with all other local communions is the full reality. The church in effect is composed of people as they exist locally but as part of a world community. There is no megachurch or mega-institution that has any greater significance than what occurs locally. Rather, it is a local community open to the totality of the world. Does this model have any relevance for business or government?
5. In light of the unity of the whole human race, who is my neighbor?
6. Does a large retailer have a right to move into a neighborhood with the likely effect of eliminating many small businesses? Make the case for each side.
7. Is it wrong to want to be rich? Is it perhaps foolish to want to be rich, if it is meant as a solution to the question of happiness? Might it, in fact, be right to want to be rich?
8. Should religion be more concerned with the creation of wealth or with the redistribution of wealth? Explain, or make the case for each position.

SUGGESTIONS FOR FURTHER READING AND STUDY

Bevans, Stephen, S.V.D., and Roger P. Schroeder, S.V.D. *Constants in Context.* Maryknoll, N.Y.: Orbis Books, 2004. On the mutual interaction of religion and culture.

Boyle, Nicholas. *Who Are We Now? Christian Humanism and the Global Market from Hegel to Heaney.* Notre Dame, Ind.: University of Notre Dame Press, 1998. A highly philosophical but eminently enlightening exploration of what is really going on in a world of global markets.

Gardner, Howard, Mihaly Csikszentmihalyi, and William Damon, *Good Work.* New York: Basic Books, 2001. An empirical study of the strategies that will allow people to maintain moral and ethical standards at a time when market forces have unprecedented power.

John Paul II, Pope. Encyclical letter, *Laborem Exercens*, On Human Work, 1981.

————. Encyclical letter, *Centesimus Annus*, On the Hundredth Anniversary of *Rerum Novarum*, 1991. These two encyclicals of Pope John Paul II are worth reading in their entirety. Most encyclicals tend to be extremely abstract. These two are much more specific and readable.

Lovett, Brendan. *A Dragon Not for the Killing*. Quezon City, Philippines: Claretian Publications, 1998. A perceptive application of the thought of Bernard Lonergan, S.J., to an analysis of contemporary culture, not only in the West but also in the East.

Miller, Vincent J. *Consuming Religion: Christian Faith and Practice in a Consumer Culture*. New York: Continuum International, 2005. An important book for anyone interested in exploring how a consumer culture impacts religious belief.

Orbis Books has a wide listing of works that highlight the needs of the poor and disenfranchised from almost every continent.

Index

access: as type of power, 78, 79
accounting, full-cost, 63, 64
achievement, ethics of, 85-88, 90
action, responsible: and decision, 93, 94
agriculture, 34
Airbus, 185
alignment, 56, 57
altruism, 87
Amazon, 35, 48
anger: and change, 171
Applied Materials, 47
Aquinas, Thomas, 220
Aristotle, 84, 184, 225, 226
   on acquisition of wealth, 27, 28
Armour, 108
Arthur Anderson, 48
Association of Southeast Asian Nations
   (ASEAN), 190
Augustine, 232
authenticity, 88-98
   growth in, 100-101

banking, deregulated, 41
bargaining: and change, 171-72
basic rights, respect for, 191
Bell Labs, 75
Bennis, Warren
   on leadership, 69, 70
   on making mistakes, 174
Berger, Peter, 205, 206, 210
Bolt, Robert, 136
Boyatzis, Richard: on goals, 162
Boyle, Nicholas, 179
   on consumer-producer identity, 185,
     186, 218, 219, 230
   on money and measuring value, 217-18
brainstorming, 97
bribes: and decision making, 199-200
Brodsky, Norm, 72
Brown, Gordon, 205
Buckingham, Marcus
   on maximizing strengths, 164
   on principles of human growth, 158

business
   as amoral, 5
   attitudes toward, 3, 6, 25, 28, 29
   containment as moral response to, 5
   as context for moral development, 153-
     58
   as contributor to society, 34
   cynicism about, 26
   and growth in prosperity, 35, 182,
     183
   as human activity, 13, 20, 21
   and human development, 156-58
   and the humanities, 224, 225, 226
   images of: in parables, 17
   as moral activity, 13, 20, 21
   moral culture of, 107, 108
   and morality: Christian reflection on,
     17-23; reconciling, 3-8
   paradigm shift in understanding, 30,
     31, 32, 37
   process, dynamics of, 215-18
   as producing goods and services, 32, 33,
     37
   as a profession, 30, 31, 37
   and profit, 11, 12
   purpose of, 8-13
   regulation by government, 4, 5, 30, 84,
     129
   as social institution, 106
   as spiritual activity, 13, 20, 21
   as a vocation, 13-17, 21, 30
businesspeople, media portrayal of, 28, 29

Carey, Ray: on ultracapitalism, 39-42
Caterpillar Corporation, 201
Catholic social teaching, 236-41
celebrations, company, 121
change: and human growth, 169-77
Citigroup, 110
Clement of Alexandria: on sacred and
   secular, 18, 19
Clifton, Donald: on maximizing strengths,
   164

244

Cloud, Henry, 85
  on empathy, 73-74
Coca-Cola, 48, 185
coercion: as type of power, 77
Coffman, Curt: on principles of human
  growth, 158
Coleman, John, S.J., on globalization and
  Catholic social thought, 236
Collins, James C.
  on company values, 107, 108
  on core values, 44, 48, 51
  on market economy and free society, 38
Columbus, Christopher, 181
command-and-control model, 52, 53, 76,
  77, 111, 206
Commodities Futures Act, 41
commoditization, 216, 217, 231, 233
common good, 226-30, 237-38
  global, 229
compensation structures, 116
compliance, ethics of, 83-85, 89, 90
consequences: as reason for moral action,
  140-41
consumer culture: and religion, 230-34
consumption, personal, 219, 220
Continuous Process Improvement, 97
core purpose, 51
core values, 44-64, 191
  and business practices, 46, 47
  and business success, 47, 48
  determining, 49-50
corporate social responsibility (CSR), 58-
  64
corporate value statements, 48
corporation
  Milton Friedman on purpose of, 9, 10,
  11
  R. Edward Freeman on responsibility
  of, 10
  and responsibility, 8-13, 59
corruption: and ethical decision making,
  199-200
cost: and price, 197
courage, 72, 73
creativity, 81
credit card, 219, 229
crucible experience, 71
Csikszentmihalyi, Mihaly: on flow experiences, 56

cultural relativism: and ethical decisions,
  191-92
cultural values: and economic development, 208-10
customer satisfaction, 45, 46

Daimler-Chrysler, 196
debt
  consumer, 219
  of developing nations, 203
Decalogue, 128, 141, 142
decision: and responsible action, 93, 94
decision making, ethical, 143-50
democracy: and market economy, 206-7
denial: and change, 170-71
derivatives, 41
despair: and change, 172
discipline, 116-17
Disney, 47, 50, 108
diversity, 123-24
Doctors Without Borders, 185
Donaldson, Thomas: on core values, 191,
  192
Drucker, Peter
  on business and humanities, 226
  and business management, 57, 58
  on responsibility, 97
DuPont, 64

eBay, 51
economic activity: types of, 34, 35
economic development,
  and cultural values, 208-10
  levels of: and ethical decisions, 193, 194
economics
  and environmentalism, 133
  free-market, issues relating to, 1-8
  global: and business ethics, 190-210
  global market: results of, 183, 184
  and short-term results, 133, 204
  zero-sum, 37, 182
economy, market: characteristics of, 38
Einstein, Albert, 170
Eliot, T. S., 68
Emerson, Ralph Waldo, 134
empathy, 73-76
Employee Retirement Income Security
  Act (ERISA), 40

employees
  as business asset, 52-58
  and core values, 49
empowerment: as type of power, 79
Engler, John, 202
Enron, 48
environmental stewardship, 62, 63, 64
Ericsson, 47
ethical culture
  and the decision-making process, 119-
    20
  formal elements of, 108-20
  leadership and, 108-10
  and organizational structures, 110-13
  and selection and training, 118-19
ethical decisions: in global context, 190-
    210
ethics
  of achievement, 85-88, 90
  codes of, 113-15
  of compliance, 83-85, 89, 90
  and corporate law, 84
  and language of, 122-23
  as organizational issue, 107
  as outside of business, 5, 6
European Union, 190
evaluations, 116
expertise: as type of power, 78
externalities, 62, 63

faith: as embodied in life in the world, 19
fear
  and change, 173-74
  of failure, 174-76
feedback: and human growth, 165-66
FEMSA, 47
Fessenden, Rol, 197, 198
flow experiences, 56, 57
Franklin, Benjamin, 134
freedom, A. Sen on, 31, 32, 37, 210, 238
Freeman, R. Edward: and stakeholder
    theory, 10
free trade
  vs. aid to developing nations, 203-5
  and price of goods, 201, 202
  vs. protectionism, 200-203
Friedman, Milton: on purpose of corpora-
    tion, 9

Fuller, Buckminster: on changing an
    organization, 169

Gardner, John W.: on role of community
    in business, 134
Gaudium et Spes
  on business and morality, 20
  on earthly activity, 19, 20, 21
Geertz, Clifford: on human being in
    nature, 105
General Agreement on Tariffs and Trade
    (GATT), 190
General Electric (GE), 47, 120
globalization, 179-212
  benefits of, 187
  as a challenge, 189
  and gains in technology, 180-81
  and interdependence, 190
  and loss of jobs, 195-96
  and national self-sufficiency, 184, 185,
    186
goals, 162
goal setting, 116
gold standard, 39, 40
Goleman, Daniel, 75
  on goals, 162
  on leadership, 69
good citizenship, 191, 192
goodwill, 48
Google, 35, 48
grapevine, 125
group norms: as type of power, 78
group think, 73
guanxi, 75

Haas, Robert, 105
Hartner, Eric, 167
hebel (futility), life as, 18
Henderson, L.: on qualities of leaders, 98-
    99
Hewlett, Bill, 56
Hewlett-Packard, 51, 56, 64
Hobbes, Thomas, 228
Hock, Dee, 83, 214
Honda, 196
human activity, levels of, 52, 53, 54
human dignity, 236-37
  respect for, 191

human growth
    hindrances to, 168-76
    principles of, 158-68
humanism, integral, 240-41
humanities: and business, 224, 225, 226
human person
    as economic unit, 218, 219
    meaning of, 223, 224
    social nature of, 237

IBM, 46, 47, 120
I Ching, 66, 69
identification: as type of power, 78
identity
    Christian: in a market economy, 235,
        236
    personal, 66-76, 218-26; as con-
        sumer-producer, 187, 188, 218, 219,
        220, 221, 222, 230; development of,
        218-26; and discovering what mat-
        ters, 67-72; and empathy, 73-76;
        and finding one's voice, 72-73; and
        success, 71
IKEA, 50
improvement, continuous, 97
incentives, 117-18
income, redistribution of, 207-8
Index of Economic Freedom, 35, 36
industry, 34
institutions, global, 190
integrity, 88-98
    and exploring intelligently, 91-92
    and leadership, 98-99
    and paying attention, 90-91
    and sound judgment, 92-93
interconnectedness: and the nature of
    business, 32
interiority, nurturing, 101-103

Jackall, Robert, 115
James, William, 153
jobs: and globalization, 195-96
John Paul II, 236, 238, 239, 240
Johnson & Johnson, 47, 48, 59, 121
judgment, sound, 92, 93
justice, 136, 137, 138
    Catholic theories of, 240
just wages, 196-98

Kaizen, 97
Kant, Immanuel, 141
Kidder, Rushworth: on ethical dilemmas,
    131, 138
Kohler, Herb, 161
Kuebler-Ross, Elizabeth: on dealing with
    change, 170-77

law, corporate: and ethics, 84
leadership, 76-81, 97, 98
    and compassion, 80
    and ethical culture, 108-10
    and integrity, 98-99
    and power, 76-80
    and team building, 80, 81
The Learning Organization, 97
Lee, Kai-Fu, 75, 76
leisure, 227, 228
L. L. Bean, 197
Locke, John, 228
Lonergan, Bernard, S.J.: on developing
    potential, 154
Lovett, Brendan, 234
loyalty, 135, 136

making money, 14, 27-33, 37, 40, 44, 45,
    46, 48, 52, 59, 71, 101, 214, 235
manipulation: as type of power, 79
market economy
    and common good, 226-30
    and consumer desire, 220
    and democracy, 206-7
    and form of government, 205-10
    and religion, 230-36
Marx, Karl, 182, 225
Maslow, Abraham: on change, 170
McCarthy, Michael, 228
McDonald's, 51, 185
McKee, Annie: on goals, 162
Merck, 50
mercy, 136, 137, 138
Microsoft, 48
Miller, Vincent: on consumer culture, 232,
    233
mission statements, 48
mistakes
    dealing with: and core values, 49
    fear of, 174-76

monetary value, 186, 187
money
    and core values, 49
    and objectifying value, 216, 217
    and religion, 221
    role of, 186, 187
moral dilemmas, 130-39
    and individual vs. community consider-
        ations, 133-35
    and justice vs. mercy, 136-38
    and short-term vs. long-term consider-
        ations, 131-33
    and truth vs. loyalty, 135-36
moral person, 85, 86, 87, 88, 89, 90
moral philosophies, 139-43
Motorola, 47
Moyers, Bill, 62
myths, company, 121-22

Napolitano, C.: on qualities of leaders, 98-
    99
National Association of Manufacturers
    (NAM), 202
negativity: as type of power, 79
neighborhood, workplace as, 155, 156
Nelson, Katherine: on moral culture of
    business, 108, 120
Nestle, 47
Nike, 59
North American Free Trade Agreement
    (NAFTA), 190, 201
Novak, Michael: on business as a calling,
    14, 15
Novartis, 196

office untouchables, 118
organizational structures: and ethical cul-
    ture, 110-13
Organization for Economic Cooperation
    and Development (OECD), 204
Organization of American States, 190
Owens, Jim, 201

Packard, David: on business as contributor
    to society, 34, 35
Parikh, Jagdish: on leadership, 69, 70
persuasion: as type of power, 79
physical force: as type of power, 77

Plato, 225
poor, 234
    preferential option for, 239-40
Porras, Jerry I.
    on company values, 107, 108
    on core values, 44, 48, 51
    on market economy and free society,
        38
power
    and leadership, 76-80
    sources of, 76-80
prayer, 70
pre-judgment, 92
price: and cost, 197
Prince, Charles O., 110
Procter & Gamble, 47
profit
    and business, 11
    meaning of, 46
    and stockholders, 9, 59
promotions, 117
Protestant ethic: and capitalism, 208

quantification, 216, 230, 231

Ratzinger, Cardinal Joseph (Pope Benedict
    XVI), 1
reality checks, 124-25
redistribution of income, 207-8
reinsurance, 41
religion
    as commodity, 231, 232
    and consumer culture, 230-34
    and market economy, 230-36
    and personal identity, 221
resignation/integration: and change, 172-
    73
responsibility, 111, 112
Rest, James: on ethical behavior in busi-
    ness, 6
results: short-term and long-term, 116,
    204
reward systems, 115-18
right vs. wrong, tests for, 128-29
rituals, 121
role models, 120
roles, organizational, 112, 113
Royal Dutch Shell, 64

Samsung, 196
Sarbannes-Oxley Act, 113
Schwab, Susan, 204
Sears, 117
self-determination, 99-100
self-interest, 46, 52, 87, 88, 227
self-renewal, 102
self-sufficiency, national: and globalization, 184, 185, 186
Sen, Amartya
    on business and freedom, 31, 32, 37, 210, 238
    on cultural values and economic development, 209-10
    on economic activity and human development, 156, 210
    on economic development and freedom, 141, 210
    on ethics in market economy, 214 15
service/information, 34
Skinner, B. F., 52
Smith, Adam, 46, 87
    and free-market economy, 26
    on economics and society, 39
Smith, Douglas K.: on balance between work and life, 12
socialism, 205, 206
Socrates, 223
solidarity, 239
Solomon, Robert, 25, 32
Sony, 47, 50
Southwest Airlines, 47
stakeholder
    interests of, 10, 11
    theory, 10
state
    as agent of social change, 225
    and self-sufficiency, 181, 184
stock: and business success, 40
stockholders
    and corporate profits, 9, 59
    relationship to corporation, 9, 60
students, business: and moral reasoning, 7
subsidiarity, 238-39
success: and core values, 47, 48
sustainable development, 61, 62

taxes: and redistribution of income, 208
Taylor, Charles: on moral self-identity, 8

teamwork, 97
Tertullian: on sacred and secular, 18
"they": as hindrance to human growth, 168-69
Thomas, Robert, 70
3M, 47, 51
Tillich, Paul, 16
Total Quality Management, 97
Towers Perrin, 47, 109
Toyota, 47
Treviño, Linda: on moral culture of business, 108, 120
truth, 135, 136
truth telling, 98

ultracapitalism, 39-42
Unilever, 47
universal principles: as reason for moral action, 141-42
utilitarianism, 140

values
    choosing among conflicting, 130-39
    cultural, 192
    individual: and business, 55
    objectification of, 216
virtue: as reason for moral action, 142-43
vision: as type of power, 77
visionary companies, 47
vocation, characteristics of, 15

Wallenda, Karl, 174
Wal-Mart, 51, 59, 120
Walton, Sam, 120
Watson, Tom, 120
wealth
    acquisition of, 27
    and social prosperity, 38
The Wealth of Nations, 26, 39, 87
Weber, Max, 208, 209
Welsh, Jack, 120, 161
    on leadership, 103
whistleblowers, 118
Witmer & Associates, 160
workaholic, 222
working conditions, human, 196-98
workplace: as neighborhood, 155, 156
World Bank, 190, 203, 204, 205
World Trade Organization, 190, 204